WINE IN THE BIBLE

And

The Scriptural Case For Total Abstinence

Wine is a mocker, strong drink is raging: and
whosoever is deceived thereby is not wise...Look
not thou upon the wine when it is red, when it giveth
his colour in the cup, when it moveth itself aright.
At the last it biteth like a serpent, and stingeth like
an adder. (Proverbs 20:1; 23:31-32)

Leighton G. Campbell

WINE IN THE BIBLE
And
The Scriptural Case For Total Abstinence

Leighton G. Campbell

Unless otherwise stated, Scripture quotations are from the King James or Authorized Version.

PUBLISHED BY:
BRENTWOOD CHRISTIAN PRESS
4000 BEALLWOOD AVENUE
COLUMBUS, GEORGIA 31904

TO THE MEMORY OF E.E. VAN DEVENTER
A CONTENDER FOR THE FAITH

And to all those who love the truth.

FOREWORD

Leighton Campbell's monumental, exhaustive but not exhausting book meets a need for Christians and non-Christians alike to understand unequivocally the consistency of Scripture in addressing the matter of total abstinence. The book is a labour of love as evidenced by the time spent in its production and the balance shown in dealing with areas that often evoke strong differences of opinion.

Too many people have thought that the Bible can be variously interpreted to justify their own lifestyle choices. Campbell exposes this fallacy and faces the reader with: a basis of seasoned support for abstainers who, though whilst abstaining on principle, will find encouragement in the rich Biblical foundation for their decision; and aid the non-abstainer in making an intelligent choice.

There is no comfort here for the so-called 'sensible' or moderate drinker. For a generation of people brought up on the popular belief that 'a little alcohol is good for your health' both the Scriptural and medical evidence shows otherwise. (The modicum of alcohol said to confer benefit on the heart is so minuscule as to be not worthy of consideration, since the same small amount can damage both the liver and the brain!)

Whilst medical considerations for abstaining are not the subject for this book the fact that alcohol affects the reasoning and discriminating powers is. The book can be read through from A to Z, or used as a commentary or reference book for specific Bible study in relation to the various aspects of the abstaining theme, and will provide answers to the various misstatements one hears concerning Jesus' use of wine, and its domestic use in ancient and early Church times.

The timely publication of this volume cannot be over-emphasised bearing in mind the UK government's concern with binge- and under-age drinking, and the fact that former abstaining faith communities are now applying for liquor licences to sell and con-

4

sume alcohol on their premises. Campbell's book is a wake-up call to sleeping communities both secular and faith-centred. It should be a 'must read' not just for people interested in healthy living but to all who claim to be enjoying the abundant life in Christ! Every Church, home and youth group should possess a copy, and act on its contents – what a witness that would be!

Richard J B Willis MA MSc FRSH FRIPH AITV MIHPE
Executive Director,
UK National Committee for the
Prevention of Alcohol and Drug Dependency

ACKNOWLEDGEMENTS

The author would like to acknowledge the following:

Dr. William Patton's excellent work on Bible wines and the laws of fermentation. This served as an invaluable source of help in preparing this book.

Albert Barnes' Commentaries on the Bible. This also served as an excellent source of help in putting this work together. Barnes is one of the few Bible commentators who fairly and thoroughly deals with this subject.

Adam Clarke's superb Bible Commentaries, which expertly and bluntly refutes the narrow-minded views concerning the drink issue.

Bible scholars, teachers, commentators and writers past and present, whose good work has helped to shed light on this most poorly understood subject.

The late Bishop E.E. Van De Venter, for suggesting and encouraging me to embark on this task. His abstinence stance and Biblical resoning on this subject, was an important factor in structuring this material.

Chris Mansfield, a faithful friend and brother in the Lord. His help in obtaining valuable material for developing this book, and his insight and general advice is greatly appreciated.

Errol Campbell, my brother in the flesh, brother in the Lord, pastor and friend, for his general encouragement and emphasis on an in depth approach to Bible study.

Maureen Campbell, sister in the flesh and sister in Christ, for the hours she sacrificed in helping with the early stages of the manuscript.

Jenny, my lovely wife, companion, and friend, for her support and patience.

The Lord Jesus Christ, for giving me the strength, wisdom, inspiration and persistent patience. Most of all, for the honoured privilege of glorifying His Name through this work.

Leighton G. Campbell

CONTENTS

INTRODUCTION

Judge not according to the appearance, but judge righteous judgment. Jesus Christ (John 7:24)

Common honesty demands that we interpret the Scriptures with the eye, the taste and the usages of the ancients, and not with the eye, the taste and the usage of the moderns. Dr. William Patton

Before approaching any study of the Holy Scriptures, it would be good for one to apply the principles of these wise opening statements. It is unfortunate that these principles have been especially lacking concerning the study of wine in the Bible.

Due to the modern day alcohol industry, the subject of wine in the Bible has sadly become an almost hidden truth. This work therefore attempts to unveil such truth, and thus counter balance the alcohol minded prejudices that we find today, even among Christians. After a thorough examination of the Biblical view of wine drinking, etc., this material comes down very strongly in favour of total abstinence from alcoholic or intoxicating beverages. The aim has been not to use purely rational and subjective arguments in seeking to uphold this stance. This is a practice that has been common among many sincere and well meaning Christians who have tried to enforce it.

Critics of the Bible and those who wish to drink, in many cases frown upon these arguments, which is most unfortunate. This is largely due to the fact that many of the arguments for total abstinence lack real conviction and Scriptural forcefulness, and sometimes even contain an optional tone to them.

It is for these reasons that the approach to this work has been to intensely scrutinize the Scriptures for the truth concerning this subject. Therefore technical facts about alcohol, or the present day substances added to intoxicating spirits are kept to an absolute minimum. Scientific facts are important and have their place. But if one examines the Bible closely enough, one will realize that it too contains important and relevant scientific facts.

9

Facts that express the evil effects of intoxicating drinks in its own terminology. Technical facts are used only to provide scientific amplification of the Biblical terms.

Throughout our study, we will see that the Bible is capable of positively speaking for itself whether it is sin to drink intoxicating drinks or not. Many today interpret this subject from their own experience, human reasoning, and their own sinful perspective, instead of the solid principles of Scripture.

Hence the wild and slanderous allegations levelled at Jesus for creating what many suggest was alcoholic and intoxicating wine at the marriage feast in Cana of Galilee. What is even more amazing, is that Bible expositors who realize the need for the study of Bible manners and customs. Along with a correct understanding of the original Hebrew and Greek words used in the Bible etc., fail to even consider that not all wines mentioned in the Bible were of the nature of the beverages we call wine today and therefore non-alcoholic.

Some expositors even belittle the idea of non-alcoholic wine. Their attitude towards Jesus is grossly inconsistent. One moment they hail Him as the glorious and Spotless Son of God. And in the next breath, claims that He was a winebibber who bestowed a large measure of alcoholic and intoxicating wine upon sinful men, of whom He came to liberate.

The problem with many readers of the Bible today, is that their minds are conformed to this evil World's system and need renewing by the Word of God. Many do not realize that this is a serious subject, and that there are important questions that must be answered fairly, and should not be ignored.

The chief aim of this work is to glorify Christ and the exceedingly high standard of His Bible. And to show that it must be treated with fear, reverence, and much thought. Rather than superficial or sinful indifference.

Because of the multiplicity of views on this subject, both for and against the abstinence cause, it has been necessary to quote from a great number of sources. This will help shed light on the Biblical facts, and to highlight erroneous convictions on the subject. All opposing views therefore, are presented clearly and fairly.

Some of the arguments presented in this book may be a bit technical, but the aim has been to keep the material as simple as possible. Where it has been considered necessary, the author has highlighted key points contained in quotes, and added explanations in brackets for greater emphasis and clarity. A simple reference chart including important word definitions is included at the back of the book. This material covers *every* New Testament reference to wine and drunkenness, with an index also at the back of the book showing the respective chapter that comments on them. The design is to help the reader to easily check any verse on drinking, etc., along with crucial words.

It is greatly hoped that this book will serve as a focusing tool for understanding the sacred Book on this "controversial" subject.

Leighton G. Campbell.

PART 1

IMPORTANT PRINCIPLES
OF INTERPRETATION

INTRODUCTION

The word "wine" in the Bible is the translation of various Hebrew and Greek words. The Old Testament generally uses two Hebrew words when referring to wine, tirosh and yayin. Tirosh refers to unfermented wine (new or sweet wine). Tirosh can also refer to the juice while still in the grape:

> *Thus saith the Lord, as the new wine (tirosh) is found in the cluster: and one saith, Destroy it not; for a blessing is in it: so will I do for my servants' sakes, that I may not destroy them all.* (Isaiah 65:8)

This is also the case in Nehemiah 10:37,39 where the words "wine" and "new wine" refers to the grapes in their natural state.

The other Hebrew word yayin, is a generic word and can refer to wine in its fermented or unfermented state (Psalms 60:3-fermented; Isaiah 55:1-unfermented).

In the Greek New Testament, two words are generally employed when referring to wine; oinos and gleukos. Oinos is the Greek equivalent to the Hebrew yayin, and refers to wine in its fermented and unfermented state (Ephesians 5:18, fermented; John 2:9, unfermented). The other Greek word, gleukos, is the Greek equivalent to the Hebrew tirosh. This refers only to unfermented sweet new wine. This corresponded somewhat to the fruit of the vine, and was the only kind of wine that Christ drank or endorsed (Acts 2:13; Matthew 26:29).

The Hebrew word translated "strong drink" is shekar (Leviticus 10:9; Numbers 6:3). The Greek equivalent to this word is sikera (Luke 1:15). Both these words are generic, and can refer to a strong intoxicating drink as well a sweet non-intoxicating drink. When used in the Bible, it usually refers to a strong intoxicating drink. This was made from ingredients other than the grape, such as vegetables, or the juice of fruits or honey. Beer would also come under this heading.

That there were different kinds of wines in Bible times, both fermented and unfermented is obvious from:

(a) The different Hebrew and Greek words used to describe them.

(b) The context of the passage (this is most important, especially for those who do not understand the meaning of the original Hebrew or Greek words).

(c) The fact that God sanctioned the use of wine as being good for man (Gen 27:28; Deut 7:13; John 2:9-10). And also condemned its use (Prov 20:1; 23:20,31-35).

John Wesley Ewing correctly explains:

> *...if a reader will just consider the context surrounding the word he can easily understand whether the fermented or unfermented grape juice was intended. Wherever the use of wine is prohibited or discouraged it means the fermented wine. Where its use is encouraged and is spoken of as something for our good it means the unfermented.*

These are solid principles of Bible interpretation, which will stand the test against the arguments of those who insist that the Bible only speaks of alcoholic wine.

Chapter 1

THE SYMBOLIC VINE

The fabricating of an intoxicating liquor was never the chief object for which the grape was cultivated among the Jews. (Rev. Henry Homes, Bibliotheca Sacra, May 1848)

The vine was cultivated from the earliest times of man's history (Gen 9:20,21). When the spies were sent to search out the land of Canaan, one of the things they brought back was a huge cluster of grapes. These were carried between two upon a staff (Numbers 13:23).

Amongst other things, Canaan itself was a land of vines (Deut 8:8). Grapes were a very important part of the diet of the Hebrews. And as well as wine, they were used for making raisin cakes (1 Sam 25:18). Grapes were an important source of sugar to the Hebrews. This was a gift from God of which they were very dependent. Wine (the fruit of the vine, unfermented and possibly in its natural state in the grape cluster) was to be presented at the altar as an offering to God (Numbers 18:11,12). This was a first fruit offering and all that was to be offered had to be pure, and leaven (fermentation) was prohibited (Lev 2:11).

Figuratively, the vine symbolized prosperity and peace among the ancient Hebrews (1 Kings 4:25; Micah 4:4; Zec 3:10). The vine also symbolized the nation of Israel throughout the Bible (Psalms 80:8-19; Jer 2:21; Ezekiel 15:2-8; 17:6-10; 19:10; Hosea 10:1; Isaiah 5:1-7; Matt 21:33-36).

The Jews themselves also realized the importance of the vine in their history. When Antiochus VII granted Simon the Maccabee permission to coin money with his own stamp (1

Macc XV.6; 140 BC); on the reverse side of one of his copper coins, was a stamp of a vine leaf with the legendary inscription, "for the freedom of Jerusalem." The Jewish historian Flavius Josephus writes of the magnificent golden vine in Herod's Temple (Book XV.Chap.XI.3). Francis H. Derk explains the significance:

> A golden vine was one of the chief ornaments of Herod's temple. On the temple door it was a symbol of the Theocracy of Israel. Israel was called the "Noble Vine." The ornament had clusters of grapes the stature of a man in length, one of the marvels of the temple. In ancient times a symbol of Israel it later became the symbol of the Messiah.

Because the vine was such an integral and important commodity in the life of the Jewish people, Christ was able to perfectly illustrate spiritual truths by saying, *I am the true vine* (John 15:1). This showed that the Jews were totally dependent upon Him for salvation.

Thus we can see that the fruit of the vine was created by God as a blessing for man's physical health, and like marriage it reveals deep spiritual truths. It was never God's intention that wine should be drunk in its fermented state. Because the physical ill effects (poor judgment, tipsiness, drunkenness) reveal the spiritual reality of sin and destruction, as Jeremiah 25:15,16 makes clear:

> For thus saith the Lord God of Israel unto me; Take the wine cup of this fury at my hand, and cause all the nations, to whom I send thee, to drink, and be moved, and be mad, because of the sword that I will send among them.

Before even approaching the subject of wine drinking, it is important that one understands the concept of wine in the Bible from a spiritual point of view, because this is how God desired Israel to understand it. Once one understands the symbolic use of wine in its pure state (unfermented) and its corrupt state (fermented), the absolute truth concerning its use becomes easy to understand.

As we focus on the Bible, these truths become startlingly clear and enables us to more fully understand and appreciate the temporal and spiritual significance of our Lord's first miracle of turning water into wine (John 2:1-11).

Let us not forget that there was a blessing in the vine (Isaiah 65:8) and also a curse (Jer 25:15,16), just as there were blessings in Jehovah for obedience and curses for disobedience (Deuteronomy 7:12-15; 28:15-19), so it was with the vine.

In the Bible we see that God expected the obedient person to appreciate and drink the pure fruit of the vine that He gave them for the benefit of their health:

> *Thus saith the Lord, As the new wine is found in the cluster, And one saith, Destroy it not; for a blessing is in it...*
> (Isaiah 65:8)

> *...and thou didst drink the pure blood of the grape.*
> (Deuteronomy 32:14)

While on the other hand, we see that God also expected the sinner even after experiencing the ill effects of drunkenness, to illogically crave after the juice of the same fruit but in its contaminated, rotten, and poisonous state:

> *They have stricken me, shalt thou say, and I was not sick; they have beaten me, and I felt it not: when shall I awake? I will seek it yet again.* (Proverbs 23:35)

These facts form the theme of wine throughout the Bible.

CHAPTER 2

ALCOHOL –
A SYMBOL OF SIN AND DEATH

Romans 5:12 states:

Wherefore, as by one man sin entered into the world, and death by sin; and so death passed upon all men, for all have sinned.

When man sinned, a vast change took place in his spiritual condition. Spiritual and physical death was sentenced upon him (Genesis 3:3). Even the animals turned wild, judging by Isaiah 11:1-8, which shows that the animals will again become tame when Jesus Christ restores peace to a sinful World.

There was also a change in the earth through God's curse:

And unto Adam he said, Because thou hast hearkened unto the voice of thy wife, and hast eaten of the tree, of which I commanded thee, saying, Thou shalt not eat of it: cursed is the ground for thy sake; in sorrow shalt thou eat of it all the days of thy life; Thorns also and thistles shall it bring forth to thee; and thou shalt eat of it all the days of thy life. (Genesis 3:17,18)

Since as this text clearly shows, that the food being brought from the earth was to bring sorrow to man, we can see that the destructive laws of fermentation was one of a number of processes that God put into operation because of man's sin. Although the above Bible text does not specifically mention fermentation, it must still naturally apply here. Seeing it is connected with death, and death with sin. It is therefore obviously clear that God did not intend that man should drink in any quantity, something which was symbolic of sin and death, and which was also harmful to his body and mind.

Alcohol is not a natural product of the creative hand of God, but rather a repulsive agent of sin which man in his unregenerate mind uses against himself. Patton quotes Dr. Henry Monroe in his lecture on alcohol, as saying:

> *Alcohol is nowhere to be found in any product of nature; was never created by God; but is essentially an artificial thing prepared by man through the destructive process of fermentation.*

Let us take a look at some of the things some well known men say about alcohol:

Shakespeare:

> *Alcohol is a poison men take into the mouth to steal away the brain.*

Abraham Lincoln:

> *A cancer in human society, eating out its vitals and threatening its destruction.*

General Robert E. Lee:

> *My experience through life has convinced me that abstinence from spirituous liquors is the best safeguard to morals and health.*

Ruskin:

> *The most criminal and artistic method of assassination ever invented by the bravos of any age or nation.*

Robert Hall:

> *Distilled damnation.*

Lord Chesterfield:

> *An artist in human slaughter.*

General Pershing:

> *Drunkenness has killed more men than all of history's wars, pestilence and famine.*

Sir Wilfred Lawson:

THE DEVIL IN SOLUTION.

After looking at these wise comments, it becomes extremely hard to imagine how any Christian can say that our Lord Jesus Christ, the greatest Man that ever walked the face of this earth. Exceedingly greater than the greatest of these men in wisdom, holiness and power would transform pure and harmless water into a deadly and harmful substance, which could potentially kill the people He created and loved so much. To make such an allegation is not only outrageous, but is also a slur on the reputation of our Lord.

It is thus self-evident that due to the destructive nature of alcoholic beverages to man's health, that it is a fitting symbol of spiritual death. Alcoholic wine is used in Scripture as a symbol of God's divine wrath:

> *You have made your people suffer hard things; You have given us to drink wine that made us reel and be dazed.* (Psalms 60:3, Amplified Bible)

> *For thus says the Lord, the God of Israel, to me: Take this cup of the wine of wrath from My hand, and cause all nations to whom I send you to drink it. They shall drink and reel to and fro and be crazed, because of the sword that I will send among them.* (Jeremiah 25:15,16 Amp Bible)

> *For in the hand of the Lord there is a cup [of His wrath], and the wine foams and is red, well mixed; and He pours out from it, and all the wicked of the earth must drain it and drink its dregs.* (Psalms 75:8, Amp Bible)

> *He too shall [have to] drink of the wine of God's indignation and wrath, poured undiluted into the cup of His anger, and he shall be tormented with fire and brimstone in the presence of the holy angels and in the presence of the Lamb.* (Revelation 14:10, Amp Bible)

A paper published by the Teachers Advisory Council on Alcohol and Drug Education, quoted the following statistics:

21

When a person is under the influence of alcohol he is more prone to accidents on the roads or with machinery. In 1974 35% of all drivers who died in road accidents had been drinking.

In 1977, a working party on alcohol and work reported the following:

Three times as many people with a drinking problem are involved in accidents at work than other people.

People with a drinking problem on average lose 2 to 3 times as many working days through sickness than do other workers.

The cost to British Industry through alcohol problems is estimated to be getting close to £350 million.

The report went on to say:

The latest known research indicated that 89 per cent of heavy drinkers in prison claimed that alcohol had played an important part in causing their last crime.

Alcohol is also responsible for numerous deaths in America and other countries all over the World, it is plain to see that, *the wages of sin is death.* People would do well in heeding God's warning:

Then when lust hath conceived, it bringeth forth sin: and sin, when it is finished, bringeth forth death. (James 1:15)

CHAPTER 3

NEW WINE – GOD'S BLESSING

Throughout the Bible new wine or unfermented grape juice was classed as a blessing and a gift from God for the well being of man:

> *Therefore God give thee of the dew of heaven, and the fatness of the earth, and plenty of corn and wine...And Isaac answered and said unto Esau, behold, I have made him thy lord, and all his brethren have I given to him for servants; and with corn and wine have I sustained him.* (Genesis 27:28,37)

> *And he will love thee, and bless thee, and multiply thee: he will also bless the fruit of thy womb, and the fruit of thy land, thy corn corn, and thy wine, and thine oil, the increase of thy kine, and the flocks of thy sheep, in the land which he sware unto thy fathers to give thee.* (Deuteronomy 7:13)

> *So shall thy barns be filled with plenty, and thy presses shall burst out with new wine.* (Proverbs 3:10)

> *Thus saith the Lord, As the new wine is found in the cluster, and one saith destroy it not; for a blessing is in it: so will I do for my servants' sakes, that I may not destroy them all.* (Isaiah 65:8)

> *And it shall come to pass in that day, that the mountains shall drop down new wine, and the hills shall flow with milk, and all the rivers of Judah shall flow with waters, and a fountain shall come forth of the house of the Lord...* (Joel 3:18)

And the vine said unto them, Should I leave my wine, which cheereth God and man, and go to be promoted over the trees. (Judges 9:13)

He causeth the grass to grow for the cattle, and herb for the service of man: that he may bring forth food out of the earth; And wine that maketh glad the heart of man, and oil to make his face to shine, and bread which strengtheneth man's heart. (Psalms 104:14,15)

Behold, the days come, saith the Lord, that the plowman shall overtake the reaper, and the treader of grapes him that soweth seed; and the mountains shall drop sweet wine, and all the hills shall melt. And I will bring again the captivity of my people of Israel, and they shall build the waste cities, and inhabit them; and they shall plant vineyards, and drink the wine thereof; they shall also make gardens, and eat the fruit of them. (Amos 9:13,14)

The new wine mourneth, the vine languisheth, all the merryhearted do sigh. (Isaiah 24:7)

Albert Barnes commenting on this verse writes:

New wine (tirosh) denotes properly must, or the wine that was newly expressed from the grape and that was not fermented, usually translated new wine or sweet wine.

H.C Leupold also states concerning this verse:

The "juice of the grape" would seem to refer to the juice within the skin of the berry while the clusters still hang on the vine..."All those who were merry of heart will sigh," apparently over the loss of the wine and the vine.

Notice how the Scriptures continually refer to corn, oil and wine. In actual fact, the word `corn' was a generic word for grain. This could include wheat from which bread was made, which was to symbolize the body of our Lord Jesus Christ. Oil is used in Scripture to symbolize the Holy Spirit (Hebrews 1:9) and new wine (the fruit of the vine) represents the precious atoning blood of Christ (Matthew 26:28).

24

Apart from the spiritual significance, oil and wine also had physical benefits too. In the parable of the good Samaritan, Christ said:

> *But a certain Samaritan, as he journeyed, came where he was: and when he saw him, he had compassion on him, And went to him, and bound up his wounds, pouring in oil and wine...* (Luke 10:33,34)

This was an external and medicinal application. The mixture of the two formed a healing ointment. Pliny, Roman official, Latin historian and scientist (AD 23 or 24-79) mentions, "Oleum gleucinum", which was compounded of oil and gleucus (sweet wine), as an excellent ointment for wounds. Here we can see the wonderful providence of a God of infinite wisdom, knowledge and love.

CHAPTER 4

ALCOHOL – A MENACE NOT A MEDICINE

Many Christians and unbelievers alike today are under the illusion that some alcoholic beverages are beneficial as a tonic for various ailments. Today there are so many "remedies" for all kinds of sicknesses, from fevers to colds. Many people believe them even though medically, there is no grounds for such action. The real fact is that man is so sinful that he likes to believe that the sinful things that bring him "pleasure" can cure him of his physical and mental problems.

Consequently, tradition has produced all sorts of "tonics" and old wives "remedies" which have included rum, whiskey, brandy, and others. These are nothing more than folklore which have been passed around for generations doing more harm than good. God's Word is clear concerning this:

> But refuse profane and old wives' fables, and exercise thyself rather unto godliness. (1 Timothy 4:7)

Our Lord was well aware of man's lack of appreciation of the things God have provided both for his physical and spiritual well being. In Luke 5:39, He says:

> No man having drunk old wine (legalism) straightway desireth new (salvation): for he saith, the old (legalism) is better.

In this parable Christ likens new wine (non-alcoholic grape juice) to salvation, or His powerful Kingdom, and old wine (alcoholic) to legalism or pharasaic tradition. Christ's analogy is perfect as usual. We know that Jesus' offer of salvation meant

26

eternal life and blessings to man. Something which legalism could never bring, because without Christ, man could never live up to the standards of the law.

Those who were unwilling to accept Christ would die in their sins (John 8:21). Thus we can see how Christ knowing of the ill effects of alcoholic wine, was able to effectively show the great contrast between legalism and grace.

Salvation or the blessings of the Kingdom, like new wine being healthy and beneficial to man. And legalism or pharasaic tradition, like old wine is harmful and would bring spiritual death.

It is clear from the context of the parable that not only is new wine superior to old wine, but that also old wine just like legalism is useless. And as the Master said, those who are used to drinking old wine prefer it to the new.

Today we can see by the amount of alcoholics, social drinkers, and tonic takers, that this is very much true. Those who are Christians should take a lesson from this.

There are many other misconceptions concerning the so-called benefits of alcohol. Including the common notion that it keeps the cold out. Those who give credence to such an idea should consider these facts from Black's Medical Dictionary:

> *The popular habit of taking spirits `to keep the cold out' is a delusion. Alcohol gives a sense of warmth to the skin by bringing the blood there; but, as the blood is rapidly cooled in cold air, the risk of frostbite and even death by freezing is increased, so that experienced hunters and mountaineers will on no account touch spirits on biting cold days or at high altitudes.*

> *In health, there is no necessity for alcohol, and, as so many persons contract the alcohol habit, it would be well for every one to consider the question carefully before embarking on its habitual use.*

Here we can see one of the many examples of the lack of understanding concerning the effects of this deadly substance.

This now is being realized, because during the past fifty or so years the use of alcohol as a medicine has rapidly declined.

Dr. William Patton writing long ago on this subject quoted Dr. J.W. Beaumont, Lecturer on Materia Medica in Sheffield Medical School, England, as saying:

> *Alcoholic liquors are not nutritious, they are not a tonic, they are not beneficial in any sense of the word.*

The recent claims today that red wine is beneficial because it reduces the chances of one contracting heart disease is misleading and contradictory to the message of the Scriptures. The French are often cited as an example of this because they eat a lot of fatty foods, consume a high amount of red wine, yet have a considerable reduced rate of heart disease when compared with other countries. However these claims are really inconclusive. Let us consider the following from the BBC's web site (www.bbc.co.uk/health/nutrition/drinks_alcohol.shtml) under the heading of, *Alcohol — the benefits and the risks:*

> *Alcohol consumed in moderation is **thought** to be beneficial in reducing the risk of coronary heart disease. Indeed, alcohol consumption, in conjunction with high intakes of fruit and vegetables, or red wine, may well explain the so-called 'French paradox.' The French diet is considered to be very high in fat, especially saturated fat, and yet the death rate from coronary heart disease is apparently lower than that of any other developed country.*
>
> *So what are we saying? Reach for your wine glass? The key word here is moderation. The World Health Organisation in 1997 concluded that the reduced risk from coronary heart disease was found at the level of one drink, consumed every second day.*
>
> *Alcohol, even when consumed in moderation, has been linked to a very wide range of other ailments and diseases, such as increased risk of mouth, pharyngeal and oesophageal cancers (this risk being greatly*

increased if combined with smoking). Furthermore, alcohol probably increases the risk of colorectal and breast cancer.

The list doesn't stop there: high blood pressure; gastrointestinal complications, such as gastritis, ulcers, and liver disease; and a depletion of certain vitamins and minerals are all caused by alcohol consumption. Of course, excessive alcohol can also have detrimental social and psychological consequences.

This clearly shows that any so-called benefits derived from drinking alcoholic wine are massively outweighed by the risks. You might not die of alcohol induced heart disease, but you will probably die of cirrhosis of the liver or some other alcohol related disease!

In proclaiming the fact that the French suffer a low rate of heart disease, it is not mentioned in the same degree that they have a high rate of deaths from cirrhosis of the liver as compared to other countries! The question that must be asked is what is it in the red wine that is beneficial? It is certainly not the alcohol! Any benefit derived is clearly from the fruit used to make the wine!

If one wants to be healthy, they would be better served if rather than drinking an alcoholic beverage, they would sample the many variety of pure healthy fruit juices on offer. If one wants to avoid the risk of alcohol related diseases, one shouldn't drink alcohol!

When alcohol enters the blood stream it is undigested (neither can it be, for the body tries to get rid of it), it then attacks the entire nervous system and the whole body structure, causing damage everywhere it goes. And if enough is ingested it will eventually result in death. God in His infinite wisdom directly and implicitly commands us to abstain from this deadly substance:

Wherefore do ye spend money for that which is not bread? and your labour for which satisfieth not?... (Isaiah 55:2)

The Moffatt Translation reads:

29

Why spend your money on what is not food, your earnings on what never satisfies?

John N. Moore and Harold Slusher writing on the subject in their book, *A Search for Order in Complexity*, states:

Alcohol is seldom consumed for its food value, although when drunk regularly in small amounts it seems to build up fat. It may seem to be a stimulant, but actually it is a narcotic. All of its effects interfere with some bodily process. If it seems to make a person more active, it is because the normal controls are stopped.

After a drink, a person may feel warm because the arteries leading to the skin dilate and let more blood through. But this process causes the body to cool off rapidly. The principle effect of drinking alcohol is on the nervous system, and the higher centers are affected first. For example, a person may not distinguish between what is funny and what is obscene. He may be friendly, but then suddenly change from affability to unprovoked rage. Thus he can become an unpredictable and dangerous person, even when he might not admit that he is drunk.

Having looked at all these facts, let the reader take a closer look at God's Word, which contains the best instructions for health:

My son, attend to my words; incline thine ear unto my sayings. Let them not depart from thine eyes; keep them in the midst of thine heart. For they are life unto those that find them, and health to all their flesh. (Proverbs 4:20-22)

The margin of a good reference Bible quotes the last phrase,...*and medicine to all their flesh.* God's Word is medicine for the believer:

Bless the Lord, o my soul...and forget not all his benefits: Who forgiveth all thine iniquities; who healeth all thy diseases. (Psalms 103:2-3)

Christians today should seek their healing in Christ and not in the bottle!

CHAPTER 5

ALCOHOL –
A TOOL OF THE ENEMY

There is a section in the Jewish Talmud, which reads:

The tree from which Adam ate from was the vine, for there is nothing which brings lamentation upon man so much as wine. (San.70a,b)

Whether the tree that Adam ate from was the vine or not is another matter, but the point of human suffering brought about by the consumption of fermented wine is certainly true. Alcohol is merely a tool that Satan uses against man whom he so much hates.

The great evangelist, Smith Wigglesworth told the story of a man whom he had met who was addicted to whiskey. The man said that he was told that the inside of him was shrivelled up and that he knew he was dying but he could not stop himself from drinking. Wigglesworth tells of how he brought deliverance to the man by laying his hands on him and cursing the drink demon that was taking his life. Obviously this does not apply to every drink problem case, but whether people are aware of it or not, there are invisible evil forces which drive people into slowly or rapidly destroying their bodies and minds with alcohol and other drugs, and eventually damning their souls in hell:

For we wrestle not against flesh and blood, but against principalities, against powers, against the rulers of the darkness of this world, against spiritual wickedness in high places. (Ephesians 6:12)

31

Let us again consider this passage:

...Behold, the husbandman waiteth for the precious fruit of the earth, and hath long patience for it, until he receive the early and latter rain. (James 5:7)

Chapter 1:17, of the same book reads:

Every good gift and every perfect gift is from above, and cometh down from the Father of lights...

But because Satan is the god of this World (2 Corinthians 4:4), man through satanic influence destroys the precious food of the ground that God has given to him for good health by turning it into the deadly substance of alcohol. With so many people starving in the World today (at the time of writing millions are starving in Ethiopia), it has been quoted that the grains and fruit used to make alcoholic beverages in the USA alone would feed twenty million each year! God's Word is clear concerning this:

...neither be partaker of other men's sins: keep thyself pure. (1 Tim 5:22)

Men in their ingenuity destroys the grain and fruit of the ground by cleverly manipulating the processes of fermentation to satisfy their evil desires, *...inventors of evil things..* (Romans 1:30)

When one really begins to consider the facts, one will see that the product of that so called "temperate" drink stems from a mass of gross evil. Leonard Ravenhill writing on revival stated the following:

Directed by the devil, the world has given a new injection to the flesh. One of the signs of the "last days" is that "men are lovers of pleasures." (Note that it is in the plural.) And where is hell's broth stewed? In the breweries of the world. It is a lame argument that in some cases government subsidies are granted to help the breweries keep men employed. Breweries are maternity clinics that breed men-slayers operating with guns, and men driving on the highways while drunken. Courts deal with the fruit of the liquor; revival would slay this deadly tree at the roots.

Christians today should remember and adopt the words of our Lord Jesus Christ concerning this satanically dominated world:

The world cannot hate you; but me it hateth, because I testify of it, that the works thereof are evil. (John 7:7)

BIBLE HISTORY OF DRUNKENNESS

The first recorded incident of drunkenness in the Bible is that of Noah, which is recorded in Genesis 9:20,21, which reads:

And Noah began to be an husbandman, and he planted a vineyard: And he drank of the wine, and was drunken; and he was uncovered within his tent.

Although this is the first recorded account of drunkenness in the Bible, it surely must have been rampant in the wicked antideluvian world, as Genesis 6:5 implies:

And God saw that the wickedness of man was great in the earth, and that every imagination of the thoughts of his heart was only evil continually.

Concerning this point, HC Leupold writes:

The notion that mankind took a long time to advance to the point of becoming a agriculturist does not agree with the Biblical evidence...Besides, it would seem strange indeed if the uses of wine were now first being discovered by man, whose earliest works, wherever we find them, give evidence of great ability. Besides, in the case of Noah's being the first wine-grower, Noah's drunkenness is entirely excusable; and yet the nature of this record seems to imply guilt on Noah's part. Consequently, we are rather led to the conclusion that Noah began to cultivate a plant of whose cultivation and uses he had previously known.

Regarding Noah's drunkenness, he continues:

The having of grapes led to the making of wine. The having of wine leads to the drinking of it. In all this, taken by itself, there is no wrong. We have every reason to believe, however, that Noah was not ignorant of the potency of the drink he had prepared. But he neglected caution. He who maintained his ground over against a wicked and godless world, neglecting watchfulness and prayer in a time of comparative safety, fell prey to a comparatively simple temptation, which should have been easy to meet. It is not the young and untried Noah who sins. It is the seasoned man of God, ripe in experience, who is here brought low. The sober tone of the detailed narrative points strongly to Noah's guilt. Noah drinks to excess and actually "becomes drunk" (shakhar).

The Bible Knowledge Commentary also bears out this point:

Here Noah lay drunk and naked in his tent. Intoxication and sexual looseness are hallmarks of pagans, and both are traced back to this event in Noah's life. Man had not changed at all; with the opportunity to start a "new creation," Noah acted like a pagan.

The results of this action had serious and far-reaching consequences of which we should take note of today. Genesis 9:22-25 explains:

And Ham, the father of Canaan, saw the nakedness of his father, and told his two brethren without. And Shem and Japheth took a garment, and laid it upon both their shoulders, and went backward, and covered the nakedness of their father; and their faces were backward, and they saw not their father's nakedness. And Noah awoke from his wine, and knew what his younger son had done unto him. And he said, Cursed be Canaan; a servant of servants shall he be unto his brethren.

Had not Noah been drunken in the first place, this event would have never occurred. The drastic outcome of this incident changed the course of human history. We can be sure that after this episode that Noah must have considered it wise to have followed a course of total abstinence from intoxicating wine!

The next godly man to fall prey to the deceitfulness of wine was Lot, whose incestuous acts gave birth to the tribes of the Moabites and Ammonites who became a constant source of irritation to the Israelites. In Genesis 19:30-36, we read of the incident:

> *And Lot went up out of Zoar, and dwelt in the mountain, and his two daughters with him; for he feared to dwell in Zoar: and he dwelt in a cave, he and his two daughters.*
>
> *And the firstborn said unto the younger, Our father is old, and there is not a man in the earth to come unto us after the manner of all the earth:*
>
> *Come, let us make our father drink wine, and we will lie with him, that we may preserve seed of our father.*
>
> *And they made their father drink wine that night: and the firstborn went in, and lay with her father; and he perceived not when she lay down, nor when she arose.*
>
> *And it came to pass on the morrow, that the firstborn said unto the younger, Behold, I lay yesternight with my father: let us make him drink wine this night also; and go thou in, and lie with him, that we may preserve seed of our father.*
>
> *And they made their father drink wine that night also: and the younger arose, and lay with him; and he perceived not when she lay down, nor when she arose.*
>
> *Thus were both the daughters of Lot with child by their father.*

Such abominable acts were made possible after the first drink of wine. Let us note that the text says that Lot's daughters made him *drink* wine. The Hebrew word used for drink here is shaqah. Young's Analytical Concordance states the meaning here, "To cause or give to drink."

It is obvious that after Lot took the first drink of wine it was then easy for his daughters to get him in a high state of drunkenness; because as the text states, he did not even realize what he had done. Had Lot adopted the principle of total abstinence from intoxicating wine, such deceit would never have been possible.

The truth of the matter is that Lot was in a sense drunk from the moment he had taken the first drink, for he had lost self discipline. The Oxford Dictionary gives us the definition of the word "drunk":

Deprived of proper control of oneself by alcoholic liquor.

One therefore does not have to be reeling to be effectively drunk.

There are numerous other references to drunkenness throughout the history of the Bible, but it is not the aim of this work to go into all of them. We will conclude however with an outline of some:

Nabal	(1 Samuel 25:36).
Uriah	(2 Samuel 11:13).
Amnon	(2 Samuel 13:28).
Elah, king of Israel	(1 Kings 16:9).
Benhadad, king of Syria	(1 Kings 20:16).

In the New Testament there is no specific reference to any particular individual being drunk, but there are numerous warnings against it with the emphasis being made that those who engage in it would be excluded from the Kingdom of God (1 Corinthians 6:10; Galatians 5:21).

CHAPTER 6

TOTAL ABSTINENCE NOT A
DOCTRINE OF DEMONS!

In this section we will examine some of the disturbing allegations against the abstinence or temperance cause put forth in G.I. Williamson's book entitled, *Wine in the Bible & the Church.* In his book he categorically dismisses any suggestions that wine in the Bible was any thing other than a fermented beverage.

After grossly distorting and manipulating several Scriptures to suit his own view-point, he comes to the outrageous conclusion through the abuse of 1 Timothy 4:1-5, that those who advocate total abstinence from intoxicants are propagating a doctrine of demons! On page 14 of his book he states:

> *Wine is one of the things created by God to be received with thanksgiving by those who believe and know the truth. Those who desire to impose a law of total abstinence upon Christians are departing from the truth of God and are following the doctrine of demons.*

We will examine the relevant arguments put forward by Williamson in the light of the Scriptures to show that such views are utterly false. It is not the purpose of this work to discuss the rights and wrongs of the Temperance movement, or the United Presbyterian Church of North America. Williamson makes a point of highlighting the errors of these movements to add further ammunition to his anti temperance or abstinence crusade.

Wrongs such as enforcing vows of abstinence, refusing to associate with those who manufacture alcohol etc., should not be allowed to cloud our judgement when we come to evaluate the drink issue in the light of Scripture.

Let us say for instance, vows were enforced to make people pray or it was encouraged that one should not associate with those who failed to carry out the practice, this would not mean that prayer in itself is wrong! The point that we are concerned with is whether or not the Bible itself upholds the teaching of total abstinence from intoxicants or not.

On page 2 of his book, Williamson asks the question whether the temperance movement arose out of a careful study of the Bible. The question the present author would like to advance, is whether Williamson's anti temperance views also arose out of a careful study of the Bible?!!! After reading his book, it is quite evident that it did not. Again on page 2, he states that the term "temperance movement" is an inaccurate description of a movement which advocates total abstinence from intoxicating liquors. This is false.

In the New Testament, the term "temperate" or "temperance" did not mean moderation, but self-restraint or abstinence. Therefore in the light of Scripture, this is an accurate or appropriate label for an organisation whose object is the promotion of total abstinence from beverages, which contain the addictive, destructive poison of alcohol!

Having said all this, we will now get to the crux of the matter by firstly examining 1 Timothy 4:1-5, in order to determine exactly what the inspired Apostle was saying, and who he was referring to in his strong denunciations. The passage reads:

> *Now the Spirit speaketh expressly, that in the latter times some shall depart from the faith, giving heed to seducing spirits, and doctrines of devils; Speaking lies in hypocrisy; having their conscience seared with a hot iron; Forbidding to marry, and commanding to abstain from meats, which God hath created to be received with thanksgiving of them which believe and know the truth. For every creature of God is good, and nothing to be refused, if it be received with thanksgiving: For it is sanctified by the word of God and prayer.*

38

Let the reader note that this text is speaking of wicked men, who have categorically denied the fundamental doctrines of the Christian faith. Men whose consciences have become cauterised or totally insensitive to the truth of salvation by grace. So that they substitute it for man made rules such as enforced celibacy and abstinence from certain *foods*. The word translated "meats" in the above text refers to any kind of food, particularly that of animal flesh. There were certain religious sects who adopted these practices such as the Judaizers, the Essenes, and more recently, Roman Catholicism.

Williamson's attempt to transpose the damning indictments of the above text on to blood bought *Christians*, who believe in total abstinence from intoxicating beverages. Even if they might be misguided in applying it, is not only wicked, but is also a gross misrepresentation of the inspired text. The text above referred to *food*, which God created for man to enjoy for the benefit of his health. In the book of Genesis we read:

> *And God said, Behold, I have given you every herb bearing seed, which is upon the face of all the earth, and every tree, in the which is the fruit of a tree yielding seed; to you it shall be for meat (food). And God saw every thing that he had made, and, behold, it was very good.*
> (Genesis 1:29,31a)

After the universal flood recorded in Genesis, man's diet was extended by God to include all animal flesh:

> *Every moving thing that liveth shall be meat for you; even as the green herb have I given you all things.*
> (Genesis 9:3)

Alcohol is not a food, and was never a part of God's original creation, and therefore cannot be applied to the text of 1 Timothy 4:1-5, which refers solely to food. Under the subject of, *Healthy Living,* on the BBC's web site, it states the following concerning alcohol:

> *Alcohol is a drug with the immediate effect of altering mood. Because drinking makes people feel relaxed, happy and even euphoric, many might find it surprising*

to learn that alcohol is in fact a depressant. As such, it switches off the part of the brain that controls judgement, leading to loss of inhibitions. As most people are aware alcohol also affects physical co-ordination.

Dr. William Patton quotes Dr. Lionel S. Beale, Physician to King's College Hospital, England long ago, as saying:

Alcohol does not act as a food; it does not nourish tissues.

He also quoted Dr. James Edmunds of London, as stating:

*Alcohol is, in fact, treated by the human system **not as food, but as an intruder and as a poison.***

Dr. Henry Monroe's statement in his lecture on alcohol is again appropriate here:

Alcohol is nowhere to be found in any product of nature; was never created by God; but is essentially an artificial thing prepared by man through the destructive process of fermentation.

These facts merely confirm the truth of the Biblical account of creation. Williamson's suggestion on page 14, that God created alcoholic wine is totally in error and contrary to *true* science. How blasphemous then to suggest that God would have Christians receive such with thanksgiving, and that such poison could ever be sanctified by the Word of God and prayer!

Albert Barnes gives us a correct interpretation of the clause, *For every creature of God is good* in 1 Tim 4:4, which categorically refutes Williamson's narrow-minded interpretation. It reads:

It is good in its place; good for the purpose for which he made it. But it should not be inferred that a thing which is poisonous in its nature is good for food, because it is a creation of God. It is good only in its place, and for the ends for which he intended. Nor should it be inferred that what God has made is necessarily good after it has been perverted by man. As God made it originally, it might have been used without injury. Apples and peaches were made good, and are still useful and proper as articles of food; rye

40

and Indian-corn are good, and are admirably adapted to the support of man and beast, but it does not follow that all that man can make of them is necessarily good. He extracts from them a poisonous liquid, and then says that "every creature of God is good, and nothing to be refused." But is this a fair use of this passage of Scripture? True, they are good-they are to be received with gratitude as he made them, and applied to the uses for which he designed them; but why apply this passage to prove that a deleterious beverage, which man has extracted from what God has made, is good also, and good for all the purposes to which it can be applied? As God made theses things, they are good. As man perverts them, it is no longer proper to call them the "creation of God," and they may be injurious in the highest degree. This passage, therefore, should not be adduced to vindicate the use of intoxicating drinks. As employed by the apostle, it had no such reference, nor does it contain any principle which can properly receive any such application.

He then goes on to explain what the apostle Paul meant when speaking of food again in 1 Tim 4:4, when he says, *and nothing to be refused:*

*Nothing that God has made, for the purposes for which he designed it. The necessity of the case-the "exigency of the passage"-requires this interpretation. It **cannot** mean that we are not to refuse poison if offered in our food, or that we are never to refuse food that is to us injurious or offensive; nor can it any more mean that we are to receive all that may be offered to us as a beverage...It is not to be regarded as a religious duty to abstain from food which God has appointed for the support of man.*

The lesson we learn then from a proper understanding of the text, is that contrary to Williamson's views, those who believe and know the truth would not accept intoxicating beverages as being from God. Williamson's interpretation of the text is absolutley criminal!

THE TYRANNY OF WILFUL IGNORANCE

In this section we will examine how Williamson seeks to explain away the problem of how one could justify the use of intoxicating substances, given their destructive effects to the human body. How he attempts to do this is truly alarming. Apart from distorting certain Scripture passages, he also rejects the law of common sense and the consensus of opinion from men of science, whose research bears testimony to the fact that alcoholic beverages are totally destructive and useless as far as good health is concerned.

Any calls for total abstinence from such on the grounds of medical knowledge, is termed by Williamson as, *the tyranny of experts,* a phrase which he borrowed from Professor J.G. Machen. The present author would like to state that Williamson's stance should also be described as, *the tyranny of wilful ignorance.* His argument is that all such information must be judged in the light of Scripture. This is true, but this is merely an attempt by Williamson to avoid facing up to the obvious.

One doesn't have to be an expert in medical science to know that alcoholic beverages are harmful, this is not a matter of opinion but a matter of fact! To try to evade the issue as he does on page 29, by stating an example in the past where medical experts were in error, really bears no relevance to the alcohol issue. Also, by stating that not all doctors agree that wine is harmful, is a misleading statement which seems to be designed to give the impression to the reader that the effects of alcohol are far from understood. There are somethings in the field of medicine which laymen and medical men alike did not know in the past and still don't know even today, but there are other things we **do** know for certain. And one of those things that we all know is that alcohol ingestion even in small amounts is not good for the body.

One recalls an experiment carried out on television fairly recently, in which people were given alcoholic drinks to see how it affected their driving. First of all, they had to drive around a course without any drinks while their performances were monitored. Then they were asked to drink each time they went around the course to see just how much their driving deteriorated with respect to the amount of drinks they had. It was clearly evident that only after *one* glass of wine, co-ordination and reaction time was affected significantly.

Such contrasts in performances between not being under the influence of alcohol and being under its influence, could mean the difference between causing or avoiding a fatal accident. Shall we call such facts *the tyranny of experts?!!!*

It has long been the opinion of the police who have to witness the effects of terrible accidents on the road as a result of drinking, that people should **not** drink at all before driving. But because of the attitudes of certain people the authorities have been reluctant to try to enforce such a law, and have hence made a compromise by setting a legal limit.

When we allow our minds to become so prejudiced that we become wilfully blind to truth, we are a danger to ourselves and to others. Irrespective of what our views may be on a particular subject, we still have an awesome responsibility to those whom we minister to be fair and honest. To almost pretend that a substance which Proverbs 20:1 unconditionally describes as *a mocker* of which men of science in confirmation of the Scriptures and common sense experience, have conclusively proved to be damaging to the human system is not harmful, is not only a gross act of wilful ignorance, but it is also an act of deceit.

Another thing he does is to introduce useless and irrelevant information into the argument. He also employs the tactic of playing with words in order to substantiate his anti abstinence views. From a misinterpretation of Paul's statement in Romans 14:14, where when referring to food he says, *that there is nothing unclean of itself,* he seeks to build an argument from this that there can be no Scriptural force for total abstinence from intoxicants. On pages 27-28, he quotes Prof. J.G. Vos' remarks about carbolic acid, in which he states that if the use of it were sinful in itself, then even if the slightest drop diluted in a thousand gallons of water were drunk, then according to Scripture, this would violate the whole moral law, thus being a sin worthy of eternal death.

Vos himself states that no one should say that his arguments are a *reductio ad absurdum,* but that is exactly what it is. His arguments are nothing more than irrelevant, absurd nonsense. Such "clever" arguments are merely designed to pour scorn and ridicule upon those who believe that it is sin to drink and to abuse themselves with other drugs.

The believer would do well to spend his time occupying his mind with the plain, simple and practical message of the inspired Word. In the apostle Paul's letter to Titus he states:

> *This is a faithful saying, and these things I will that thou affirm constantly, that they which have believed in God might be careful to maintain good works. These things are good and profitable unto men. But avoid foolish questions, and genealogies, and contentions, and strivings about the law; for they are unprofitable and vain.* (Titus 3:8,9)

Williamson's continual focus on the idea of nothing being sinful or evil in itself, appears to be nothing more than a smoke screen to divert attention away from the real moral issues relating to alcohol.

We will now take a closer look at Romans 14:14, where the apostle Paul states that there is nothing unclean in itself to properly understand its meaning. We will also answer the charges made by Williamson in his book against temperance men, that they locate evil in material things and hence reject the Scriptural teaching that evil in man stems from his depraved heart.

When we examine Williamson's interpretation of the apostle Paul's statement in Romans 14:14, when he states, *that there is nothing unclean in itself,* we learn that he is taking the Scripture out of context. The apostle Paul here is dealing with the issue of different kinds of *foods.* This truth is made clear near the end of the chapter, where the Apostle states:

> *For the kingdom of God is not food and drink but righteousness and peace and joy in the Holy Spirit.* (Romans 14:17, Revised Standard Version)

44

Here Paul makes it absolutely clear that the subject that he was dealing with in the chapter related solely to food and nothing else, as was also the case in 2 Timothy 4:1-5. Again, this is obvious from the statement the inspired Apostle makes in 2 Corinthians 6:17, where he states, *touch not the unclean thing.* The Amplified Bible states *touch not [any] unclean thing.*

The reason why Paul could make two statements which appear to be contradictory, is that in Romans 14:14, he is making it clear that there is no food which can be considered impure. While in 2 Corinthians 6:17, he makes it clear that when speaking relative to sin, there are things that can be considered unclean. So we see that Williamson's attempt to use the Apostle Paul's statement in Romans 14:14, to justify the use of alcohol, is refuted by the inspired Apostle himself!

Now in answering the charges against temperance men that they erroneously consider material things such as alcohol as intrinsically evil, rather that pin-pointing the real problem of the depraved human heart, a point which Williamson and others have blown out of all proportions in dealing with this subject. We will now examine the charges he makes on page 27 of his book, which states:

> *How then does it happen that Christians commonly think of some things as inherently evil? Is it not the failure to make an important distinction? If a certain material thing is dangerous, and potentially harmful, to man, then it is assumed that it must be sinful to use it. Hence the slogan of the proponents of total abstinence defining temperance as "a moderate use of things that are good and total abstinence from things that are harmful." If a thing is harmful or dangerous to man then it is thought of as evil. Yet the truth is that the two are quite distinct. The one does not automatically follow from the other. It is not true that it is always a sin to use something that may be harmful or dangerous. It is not the nature of a thing that determines whether or not its use is sinful, but the way in which it is used.*

In the light of the above remark, suggesting that there are Christians who wrongly assume the use of some things as evil just because they are harmful, it must be stated that it is Williamson himself who makes the erroneous assumptions. When temperance men state that alcohol is evil, they are not saying that the chemical substance of alcohol is wicked by itself, but that alcoholic beverages are evil relative to their sinful abuse by man.

To automatically make the assumption from such a statement that the proponents of total abstinence are saying that alcohol itself is sinful, or that its industrial use etc. is sinful, is a gross injustice. The fact that not all temperance men think in the way in which Williamson assumes, is reflected in the booklet entitled, *Alcohol and you,* which upholds the cause of total abstinence. On the front cover it states:

> *Alcohol has very valuable antiseptic properties, and when used outside the body is a very useful chemical.*

Alcohol is also used for industrial purposes, it is used as a solvent, fuel, etc. The present author also possesses and uses a substance with a concentration of 99.7% pure isopropyl alcohol, which is used for a wide range of technical maintenance applications, but certainly wouldn't consider sniffing or drinking it! The use of alcohol in this way would certainly be a foolish and sinful act. It is in this sense that temperance men are speaking, when they state that the use of alcohol is evil. It is only fair that their opponents at least give them the benefit of having some sense, instead of trying to build a massive argument against them, based on a naive or condescending interpretation of their terminology.

Indeed when temperance men state that alcohol is evil, they are simply speaking of alcohol in the same way as the Apostle Paul does when referring to sinful contamination in 2 Corinthians 6:17, when he states:

> *and touch not the unclean thing.*

Shall we accuse the inspired Apostle of the abuse of Scripture?!

Again, if we turn to the book of James, we read:

46

And the tongue is a fire, a world of iniquity: so is the
tongue among our members, that it defileth the whole
body, and setteth on fire the course of nature; and it is set
on fire of hell. For every kind of beasts, and of birds, and
of serpents, and of things in the sea, is tamed of mankind:
But the tongue can no man tame; it is an unruly evil, full
of deadly poison. (James 3:6-8)

The opponents of the temperance cause would not for one moment seriously imagine that the writer here is suggesting that we all have our tongues cut out! This is because it is a matter of common sense that he is speaking of the tongue relative to a sinful heart, but when it comes to the alcohol issue, there are those such as Williamson who fail to apply the same common sense rule!

WHAT DEFILES A MAN

Another dangerous misinterpretation of Scripture by Williamson which gives serious cause for concern, is the way in which he takes completely out of context Jesus' statement concerning the sinful human heart. On page 14, he states

It was Paul who said "all things are lawful for me" (1 Cor.
6:12;10:23). True, they are not always expedient, and Paul
emphasizes the fact that he will not be mastered by any-
thing. Yet the fact remains that "nothing is unclean of itself"
(Ro. 14:14). For, as our Lord stated so clearly: "there is
nothing outside the man which going into him can defile
him; but the things which proceed out of the man are what
defile the man" (Mk. 7:15). Wine is not the cause of drunk-
enness, exactly as food is not the cause of gluttony. The
truth is that all sin proceeds from the sinful heart of man. To
treat wine as the cause of sin - in any way shape or form -
is to deny the real teaching of Scripture concerning the
depravity of man. It is, in effect, to say that there is fault in
the handiwork of God. There is no greater need in the
Church today than to reject this doctrine of devils.

47

First of all, before we come to the main point of this argument, a fact which must be stated is that Paul's statement in 1 Corinthians 6:12; 10:23, stating "All things are lawful unto me," taken in context, again referred to the eating of food. The Apostle's immediate remarks in the following verse of the former statement, makes this absolutely clear:

> *Food (is intended) for the stomach and the stomach for food, but God will finally end [the functions of] both and bring them to nothing.* (1 Corinthians 6:13, Amplified Bible)

The conclusion we come to then, from a correct interpretation of the Scriptures, is that 1 Timothy 4:1-5, along with Romans 14:14, which we earlier examined; and 1 Corinthians 6:12; 10:23, when speaking of things which are permissible to the Christian, all refer to the use of *food*. Willamson's attempt to try to use these passages to justify the use of the addictive and dangerous drug called alcohol is Scripturally unjustified and extremely dangerous.

Now in coming to the main point of the argument, concerning our Lord's statement about what defiles a man, it is important for us to read the passages in context, to properly understand exactly what Jesus was saying. The accounts are found in Matthew 15:10-20, and Mark 7:14-23. We will quote Mark's account because it gives us a little more detail. Before doing so, we must realize that it is wrong to quote Scriptures to prove a point, without explaining the context of the passage. Scripture stands or falls as a unit, if this were not the case, one could quote isolated passages to "justify" anything. In Mark 7:14-16, we read:

> *And when he had called all the people unto him, he said unto them, Hearken unto me every one of you, and understand: There is nothing from without a man, that entering into him can defile him: but the things which come out of him, those are they which defile the man. If any man have ears to hear let him hear.*

The circumstances surrounding this statement concerned the teaching of the rabbi's, that one had to go through a process of

48

ceremonial washing before eating. Here our Lord explains that if one failed to go through this ritual, it could not make him a sinner. Jesus here is not endorsing the abandoning of cleanliness and hygiene, or the abuse of one's body, but is specifically referring to the fact that ritualistic ceremonies of purification cannot purify a man's heart.

Those who try to use this account to justify the use of alcoholic beverages, completely fail to understand that Jesus was dealing solely with the spiritual aspect of man; i.e., that which makes him sin, namely, an evil heart. Later, He made this point absolutely clear:

> *And when he was entered into the house from the people, his disciples asked him concerning the parable. And he saith unto them, Are ye so without understanding also? Do ye not perceive, that whatsoever thing from without entereth into the man, it cannot defile him;* **Because it entereth not into his heart, but into the belly...** (Mark 7:17-19)

Jesus then goes on to categorically explain that which defiles a man:

> *And he said, That which cometh out of the man, that defileth the man. For from within, out of the heart of men, proceed evil thoughts, adulteries, fornications, murders, Thefts, covetousness, wickedness, deceit, lasciviousness, an evil eye, blasphemy, pride, foolishness: All these evil things come from within, and defile the man.* (Mark 7:20-23)

What Williamson fails to understand from Jesus' above description of the sinful human heart, is that if a man's heart is evil he will defile his body!

The Apostle Paul, who had a far greater understanding of holy Scripture than Williamson or anyone else will ever have, makes this clear:

> *Know ye not that ye are the temple of God, and that the Spirit of God dwelleth in you? If any man defile the tem-*

ple of God, him shall God destroy; for the temple of God is holy. which temple ye are. (1 Corinthians 3:16,17)

Since the word translated "defile" in verse 17, can also mean to destroy, many scholars interpret this passage to mean that if any one attempts to destroy the body of Christ with false doctrine, God would destroy him. This however cannot be the sole meaning here, because the Spirit of God dwells in each individual and hence in the Church collectively. Therefore if we take the Apostle's statement literally, we have to accept the fact that he is speaking of both physical and spiritual contamination. This truth concerning individual responsibility for the treatment of one's own body, is again stated by Paul:

What? know ye not that your body is the temple of the Holy Ghost which is in you, which ye have of God, and ye are not your own? For ye are bought with a price: therefore glorify God in your body, and in your spirit, which are God's. (1 Corinthians 6:19,20)

Again the inspired Apostle makes it clear in no uncertain terms, that contrary to Williamson's nonsense interpretation of our Lord's remarks in Mark 7:15,18, there *are* certainly things which entering into a man that *can* definitely defile him physically:

Therefore, since these [great] promises are ours, beloved, let us cleanse ourselves from everything that contaminates and defiles body and spirit, and bring [our] consecration to completeness in the (reverential) fear of God. (2 Corinthians 7:1, Amplified Bible)

Thus we have before us then, clear Scriptural proof that Jesus' remarks in Matthew 15, and Mark 7, concerning the defilement of man, referred only to his heart and not his body. Here the Christian is commanded to cleanse himself from *anything*, which might pollute both body and spirit in order to be completely holy. Williamson's interpretation of our Lord's words can only be described as a gross narrow minded and liberal distortion of the context in which He was speaking. This kind of interpretation creates a dangerous seedbed for all kinds of sinful abuses of one's body.

What Christians must realize is that God places a high value on the importance of the body as well as the heart or spirit. The following Scriptures drives this point home:

> *I beseech you therefore, brethren, by the mercies of God, that ye present your bodies a living sacrifice, holy, acceptable unto God, which is your reasonable service.* (Romans 12:1)

> *And the very God of peace sanctify you wholly; and I pray God your whole spirit and soul and body be preserved blameless unto the coming of our Lord Jesus Christ.* (1 Thessalonians 5:23)

> *Let us draw near with a true heart in full assurance of faith, having out hearts sprinkled from an evil conscience, and our bodies washed with pure water.* (Hebrews 10:22)

WINE IN THE OLD TESTAMENT

When we examine Williamson's interpretation of the nature of wine in the Old Testament, we get a true measure of his prejudice and hypocrisy on this subject. Passages such as Deuteronomy 14:26; 32:14, Hosea 4:11, and Isaiah 25:6; 49:26, which Williamson misinterprets to accommodate his narrow minded views, are given their full and proper explanation in Part 1, Chater 7.

The first point of error we will examine from the Old Testament perspective, is Williamson's scandalous attempt to use the Septuagint to uphold his theory that the Old Testament only speaks of fermented beverages. On pages 11-12, he makes this erroneous statement:

> *...the Greek Septuagint (abbreviated LXX) used the common word wine (Greek **Oinos**) to translate various Hebrew words. Since virtually all the Hebrew terms (as shown above) referred to various kinds of fermented wine, it was natural that the Greek translators should employ the common Greek term for fermented grape*

51

*juice. It must be remembered, furthermore, that this Greek version was the Bible of the Gentile Church in the Apostolic Period. If the writers of the New Testament had wished to speak of unfermented grape juice the one word that they never could have used in their writings was the term **Oinos**.*

As stated earlier, this statement is totally erroneous. The meaning of the Greek word oinos used in the Septuagint (Greek Old Testament) and in the Greek New Testament is not restricted to fermented wine at all. Concerning the meaning of this word, Young's Analytical Concordance states, *Wine, grape juice.* Also, the Greek word oinos, is used several times in the Greek Septuagint to describe grapes in their natural unharvested state. One example of this can be found in Deuteronomy 11:14:

That I will give you the rain of your land in his due season, the first rain and the latter rain, that thou mayest gather in thy corn, and thy wine (oinos), and thine oil.

Here we see that this word refers to pure unfermented grape juice as well as fermented wine. Williamson's unsuccessful attempt to use the Septuagint to down the use of unfermented wine in the Old Testament context is ironic. In John 5:45, Jesus said:

Do not think that I will accuse you to the Father: there is one that accuseth you, even Moses, in whom ye trust.

Here Jesus is saying to the unbelieving Jews, that even Moses whom they claim to believe, his writings point an accusing finger at their hypocrisy. The same applies to Williamson and the Septuagint. The very book he clings to in support of his arguments, is the very book that strikes a deadly blow to his theory that the Bible permits the use of fermented wine.

What he fails to realize, is that the Septuagint translates Proverbs 23:20 as, *be no wine-bibber.* Or, *be not a wine-drinker*! (See part 1, chapter 9; part 2, chapter 2, for a fuller explanation). So we can see from this, that contrary to Williamson's single minded interpretation, the New Testament believers could never have found wine drinking acceptable! This is why when speaking of early Christians on page 12, the following statement by Williamson makes nonsense reading:

> *When Christians...heard that Jesus, in contrast to John, came both "eating and drinking" (Lk. 7:34) it would not offend them. Though our Lord was accused of being "a gluttonous man and a drunkard" (Lk. 7:34) they knew, from the teaching of the Old Testament, that one could lawfully eat without being a glutton and drink without being a drunkard. It would not offend them to hear that their Lord made wine for a wedding feast (John 2:1-11) because they already knew from Scripture that wine is a blessing that God provides for His people (Deut. 14:26). They did not attempt to rewrite Scriptures so as to make the word wine stand for grape juice, since they knew from Scripture that even strong drink was permitted.*

Before saying anything else, it must be stated categorically that our Lord's statement that He came eating and drinking, had no reference to Him drinking intoxicating drinks whatsoever. It was merely a statement contrasting His more open life style to the secluded Nazarite life style of John the Baptist.

As a Nazarite, John the Baptist was not permitted to eat or drink anything from the vine. When speaking of this, Williamson himself on page 16, admits this:

> *...it was not abstinence from wine alone that was reqiured. No, it was abstinence from anything and everything that came from grapes.*

Since this was the case, why then does Williamson automatically assume that it was fermented wine that Jesus was speaking of when He said that He came eating and drinking!? The following remark by Williamson on page 44, is therefore totally unjustified:

> *So even in Jesus' day there were those who did see Jesus drinking wine, and they were quite prepared to accuse Him of being a drunkard for it.*

53

It must be stated that this attempt by Williamson to make the text say such, when there is no Scriptural justification, is absolutely disgraceful. Another thing that must be stated, is that Jesus' enemies did not call Him a drunkard as Williamson would have us believe, but rather they call him a wine drinker! The Good News Bible, which is one of many, clearly reflects this:

> The Son of Man came, and he ate and drank, and you said, `Look at this man! He is a glutton and a drinker, a friend of tax collectors and other outcasts!' God's wisdom, however, is shown to be true by all who accept it. (Luke 7:34, Today's English Version)

Concerning this, Parsons states:

> It should be observed that the word rendered "wine-bibber," simply means a "wine-drinker;" yet in this passage a wine-drinker and a glutton are placed on a par, plainly showing that in those days it was a disgrace for a man to be an habitual drinker of wine...

Here we can see that when we examine the Old Testament, and indeed the whole Bible, we learn that concerning drinking, it states exactly the opposite from what Williamson claims.

Indeed, again contrary to Williamson's claims, the early Christians would have found drinking offensive as is made clear by the accusations of Jesus' enemies. Thus we can see that all Williamson's talk about the Septuagint reflecting an acceptability of drinking, is totally contradicted by the Scripture itself.

The truth of the matter is, that when one takes a closer look at the Scriptures themselves, rather than accepting what Williamson states that it says, one realizes how far from the truth and incredibly prejudiced his work really is.

On reading Williamson's book, one couldn't help noticing how he makes much of blowing his own trumpet concerning his regard for the authority and sufficiency of Scripture. Let us consider this statement of his, on page 43:

> Nothing is so important to the well-being of the Church as to acknowledge the proper authority of the Word of

*God. If the Bible is reverenced as the only infallible **and** wholly sufficient rule of faith and practice, then all is well. But when the Church begins to bind the consciences of men with man-made rules it no longer treats the Bible as the one infallible and sufficient rule.*

This statement is correct, but the unfortunate thing about this, is that Williamson himself ignores the clear and emphatic message of those same Scriptures when they differ from his viewpoint!

The first example of this that we will look at, is how Williamson interprets Genesis 40:10-11, a passage which clearly shows that pure, unfermented, and freshly squeezed grape juice was drank in Bible times. Let the reader read the plain and simple truth of the inspired text for themselves:

And in the vine were three branches: and it was as though it budded, and her blossoms shot forth; and the clusters thereof brought forth ripe grapes: And Pharaoh's cup was in my hand: and I took the grapes, and pressed them into Pharaoh's cup, and I gave the cup into Pharaoh's hand. (Genesis 40:10,11)

On reading this passage, even the most strongest and obstinate proponent of fermented wine in the Bible context, on reading this, couldn't deny without tampering with the text, that this account definitely does not refer to fermented or intoxicating wine! Now let the reader look at Williamson's interpretation of this on page 11, which reads:

The only mention of the drinking of the blood of grapes immediately after the grapes were crushed is in the vision of Pharaoh (Gen. 40:10,11), but it is probable that even here it is to be understood as fermented wine. (Cf. Deut. 32:14).

It goes without saying that Williamson's prejudice here is really incredible! The present author must confess to being unaware that there are such things as fermented grapes! The point which makes his interpretation even more farcical, is that he bases his argument for the fermented nature of the wine in the above Scriptural passage, on the strength of Deuteronomy 32:14, a text which speaks of Israel drinking the pure blood of the grape!

When we continue to examine Williamson's book, things get even worse. Especially when we consider this noble statement of his on page 33:

> *Our thesis is this, then: the true source for the conquest of sin in the heart is the power of God's Spirit...It is promoted when the Church teaches the truth of God without addition or subtraction.*

Now bearing this statement in mind, let us consider another apparently innocent statement by Williamson, which blatantly contradicts his above remarks. On page 12, he states:

> *A member of the Apostolic Church who searched the Scriptures...would also find examples of (1 Sa. 25:37) and warnings against drunkenness (Prov. 20:1; 23:29-35).*

If one takes the trouble to read the actual texts of the Scripture references given, one will find that none of them fully gives a true representation of the ideas Williamson suggests, and as he would have the reader to believe. Take for instance, the first reference, 1 Samuel 25:37, which he claims is an example of drunkenness. The verse reads:

> *But it came to pass in the morning, when the wine was gone out of Nabal, and his wife had told him these things, that his heart died within him, and he became as a stone.*

Here we see that this text is not a reference to drunkenness at all, but to completely the opposite. Admittedly Nabal had been drunk, but the above text simply states that the wine had gone out of Nabal, that is, he was now completely sober! There may be some that might say that this is being hypercritical, but this is not the case. The Bible is a sacred Book, whose ultimate purpose and goal is the transmission of *truth*. Those who seek to expound it should take the trouble to make sure that what they say about it is true.

The above example may be termed by some as a minor error, but Williamson's treatment of the other two passages is much more serious. In his above statement, he states that Proverbs 20:1, is a warning against drunkenness. Let us again read the text for ourselves:

> *Wine is a mocker, strong drink is raging: and whosoever is deceived thereby is not wise.*

Again, when we read this text, we see that it contains no warning against drunkenness whatsoever, but rather a stern condemnation of the nature and character of intoxicating beverages. It makes it clear that intoxicating beverages mocks those who *drink* them, and makes them noisey or aggressive. An exctract from John N. Moore, and Harold S. Slusher's study on alcohol, confirms the truth of this inspired text:

> *The principal effect of drinking alcohol is on the nervous system, and the higher centers are affected first. For example, a person may not distinguish between what is funny and what is obscene. He may be friendly, but then suddenly change from affability to unprovoked rage. Thus he can become an unpredictable and dangerous person, even when he might not admit that he is drunk.*

We see here that true science will always uphold the truths of Scripture. The reader therefore should heed these Scripturally based implications, instead of trying to evade them by dismissing them as *the tyranny of experts*!

The message of Proverbs 20:1 therefore, is a clear command to *abstain* from intoxicating beverages. The text does not even remotely refer to drunkenness. The fact that the inspired text *unconditionally* condemns intoxicating beverages, makes it obvious as the passage itself states, that one is deceived by such when one *drinks* of them.

The above scientific facts in confirmation of the inspired text, makes this absolutely clear. Williamson therefore is guilty, as is the case with many others, when it comes to this text, of adding to it a meaning that is totally foreign. Since his book claims that the Bible encourages the use of alcoholic beverages, and hails them as a so-called blessing, such a distortion of a passage that totally refutes this error, is hardly surprising.

The comments that Williamsomn makes concerning the final Scripture reference under examination, is only a partial reflection of the truth. Again, he claims that Proverbs 23:29-35, is a warning against drunkenness; but when we read the actual text for ourselves we get a different picture:

> *Who hath woe? who hath sorrow? who hath contentions? who hath babbling? who hath wounds without cause? who hath redness of eyes? They that tarry long at the wine; they that go to seek mixed wine. Look not thou upon the wine when it is red, when it giveth his colour in the cup, when it moveth itself aright. At the last it biteth like a serpent, and stingeth like an adder. Thine eyes shall behold strange women, and thine heart shall utter perverse things. Yea, thou shalt be as he that lieth down in the midst of the sea, or as he that lieth upon the top of a mast. They have stricken me, shalt thou say, and I was not sick; they have beaten me, and I felt it not: when shall I awake? I will seek it again.*

This passage is very interesting. The inspired writer merely gives a graphic description of the different approaches relating to drinking, and the effects of it.

The most important point is the first clause of verse 31 which states, *Look not thou upon the wine.* The writer here clearly commands that one should abstain from intoxicating wine, lest they run the risk of drunkenness and alcohol addiction, of which he again goes on to graphically describe. Concerning this, Adam Clarke's Commentary states this important truth:

> *Let neither the colour, the odour, the sparkling, &c., of the wine, when poured out, induce thee to drink of it. However good and pure it may be, it will to thee be a snare, because thou art addicted to it, and hast no self-command.*

Thus we see here that contrary to Williamson's statement, Proverbs 23:29-31, is rather more accurately a warning against *drinking!* This stance according to the passage, is the only safe way to avoid the examples given, showing the disastrous effects of drunkenness and alcohol addiction. This automatically rubbishes Williamson's statements on pages 11 and 12, that the strongest kind of wine was a blessing from God.

Another example of what appears to be another deliberate and scandalous misrepresentation of a Scripture reference by Williamson, can be found on page 10 (as stated earlier, a fuller explanation concerning this text is given in Part 1, Chapter 7). It reads:

> *Yet new wine did not mean unfermented grape juice. Hosea clearly speaks of its intoxicating properties (Hos. 4:11).*

Again, it is not until one reads the text for themselves, that one realizes that this statement is completely false. At best it is either a deliberate attempt to use the inspired text to con the non-enquiring reader into accepting his tunnel vision views as fact, or just sheer ignorance. At worst it is absolute fiction!

Hosea 4:11 does *not* speak of the intoxicating properties of new wine at all. In actual fact, the passage mentions *nothing* concerning intoxication or drunkenness whatsoever. Let us now read the text for ourselves:

> *Whoredom and wine and new wine take away the heart.*

Here we can see that regarding Williamson's remarks concerning this text, nothing can be further from the truth.

Here we can see that this text quite plainly speaks of the sins of prostitution, luxurious, and sensual appetites. The remark that these things *take away the heart* had no specific reference to drunkenness, but to the fact that these sins of indulgent living were responsible for the taking away of Israel's understanding of the true and living God. Even if this remark did specifically refer to drunkenness, the text says that whoredom (prostitution) *and* wine (Hebrew, yayin; usually intoxicating wine) *and* new wine

59

(tirosh, fresh grape juice) was responsible for this. And not solely new wine or grape juice!

If drunkenness is the subject of this text as Williamson would have us believe, and since three different things are mentioned in the text that could cause this, one is amazed why he singles out new wine as being the cause! Why not suggest that it was the obvious thing that could cause this, namely the intoxicating wine?! Or further still, why then does he not conclude that prostitution could be the cause of the so-called drunkenness mentioned. Instead he concludes from the text that drunkenness was due to new wine!

This is all the more strange when one considers the fact that neither prostitution or grape juice can make a person drunk! The reason why he singles out new wine as the cause, is clearly due to the fact that he does not want to admit that there was wine consumed in Bible times that was unintoxicating or unalcoholic. Williamson's treatment of this verse is totally erroneous. Whichever way one looks at it, this text in no way testifies that new wine had any intoxicating properties.

Williamson says what the text does *not* say, and therefore again contradicts himself. On examination of the facts, he is clearly guilty of adding his own false opinions or wishes to that of Scripture.

We can thus conclude from these examples shown, that Williamson contradicts his own above remarks, in which he states that the Church should teach the truth of God without addition or subtraction. This is due to the fact that he himself is infected with an unbelievable amount of prejudice. A prejudice which refuses to acknowledge the plainest and simplest truths of Scripture. If one claims to believe in the sufficiency, finality, and absolute authority of Scripture, and then grossly misinterprets it to suit one's own bias, then one is just as guilty as those who overtly add to or subtract from it. It has to be said, with all the passages taken out of context by Williamson, that his book is high on pretext, but low on context!

Indeed, if we adopt Williamson's own call for non-addition or subtraction to or from Scripture, as off course we should. We see that it is rather the moderation argument, and not the abstinence one that comes under fire. A further example of this can be seen from Isaiah 28:7:

> *But they also have erred through wine, and through strong drink are out of the way; the priest and the prophet have erred through strong drink, they are swallowed up of wine, they are out of the way through strong drink; they err in vision, they stumble in judgment.*

Here this text simply states that the priests and prophets erred in vision and judgment because of the use of wine and strong drinks, as well as being swallowed up with it, which could be legitimately understood as referring to drunkenness. It is not said that it was solely drunkenness that was responsible for the problem of poor vision and judgment, but rather the *use* of intoxicating beverages. The same thing is made absolutely clear in Leviticus 10:8-11:

> *And the Lord spake unto Aaron, saying, Do not **drink** wine nor strong drink, thou, nor thy sons with thee, when ye go into the tabernacle of the congregation, lest ye die: it shall be a statute for ever throughout your generations: And that ye may put difference between holy and unholy, and between unclean and clean. And that ye may teach the children of Israel all the statutes which the Lord hath spoken unto them by the hand of Moses.*

Here we can clearly see from the inspired text itself, that the priests were forbidden to minister under the influence of intoxicants because it would affect their powers of vision and judgment. Thus preventing them from being able to discriminate between what was clean and unclean. Again, nothing is mentioned concerning drunkenness, for it is the *use* of intoxicants that is the danger here.

Another important point that must be noted, is that there is also nothing said in the Scriptures that the priests were *ever* permitted to drink while *not* ministering in the tabernacle of the congregation either! Williamson is therefore again guilty of saying what the Scripture does *not* say, when he states the following concerning this text on page 15:

> *...the prohibition against the use of wine and strong drink is limited. It was only **when** the priests came to the tent of meeting to perform their duties that they were forbidden to use alcoholic beverages.*

Let the reader again read the above Scriptute text (Lev 10:8-11), and note how erroneous Williamson's statement really is. As previously stated, the Scripture passage does *not* say that the priests were ever permitted to drink at any other time. It merely makes it clear that if the priests dared to drink while ministering in the tabernacle of the congregation, the penalty would be death. When we read Isaiah 28:7 above, the clear implication we derive is that it was *never* an acceptable thing for the priests of Israel to drink.

Again, we read in Proverbs 31:4-5:

> *It is not for kings, O Lemuel, it is not for kings to **drink** wine; nor for princes strong **drink**: Lest they drink, and forget the law, and pervert the judgment of any of the afflicted.*

Here again, Lemuel is commanded to abstain from intoxicants, because *drinking* not drunkenness would cause him to err in judgment.

TOTAL ABSTINENCE A BIBLICAL PRINCIPLE

Contrary to Williamson's tunnel vision views, we learn that total abstinence is indeed an established principle which runs throughout the Bible. Concerning the subject of Abstinence, The Zondervan Pictorial Bible Dictionary correctly states:

> *The injunctions regarding drunkenness and sobriety (Eph. 5:18, 1 Tim. 3:3,8, Tit. 2:2-4, 1 Cor. 5:11, 6:9,10, etc.) point to the wisdom of total abstinence from alcoholic beverages if one would be at his best for the Lord. They are reinforced by the fact that the believer's body is the temple of the Holy Spirit (1 Cor. 6:19, II Cor. 6:16),*

and by such words as Colossians 3:17. Paul's advice to Timothy (1 Tim. 5:23) sanctions no more than medicinal use of wine mixed with water.

Abstinence is not a virtue in itself, but a means to make virtue possible.

What we learn from these facts, is that all Williamson's talk about wine not being the cause of sin, is not correct when viewed from a Scriptural perspective. We know from Scripture that man's sinful conduct emanates from his evil heart, but to say that wine does not cause sin is to be naive and simplistic. Let us consider the apostle Peter's statement in 1 Peter 2:11:

Dearly beloved, I beseech you as strangers and pilgrims, abstain from fleshly lusts, which war against the soul.

Ephesians 4:27 also warns:

Neither give place to the devil.

Williamson's suggestion that one should encourage converted alcoholics to drink at the Lord's Table on the grounds of the so-called Spirit's power, is again totally refuted by Scripture. On page 25, he states:

Those who argue that wine at the Lord's Table threatens the converted alcoholic virtually deny the power of the Holy Spirit. "They fail," as Prof. J.G. Vos puts it, "to take the power of the Holy Spirit into their reckoning." What the Church should do, in dealing with such persons, is not to educate them in falsehood - by making them think that there is more power in a little wine than there is in the third person of the God-head. No, it should teach them the truth. The truth is that there is not - and never was - any destructive power in wine.

The same Spirit whom Williamson refers to, refutes his erroneous statement when He inspired these words:

Wine is a mocker, strong drink is raging: and whosoever is deceived thereby is not wise. (Proverbs 20:1)

63

Those today who have ended up ruining themselves through alcohol, obviously failed to take the power of intoxicating spirits into their reckoning! They would not have done so if they had heeded the wise warnings of this Spirit inspired text. The same Spirit also states, *Look not thou upon the wine when it is red...* (Prov 23:31) The same Spirit goes on to explain (Prov 23:31-35) that the reason one should do this, is to avoid drunkenness and alcohol addiction! The Spirit inspired text also makes it plain that abstinence is imperative because the power to make one an alcoholic lies within the alcohol itself!

Admittedly, not everyone who drinks gets drunk, but the deceptive effects on someone who is under the influence of alcohol is sometimes worse than when one is obviously drunk. The Scriptures relegate Williamson's arguments to mere simplistic nonsense.

Alcohol addiction is really no different to being addicted to cocaine, marijuana, or any other dangerous drug. Should we then encourage Christians to regularly take these drugs as proof of the Spirit's power, as Williamson suggests on page 26, in the case of wine?! Or should we also encourage converted drug addicts to go back to taking these drugs, assuring them that addiction would not occur because of the Spirit's power?

Alcoholic beverages are dangerous and destructive. The Scriptures command that we abstain from such. God will only help us when we fill ourselves with the right Spirit!

These passages clearly settle the question as to the nature of the wine our Lord created at the marriage feast in Cana, recorded in John 2:1-11. It obviously was a pure unfermented wine or grape juice. Ironically, Williamson himself unwittingly reasons out this Scriptural truth on page 25! His statement reads:

> *If even a little wine could cause the sin of drunkenness, then surely our Lord would never have done this thing.*

SUMMING UP THE ERRORS OF
THE DEMON DOCTRINE CHARGE

In summing up Williamson's book in the light of Scripture, the conclusion that we come to is that his main argument is false. To suggest that those who advocate total abstinence from alcoholic beverages are espousing a doctrine of demons is indeed outrageous.

His arguments against the so-called prohibitionists can only be described as wild sensationalism, to put it mildly. His attempt on page 8, to put the temperance movement on parallel with the movement for enforced celibacy in the medieval Church, is again an outrageous charge. This combined with his talk of Protestantism and the Reformation on page 29, his reference to the noble convictions of Luther on page 2, and his continual appeals to the Westminster Confession, appears to be nothing more than a "subtle" attempt to gain support for his arguments from hard core Protestant evangelicals.

By smearing the temperance movement as a popish like regime, and by appearing to have the backing of those who only submit to the voice of Scripture, one can be easily conned into automatically thinking his views are right without even looking at Scripture!

All his talk seems good at face value, until one puts them under the scrutiny of Scripture. If Williamson had given as much attention to Scripture as he did in quoting the Westminster Confession, then his arguments would have certainly been more accurate.

One can quote great sounding creeds affirming one's faith in Scripture as much as one likes, but actually applying that faith is another thing. One must not forget that despite the great contribution that Luther made towards the Reformation, he himself on occasions fell short of his own noble calls that Scripture alone should govern our conduct!

To use Williamson's own words on page 39, his book is basically a thesis of one-sided propaganda!

CHAPTER 7

AN IN DEPTH DEFENCE OF
THE ABSTINENCE POSITION

Judge not according to the appearance, but judge righteous judgment. Jesus Christ (John 7:24)

Ye judge after the flesh. Jesus Christ (John 8:15)

But in vain do they worship me, teaching for doctrines the commandments of men. Jesus Christ (Matthew 15:9)

Ye do err, not knowing the scriptures. Jesus Christ (Matthew 22:29)

One must bear these Scriptures in mind from the lips of our Lord Himself when seeking to correctly interpret and understand God's precious Word. In preparing this material, the author has read various books and commentaries, including the Jewish Talmud, on the subject of drink. Unfortunately, many scholars and commentators are guilty of the sharp rebukes of the above Scriptures in their interpretation of the sacred Book.

We are grateful for other useful literature that can be used to aid our understanding of the Bible, but they must not be taken as totally authoritative. The Bible, God's revelation of Himself and His perfect holiness in Jesus Christ is our sole and absolute authority. The way some scholars write, one would think that the Talmud was the Bible!

There are many things in the Talmud that are wrong and out of line with Scripture, they are merely the traditions of men. One only has to open the Bible and read Jesus' word's to know that.

Many scholars today *err, not knowing the Scriptures,* despite their learning, just like the rabbis in Christ's time. The present author is well aware of the fact that not all those who believe that the Bible and indeed Christ Himself, endorses the drinking of alcoholic beverages are deliberately sinful, as much of it is just down to a lack of understanding of the subject, and the sinful influence of society today. This is why when one suggests that the Bible speaks of unalcoholic wine or grape juice as well as the fermented kind, it is scoffed at and frowned upon by many.

The purpose of this section is to defend the cause of total abstinence and to put right some of the narrow minded errors that have been taught and written on this subject.

The first set of arguments that we will examine, are from an article entitled *Wine-Drinking in New Testament Times,* written by Robert H. Stein, which was published in the magazine "Christianity Today" in 1975. In introducing his subject, he states:

> *My subject here is the use of the term "wine" in the New Testament. Some readers may already be thinking, "Is he going to try to tell us that wine in the Bible means grape juice?..." ...No, the wine of the Bible was not unfermented grape juice. Yes, it was different from the wine of today.*

Basically this statement is erroneous, for it is not accurate to make a general and sweeping statement concerning the nature of wine in the New Testament, because people drank many different kinds of wines.

His argument is that "wine" in New Testament times was a fermented beverage that was mixed with water. He quotes various ancient authorities in support of his argument. Speaking of wine, he states:

> *The ratio of water might vary, but only barbarians drank it unmixed, and a mixture of wine and water of equal parts was seen as "strong drink" and frowned upon. The term "wine" or oinos in the ancient world, then, did not mean wine as we understand it today but wine mixed with water.*

Certainly these views were held by many ancient writers, but these views conflict with the teachings of Scripture. Isaiah 1:21,22 explains:

> *How is the faithful city become an harlot! it was full of judgment; righteousness lodged in it; but now murderers. Thy silver is become dross, thy wine mixed with water.*

Wine as well as other things, is used here to figuratively condemn the corrupt and rebellious condition of the inhabitants of the city of Jerusalem. Albert Barnes' comments give us a clear insight into this:

> *Wine was regarded as the most pure and valuable drink among ancients. It is used, therefore, to express that which should have been most valued and esteemed among them-to wit, their rulers...According to Gesenius, the word rendered mixed-mahul-is from mahal, the same as mul, to circumcise; and hence, by a figure common with the Arabians, to adulterate, or dilute wine...Wine mixed with water is that which is weakened, diluted, rendered comparatively useless. So with the rulers and judges, they had lost the strength and purity of their integrity, by intermingling those things which tended to weaken and destroy their virtue, pride, the love of gifts, and bribes, &c. Divested of the figure, the passing means, that the rulers had become wholly corrupt.*

Here we can see that the Scriptures and indeed the Jews do not regard fermented wine mixed with water as being "wine" at all, but rather the opposite. If this were the case in the Old Testament then this would certainly be the case in New Testament times, irrespective of certain opinions and customs. In actual fact, the Jews were so unaccustomed to mingling their wine with water, that when they spoke of mixing wine they referred to the strengthening of wine by the addition of certain ingredients. Adam Clarke's comments on Isaiah 1:22 explains:

> *It is remarkable that whereas the Greeks and Latins by mixed wine always understood wine diluted and lowered*

with water, the Hebrews on the contrary generally mean by it wine made stronger and more inebriating by the addition of higher and more powerful ingredients, such as honey, spices, defrutum (or wine inspissated by boiling it down to two-thirds or one-half of the quantity), myrrh, mandragora, opiates, and other strong drugs.

We learn here that to the Hebrew mind which was conditioned by God in order to be instrumental in the revelation of holy Scripture, *to whom pertaineth the adoption, and the glory, and the covenants, and the giving of the law, and the service of God, and the promises;...* (Romans 9:4), that Stein's arguments concerning "wine" totally collapses. All he can appeal to is gentile tradition and unscriptural opinions of the rabbis in support of his argument. He again states the following:

And we do have examples in both Jewish and Christian literature and perhaps in the Bible that wine was likewise understood as being a mixture of wine and water. In several instances in the Old Testament a distinction is made between "wine" and "strong drink."

We have already seen from examination of the Scriptures that this statement is incorrect. As to the point concerning the Bible's reference to "wine" and "strong drink," it must be stated categorically that this does not at all refer to wine mixed with water and unmixed wine respectively.

The Hebrew word for wine (yayin) corresponds to the Greek word for wine (oinos). Young's Analytical Concordance says of yayin, "Wine, grape juice." This refers to a fermented or unfermented beverage, depending on the context. The word usually translated "strong drink" in the Bible (Hebrew, shakar, shekar) has no reference to undiluted wine whatsoever. In actual fact, it is a generic term for a fermented or unfermented solution that did not come from the grape! However, it generally referred to a strong fermented beverage. Kitto's Cyclopedia explains:

Shakar is a generic term, including palm-wine and other saccharine beverages, except those prepared from the vine.

The Scriptures therefore do not support Stein's arguments, which are built on the opinions and traditions of men. Scriptures such as Leviticus 10:8,9; Numbers 6:3; Deuteronomy 14:26; 29:6; Judges 13:4,7,14; 1 Samuel 1:15; Proverbs 20:1; 31:4,6; Isaiah 5:11, 22; 28:7; 29:9; 56:12; and Micah 2:11, when referring to wine and strong drink respectively, meant just that, with the above Scriptural definitions.

Again, in support of his argument, he mentions the fact that the 1901 Jewish Encyclopedia states that in the rabbinic period at least, wine (yayin) is that which is mixed with water, and strong drink (shekar) is diluted wine. Again this is irrelevant. The Bible was completed centuries before the Jewish Encyclopedia of 1901, which has obviously been heavily influenced by the teachings of the rabbis. The point to be taken note of here, is that irrespective of what the definitions were during the rabbinic period, it does not make an ounce of difference to the teachings of Scripture.

From these traditions and opinions he then seeks to build an argument for the nature of the wine that Jesus used when He instituted the Lord's Supper. He states:

> *In the Talmud, which contains the oral traditions of Judaism from about 200 B.C. to A.D. 200, there are several tractates in which the mixture of water and wine is discussed. One tractate (Shabbath 77a) states that wine that does not carry three parts of water well is not wine. The normal mixture is said to consist of two parts water to one part wine. In a most important reference (Pesahim 108b) it is stated that the four cups every Jew was to drink during the Passover ritual were to be mixed in a ratio of three parts water to one part wine. From this we can conclude with a fair degree of certainty that the fruit of the vine used at the institution of the Lord's Supper was a mixture of three parts water to one part wine.*

This method of hermeneutics (the method of interpreting the Bible text) seems very suspect indeed. The traditions of men is not the way of truly determining the actions of our Lord, since as stated earlier, many of them were out of line with Scripture. This fact is very important. Brian H. Edwards gives us a clear insight into Christ's view towards this:

> *The Jewish Rabbis, or teachers, had added six hundred and thirteen laws of their own to God's laws. Two hundred and forty-eight of these were positive and three hundred and sixty-five were negative. Many of them were ridiculous...Our Lord gave no authority to such nonsense as this, and never at any time did he discuss or quote approvingly the foolish teaching of the Rabbis. But even on a more serious note He refused to accept the way the Pharisees mis-interpreted and abused Scripture.*

Let us consider Christ's words again:

> *This people draweth nigh unto me with their mouth, and honoureth me with their lips; but their heart is far from me. But in vain do they worship me, teaching for doctrines the commandments of men.* (Matthew 15:8,9)

Since Jesus did not recognise the subjective teachings of the rabbis, and thus blatantly and openly disregarded their laws. It is amazing how Stein can attempt to build a case for Christ's teaching or conduct with as he puts it, *a fair degree of certainty,* from these same man made laws!

He also appeals to the writings of the early church fathers in support of his theory that the wine Jesus used at the Lord's Supper was a fermented beverage, which was mixed with water. A typical example is his quote of Cyprian (approx A.D. 250), which reads:

> *Nothing must be done by us but what the Lord first did on our behalf, as that the cup which is offered in remembrance of Him should be offered mingled with wine....Thus, therefore, in considering the cup of the Lord, water alone cannot be offered, even as wine alone cannot be offered. For if anyone offer wine only, the blood of*

71

Christ is dissociated from Christ....Thus the cup of the Lord is not indeed water alone, nor wine alone, unless each be mingled with the other. (Epistle LXII,2,11 and 13)

He also quotes Justin Martyr (approx. A.D. 150), Hippolytus (approx. A.D. 215), and Clement of Alexandria (early 2nd. century), all of which state that the wine used at the Lord's Supper (Eucharist) was to be mixed with water. It must be again stated categorically that these are all the opinions and traditions of men, which are not to any degree substantiated by Scripture. No matter how noble the intent of these or any traditional practices, they are of no binding authority or relevance if their origin is not from Scripture. In Jack Cottrell's book *The Authority of the Bible,* he explains this point:

> *Traditional practices are not necessarily wrong, of course. What is wrong, and what must be avoided, is elevating fallible human applications of Biblical principles to the level of Scripture itself. Scripture alone has binding authority.*

According to Ephesians 2:20, the church is *built upon the foundation of the apostles and prophets, Jesus Christ himself being the chief corner stone,* and not upon the early church fathers! The writings of the early church fathers was written years after Jesus' institution of the Lord's Supper, and thus has no real authoritative significance in the application of Scriptural truth, despite the established custom in the ancient world of mixing water with wine, as Stein irrelevantly mentions:

> *Unmixed wine and plain water at the Lord's Supper were both found unacceptable. A mixture of wine and water was the norm.*

Cottrell again ably gives the Biblical principle of exactly how to treat or react to this or any other custom:

> *Recognising the Bible's sufficiency as the sole **norm** for faith and life does not mean that we exclude and ignore completely the use of human reason, traditions, and*

*interpretations. On the contrary, we should continue to use them even more than ever, but only as **aids** to **understanding** the Bible and applying it to our lives, not as authoritative norms.*

He goes on to explain how any information should be viewed in the light of the Bible's absolute authority:

Books, commentaries, sermons, lessons, and informed opinions and interpretations of all kinds may help us to understand the meaning of the Bible, even though the Bible alone is the final authority. We do not use such things in order to judge the Bible; the Bible must always judge them.

Indeed when we allow the Scriptures to judge the teachings of the rabbis, the practices of the ancient Greeks, and the writings of the early church fathers, we have to reject the diluted wine theory as a suitable explanation of the nature of the wine used at the Lord's Supper.

If Christ had intended that the wine, which was to symbolise His precious blood, was to be diluted with water as a Biblical principle, He would have clearly stated it. In Paul's discourse on the Lord's Supper in 1 Corinthians 11, which he *received of the Lord,* he mentions nothing about diluting wine. Here we can see the danger of trying to build a doctrine on something, which the Bible is silent about. Stein himself admits:

When we come to the New Testament the content of the wine is never discussed.

Evangelicals are supposed to believe in the sufficiency and finality of Scripture. Trying to make the Scriptures fit a multiplicity of views from extra Biblical material, leads to nothing but confusion.

In the Old Testament accounts of the Passover, nothing is mentioned concerning the cup. Alfred Edersheim, eminent Jewish scholar expains:

The use of wine in the Paschal Supper, though not mentioned in the Law, was strictly enjoined by tradition.

73

Jesus attached a new, spiritual, and authoritative meaning to the Passover cup, which he calls the *fruit of the vine*. Which is naturally the pure unfermented juice of the grape. Proverbs 20:1 states, *Wine is a mocker,* not, *mix it with water.* Therefore Christ would not have used alcoholic and intoxicating wine. The Lion Concise Bible handbook ably explains this principle:

> *It is interesting that the New Testament makes no distinction between what `Scripture' says and what God says. Old Testament quotations are given as what God said, even though God was not the speaker in the Old Testament context. Conversely, words spoken by God in the Old Testament narrative are ascribed to `Scripture'. Where Jesus led the way in His acceptance of the Old Testament as the word of God, the New Testament was content to follow. If we Christians set our own judgement or our own inherited traditions above the Old and New Testament scriptures, we part company with the Lord and the apostles, and cut ourselves off from our one source of knowledge of God.*

Here we can see the vital need to stick strictly to the Scriptures for rules of Biblical interpretation. If we use the Bible as our fixed reference point everything falls into place.

To say that the only kind of wine that was drank in New Testament times was fermented shows wilful ignorance and unfairness, as there is an abundance of evidence (if one looks for it) to show that sweet and unfermented wine was also used. The Zondervan Pictorial Bible Dictionary states:

> *Means for preserving grape-juice were well known: Cat, De Agri Cultura CXX has this recipe: "If you wish to have must (grape-juice) all year, put grape-juice in an amphora and seal the cork with pitch; sink it in a fishpond. After 30 days take it out. It will be grape-juice for a whole year."*

Also, another important point that we must not forget is that just because wine was mixed with water, is not a sufficient argument to prove that it was fermented. It must be remembered that the ancients also used to boil their wines down to a thick treacle or syrup to prevent fermentation. Patton explains:

> There is abundance of evidence that the ancients mixed their wines with water; not because they were strong, with alcohol, as to require dilution, but because, being rich syrups, they needed water to prepare them for drinking. The quantity of water was regulated by the richness of the wine and the time of year.

Edersheim also gives us an extensive list of a variety of fermented and unfermented wines used in New Testament times (See part 2, "Introduction").

It is clear that Stein's arguments are well intentioned, this cannot be denied. But they are unsatisfactory because they lack real Scriptural force and create more problems than they solve.

Stein concludes his arguments by implying that one should abstain from today's intoxicating beverages on the grounds that they are stronger than the diluted fermented beverages of the ancients. He writes:

> If the drinking of unmixed wine or even wine mixed in a ratio of one to one with water was frowned upon in ancient times, certainly the drinking of distilled spirits in which the alcoholic content is frequently three to ten times greater would be frowned upon a great deal more.

There were many things that Jesus did that were frowned upon by many, but they certainly weren't wrong! All Stein has succeeded in doing is to relegate total abstinence to something optional. One will have to produce a stronger argument to uphold total abstinence than that!

In the opinion of the author, Stein's arguments are basically an attempt to reach a compromise between those who flatly reject and scorn the idea of unfermented grape juice in the Bible context. And those who do accept it as a reasonable explanation in the light of the Bible's condemnation of intoxicating beverages. As we have seen, this attempt to soft pedal the principle of total abstinence has proved to be confusing, as one is left to decide from a multiplicity of subjective views quoted from ancient writers (at least 10), as to what ratio of water mixed with fermented wine was acceptable. One is also left with the problem of how a God of wisdom and love could sanction the use of a drug, which is dangerous and addictive, whether it is mixed with water, or not.

There really isn't any other way of explaining away the alcohol problem. Either the Bible is for the use of this drug or it is against it. In upholding the cause of total abstinence, one must take a stand against alcohol *totally* as is the case with Proverbs 20:1:

> *Wine is a mocker, strong drink is raging...*

One must understand that the uncompromising stance, and the unambiguous message of the Bible alone, must be our sole guide in determining what is right and what is wrong. One must not feel intimidated by liberal minded critics into seeking to find an explanation which might not offend them, and which may basically suit everyone.

Contrary to the views of the narrow-minded critics, grape juice *was* drunk in Bible times as an alternative to fermented wine. In the same way it is available today for those who desire it.

We will now take a look at some arguments of those who either seek to dismiss the possibility of the drinking of unfermented grape juice, or call into question its feasibility or usefulness in the Bible context.

THE FRUIT OF THE VINE

In order to reduce to nothing the arguments of those who rightly say that Jesus' reference to the "fruit of the vine" in Matthew 26:29, obviously refers to unfermented grape juice, it is stated that the Greeks also used the term "fruit of the vine" as a synonym of wine which was capable of producing intoxication (Herod.i.211 f.).

The answer to this "problem" is very simple. The institution of the Lord's Supper was a perfection of its Old Testament type, the Passover (Exodus 12). During the Passover **no** fermented things were permitted (Exodus 12:15, see Part 2, Chapter 2, for a fuller explanation). The revelation of this concept to the Jewish mind is fundamental to our understanding of this truth. Thus when Jesus referred to the fruit of the vine, it was even more obvious to the Jewish mind that this was an unfermented substance than it was to the non-Jew.

Even though the Jews strayed concerning Christ, their importance in the transmission of Scriptural truth was vital, as the Scripture itself states concerning them:

> *...to whom pertaineth the adoption, and the glory, and the covenants, and the giving of the law, and the service of God, and the promises; Whose are the fathers, and of whom concerning the flesh Christ came, who is over all, God blessed for ever. Amen.* (Romans 9:4,5)

The Greeks were simply ignorant of the truths of God's Word right throughout their history. If the Jews strayed concerning Christ, shall we rely on Greek interpretation? This is why the Greeks could not understand the conception of an infinitely holy God revealed in His Son Jesus Christ:

> *But we preach Christ crucified, unto the Jews a stumblingblock, and unto the Greeks foolishness*
> (1 Corinthians 1:23)

Again, using Scripture is the best way of interpreting Scripture.

Another way in which some seek to down grade the use of grape juice or unfermented wine in the Bible context, is by stating that the ancient writer Pliny, regarded must (sweet wine) as hurtful to the stomach (Hist. Nat. XXiii. 18). Along with this, Luke 5:39 is often quoted to give strength to the conception that old wine (fermented) was better. But if anyone ever takes the trouble to read Pliny's, or any other of the accounts of ancient writers on the subject of wine for themselves, they will find that there were many different types of must (sweet wine) which varied in strength, mixture etc., and not all of them caused stomach aches.

Some expositors never seem to mention the accounts of the disastrous effects which some of the alcoholic wines caused. To present facts in such a fashion is unfair and deliberately misleading to the unacquainted reader. Christ does not give his approval to old wine (fermented), but rather the opposite as the text makes clear:

> *No man having drunk old wine straightway desireth new: for he saith, The old is better.* (Luke 5:39)

Christ did not say he preferred old wine, but that those who were used to drinking it did. It is obvious from the text that Jesus considered new wine to be much superior than old wine, since He figuratively uses it to present His Kingdom. This alone makes it clear that the literal wine He created was new and unfermented (John 2:1-11). Since Jesus makes it clear that new wine is better, it has to be better, for there can be no greater authority than His

DIFFICULT PASSAGES

We will now examine at length some Scripture verses, which have appeared to pose problems in terms of their consistency, regarding the use and effects of the different types of wines.

Some scholars have misinterpreted certain passages, which have caused confusion to the reader who is sincerely trying to find out God's view on this important subject. It must be remembered that "God is not the author of confusion." The Bible is consistent in its message regarding holiness and sin. It must be understood that when the Bible speaks of new or sweet wine, it always means wine that is unfermented and unintoxicating, irrespective of what some Bible scholars may think, and whoever they may be.

It must also be noted that the Bible *never* endorses the use of alcoholic drinks, regardless of how difficult the passage may be, or what it may appear to say. Professor Moses Stuart states:

> *My final conclusion is this, viz., that whenever the Scriptures speak of wine as a comfort, a blessing, or a libation to God, and rank it with such articles as corn*

and oil, they can mean only such wine as contained no alcohol that could have a mischievous tendency; that wherever they denounce it, and connect it with drunkenness and revelling, they can mean only alcoholic or intoxicating wine.

If the individual stands on these solid principles of interpretation, understanding the text becomes much easier. The first passage we will examine reads:

Whoredom and wine and new wine take away the heart. (Hosea 4:11)

Some expositors have determined from this that new wine (tirosh) must have been intoxicating as well as wine (yayin). This is not the case. Let the reader note that the verse says *nothing* specifically about drunkenness.

The text merely states that pleasure seeking acts and sensuality on Israel's part would take away their understanding of God. The Bible Knowledge Commentary explains:

*The scope of the accusation widened to include the **people** in general. Sensual pleasures had robbed them of their senses, leaving them without **understanding**. They engaged in pagan worship practices, including divination (seeking answers **by a stick of wood**), sacrificed to false gods, and engaged in cult **prostitution**.*

This clearly refutes the arguments of those who erroneously try to use this verse to prove that new wine could produce drunkenness, and was hence intoxicating.

Another truth that they fail to communicate, is that the inspired text actually says:

Whoredom (prostitution) and wine (yayin, intoxicating) and new wine (tirosh, sweet unfermented) take away the understanding.

Notice it says the three combined took away the heart! It does not say that new wine was responsible for taking away the heart. The Theological Wordbook of the Old Testament says of the word tirosh:

*...apparently the fresh juice from the vineyard, **never by itself** associated with intoxication.*

So we can see that even if the verse was actually speaking of drunkenness, no intoxicating properties can be associated with new wine (tirosh) from this text. Fausset's Bible Dictionary gives us a good explanation concerning this text:

> *the tirosh is denounced not as evil in itself, but as associated with whoredom to which wine and grape cakes were stimulants...*

The next passage reads:

> *And I will feed them that oppress thee with their own flesh; and they shall be drunken with their own blood, as with sweet wine: and all flesh shall know that I the Lord am thy saviour and thy redeemer, the mighty one of Jacob.* (Isaiah 49:26)

This is another passage that some scholars erroneously use to prove that new or sweet wine was intoxicating. On examination of the text, we will see that this error is due to a superficial understanding of the passage. There are various views regarding this verse, but one thing we must bear in mind, is that sweet wine does not intoxicate.

Some say that the juice that flowed from the grapes before they were pressed in the vat began to mildly ferment, and that this verse was likened to the fact that it would take a large amount to make one intoxicated. Such an attempt to explain away this text does not make sense, for it was impossible for one to become intoxicated from fresh juice that had just flowed from grapes. Also, if we take such an inventive view to explain this text by maintaining that new or sweet wine had intoxicating potential, we would have to admit that we would be accusing Jesus of atleast encouraging drunkenness, when He changed water into approximately 120-180 gallons of wine.

The Hebrew word for "drunken" in the above text is shakar, and can mean, to "be drunken," to be "filled with drink," "be merry," and to "drink abundantly." Young's Concise Critical

Commentary makes it clear that the word translated "drunken" (shakar) in the above text, by the Authorized Version, is an unfortunate one, given the context of the passage. It states:

> *DRINK ABUNDANTLY, or `are merry;' as in Ge. 21; 43. 24; Lam. 4. 21; Nah. 3. 11.*

Here we can see quite clearly that this text cannot be legitimately used as an argument for the intoxicating nature of new wine at all. If this word as used in this verse is taken in context, the thought is that Israel's oppressors are merry through killing as they drink abundantly (metaphorically, to thirst after blood) of their own blood.

In various places in the Old Testament we read of the joy that was experienced in drinking new wine. Here we can see that the same degree of joy that was derived from drinking sweet wine, God's precious gift, was the same degree of joy that Israel's oppressors would derive from shedding blood. Matthew Henry explains:

> *See how cruel men sometimes are to themselves and to one another. They not only thirst after blood, but drink it with as much pleasure as if it were sweet wine.*

Young's Literal Translation also echoes this thought:

> *And I have caused thine oppressors to eat their own flesh, And as new wine they drink their own blood.* (Isaiah 49:26a)

The next passage that has caused difficulty, is the accusation made against Jesus' disciples of being drunk on the day of Pentecost. The text reads:

> *Others mocking said, These men are full of new wine. But Peter, standing up with the eleven, lifted up his voice, and said unto them, Ye men of Judea, and all ye that dwell at Jerusalem, be this known unto you, and hearken to my words: For these are not drunken, as ye suppose, seeing it is but the third hour of the day.* (Acts 2:13-15)

Some have concluded from this that because of the accusation of drunkenness levelled at Jesus' disciples, that new wine was intoxicating and that Christ's disciples must have habitually drank it. This was simply not the case. New wine was not intoxicating.

The Greek word translated "new wine" is gleukos, from glukus, which means sweet, which is where the English word glucose is derived from. This showed how intensely sweet the wine was which alone refutes the argument for fermentation. Because when fermentation sets in the sugar turns to alcohol, which takes away the sweetness! Concerning this, Grindrod states:

> *Wine, moreover, is known to lose its sweetness, in proportion to the extent of fermentation; a large portion of the saccharine matter being thus converted into alcohol. This fact may be considered as demonstrative evidence of the unfermented nature of the wine under consideration.*

The evidence for this fact is overwhelming. Donnegan's Lexicon defines the word gleukos as:

> *new, unfermented wine-must.*

Professor C. Anthon's Dictionary definition reads:

> *The sweet, unfermented juice of the grape is termed gleukos.*

Green's Lexicon defines gleukos (new wine) as:

> *the unfermented juice of the grape, must; hence, sweet new wine. Acts ii.13. From glukus, sweet. Jas.iii.11, 12; Rom.x.9,10.*

Smith's Greek and Roman Antiquities states:

> *The sweet, unfermented juice of the grape was termed glukos by the Greeks, and mustum by the Romans; the latter word being properly an adjective, signifying new or fresh.*

Dr. Patton's comments on these facts states:

> *Science teaches that, when by fermentation the sugar is turned into alcohol, the sweetness of the juice is gone.*

82

> *Thus, sweet means, as the lexicons state, unfermented wine.*

Grindrod's comments on Acts 2:13, reads:

> *The false and libellous charge made by certain bystanders on the Day of Pentecost, in reference to those who were filled with the Holy Ghost, is not a sufficient proof that intoxicating wine was in use among the people of those days, as a common beverage. The word used in the original, gleucos, signifies wine, sweet and new, and consequently unfermented. It was thus understood by Plautus, who flourished about two hundred years before the birth of Christ.*

Kitto's Cyclopedia (ii.955) informs us that the ancient Jewish historian Josephus, uses the Greek word translated "new wine" (gleukos) in Acts 2:13, to apply to the fresh juice of the grape which was squeezed into Pharaoh's cup! (Genesis 40:10,11), obviously unfermented.

Unfortunately, despite these facts, there are Bible scholars who concerning this text, judge "according to the appearance" rather than by common sense reasoning. An example of this is Vincent's comments on the nature of the "new wine" in our above text, in which he says it was, "Of course intoxicating."

Dr. E. Robinson first correctly defines the meaning of the word gleukos as, "must-grape-juice unfermented," but on the strength of the false accusation levelled at Jesus' disciples in Acts 2:13, he contradicts himself by adding:

> *Acts ii.13: Sweet wine, fermented and intoxicating.*

Here we can see the danger of relying too much on the interpretations of scholars, because at times they are influenced more by their own prejudices and the prejudices of others, rather than the plain and obvious facts. Vincent's comments generally on the New Testament, show him to be a vehement opponent of the principle of unfermented grape juice.

It is only fair though that we deal with any objections to the unfermented wine principle, by giving an explanation for the word translated "new wine," as used in Acts 2:13. And to give a reasonable explanation which is certainly warranted, why this word was associated with drunkenness in the text.

One notion put forward to suggest that the "new wine" (gleukos) spoken of in Acts 2:13 must have been intoxicating, is that no grapes would be available to make fresh grape juice, because eight months had elapsed since the previous vintage. This is no problem, because means of preserving wine sweet and unfermented for up to a year were known. Means were also known for preserving fruit fresh for a long time. Concerning the capture of Masada, the Jewish historian Josephus writes:

> As for the furniture that was within this fortress, it was still more wonderful on account of its splendour and long continuance; for here was laid up corn in large quantities, and such as would subsist men for a long time; here was also wine and oil in abundance, with all kinds of pulse and dates heaped up together...These fruits were also fresh and full ripe, and no way inferior to such fruits newly laid in, although they were a little short of a hundred years from the laying in these provisions...when the Romans got possession of those fruits that were left, they found them not corrupted all that while.

For those sceptics who consider this to be somewhat exaggerated, there are others such as Swinburn, who testify to the fact that grapes were preserved fresh for at least a year, which is all that would be required at the minimum.

Having established that any objections to the obvious fact that the word translated "new wine" (gleukos) in Acts 2:13, was pure unfermented grape juice is not based on scientific facts, but due to a misunderstanding of the word and the text respectively, we will now proceed in examining the meaning of the text. Albert Barnes' comments on the use of the word gleukos (new wine) in Acts 2:13, reads:

This word properly means the juice of the grape which distils before a pressure is applied; it was called must. It was sweet wine, and hence the word in Greek meaning sweet was given to it. The ancients, it is said, had the art of preserving their new wine with the peculiar flavour before fermentation for a considerable time, and were in the habit of drinking it in the morning.

Peter's reply in Acts 2:15, stating that they were not drunk, was not an admission that "new wine" (gleukos) could intoxicate, but revealed the folly of the accusers, because it was only nine in the morning, and before this time on the Sabbaths and solemn feasts, the Jews did not eat or drink.

Another point to be noted, is that those who made the accusation did not say, "these men are drunk," which is all that would have been required to say; but they said, "These men are full of new wine," something which was impossible, thus making the laughter or mockery more sarcastic.

In effect what they were really doing was deriding the disciples of Christ for being different in that they did not drink etc. They were also saying, "these men are mad." It was the only type of foolish accusation that could be made against these men of Christ that they knew did not indulge in intoxicating drinks. The Zondervan Pictorial Bible Dictionary give us an excellent explanation of why the disciples of Christ may have been accused of being drunk on unfermented wine (gleukos):

...gleukos, new, sweet wine; or grape juice; which may imply that the disciples, known to drink only unfermented grape juice, in their exuberant enthusiasm appeared intoxicated.

If we look again into the Scriptures we will see that Christ's disciples could not have drank any intoxicating drinks. In Luke 7:34-35, it states:

The Son of Man is come eating and drinking; and ye say, Behold a gluttonous man, and a winebibber, a friend of publicans and sinners! But wisdom is justified of all her children.

Jesus' enemies call Him a winebibber (wine-drinker) which Jesus refutes by saying, "But wisdom is justified of all her children." The "But" in verse 35 is negative, thus showing that He fully denies all the false charges made against Him, and that this denial would be fully justified by the life of His disciples. This proved to be true. This is why they were accused of drinking unfermented grape juice, it proved Jesus right. This would not have come as a surprise to the disciples, but rather to be expected, taking into consideration the wise warnings of their Master:

> *It is enough for the disciple that he be as his master, and the servant as his Lord, If they have called the master of the house Beelzebub, how much more shall they call them of his household?* (Matthew 10:25)

Here we can see that we must not base our judgements upon the words of the enemies of God. As Jesus said:

> *Judge not according to the appearance, but judge righteous judgment.* (John 7:24)

The next passage reads:

> *And the drink offering thereof shall be the fourth part of an hin for the one lamb: in the holy place shalt thou cause the strong wine to be poured unto the Lord for a drink offering.* (Numbers 28:7)

The translation of this verse is unfortunate, because it misleads the reader into thinking that reference is being made to an alcoholic drink offering, when this is in fact, not the case. The original Hebrew word translated "strong wine," is shekar (sometimes written, shakar or shecar). We have already observed earlier in the section entitled, *Important Principles of Interpretation,* that this word is generic and can therefore refer to any drink, whether sweet and unfermented, or strong and intoxicating.

It can also refer to palm wine, which is unfermented wine as sweet as honey. On examination of this text, we will again learn a beautiful lesson concerning the law of context, and the self-interpreting character of the inspired Book.

First of all it is necessary to reinforce the argument that the Hebrew word shekar (shakar, shecar), usually translated "strong drink," is largely misunderstood, regarding its origin and true meaning, which does not always refer to a an intoxicating beverage such as beer. The Reverend B. Parsons explains:

> *Shacar, from the verb, to satisfy, to please, to make merry, or yield perfect satisfaction. It is highly probable that the term originally meant what was sweet or delightful either to the body or the mind. We have before stated that the Hebrew shacar, the Arabic, saccharon, the Greek, sachar, the Latin saccharum, the French sucre, and the English sugar, have all sprung from the same original root, and have all the same primary meaning; for in each language sweetness is the primitive idea. In arabic, both `honey', and palm wine, which, when first made, or before it becomes acid, is as sweet as honey, were called `saccharon.'*

These very important facts are also highlighted in Dr. F.R. Lees' Bible Commentary, which states:

> *... `saccharine drink', is related to the word for sugar in all the Indo-Germanic and Semetic languages, and is still applied throughout the East, from India to Abyssinia, to the palm sap, as well as to sugar and to the fermented palm-wine. It has by usage grown into a generic term for `drinks,' including fresh juices and inebriating liquors other than those coming from the grape.*

He also states:

> *SHAKAR (sometimes written shechar, shekar) signifies `sweet drink' expressed from fruits other than the grape, and drunk in an unfermented or fermented state.*

Now in returning to the text, we will see that the Scriptures themselves vindicate these facts, which means that erroneous interpretations of Numbers 28:7, which have caused confusion must be correctly understood. Some Bible translations which reflect these errors, translate Numbers 28:7, as follows:

> *Then the libation with it shall be a fourth of a hin for each lamb, in the holy place you shall pour out a libation of strong drink to the Lord.* (New American Standard Bible)

> *And the drink offering thereof shall be the fourth part of an hin for one lamb: in the holy place shalt thou pour out a drink offering of strong drink unto the Lord.* (Revised Version)

> *Its drink offering shall be a fourth of a hin for each lamb; in the holy place you shall pour out a drink offering of strong drink to the Lord.* (Revised Standard Version)

> *The accompanying drink offering is to be a fourth of a hin of fermented drink with each lamb. Pour out the drink offering to the Lord at the sanctuary.* (New International Version)

> *Its drink offering shall be the fourth of a hin for each lamb; in the holy place you shall pour out a fermented drink offering to the Lord.* (Amplified Bible)

Unfortunately these are not contextually accurate translations. Here too much emphasis is put on the traditional interpretation of the original Hebrew word shekar, which in the light of Scripture does not make sense.

If this verse is to be interpreted this way, it would mean that God approved of the use of alcohol, something which He Himself commanded the priests to abstain from when ministering, on penalty of death (Leviticus 10:9). Also the drink offering consisted of nothing else but wine as Exodus 29:40; Leviticus 23:13; Numbers 15:5,7,10; 28:14 make absolutely clear. Keil and Delitzsch's Commentary on the Old Testament also points out this fact, and gives us a contextually sound understanding of the Hebrew word shekar as it is used in Numbers 28:7:

> *Shecar does not mean intoxicating drink here, but strong drink, in distinction from water as simple drink. The drink-offering consisted of wine only.*

88

Here we can see that this verse did not refer to any fermented drinks at all. The Authorized or King James Version translators knew very well that the drink offering did not include strong drink but wine only. And so when confronted with the Hebrew word shekar which described this wine, they opted for a translation which maintained this fact, and so rendered shekar, "strong wine."

Although not an accurate rendering, it is certainly better than the above translations we have just looked at. The wine used in the drink offering was obviously sweet and unfermented, and that is why the word shekar is used in its unfermented sense. That is, "sweet drink." The fact that shekar is used in the Bible to refer to a sweet drink, is evident from a correct understanding of Isaiah 24:9, which reads:

> They shall not drink wine with a song; strong drink (shekar) shall be bitter to them that drink it.

The clause we are concerned with here, should be translated "sweet drink shall be bitter to them that drink it," the sharp contrast in words (from sweet to bitter) makes this an obvious fact. Unfortunately, the translation does not bring this out, and as we can see, does not make sense. Young's Analytical Concordance renders the Hebrew word shekar in this case as, "Sweet drink (what satiates or intoxicates)."

We will now take a look at two key passages concerning the drink offering which emphasizes the sweetness of the wine and the delight God took from this:

> And for a drink offering thou shalt offer the third part of an hin of wine, for a sweet savour unto the Lord. (Numbers 15:7)

> And thou shalt bring for a drink offering half an hin of wine, for an offering made by fire, of a sweet savour unto the Lord. (Numbers 15:10)

Here we can see that wine, amongst other things, was to produce a sweet smelling savour to the Lord, this naturally ties in with the fact that a sweet unfermented wine would produce a sweet smelling effect! How incongruous to suggest that a strong and intoxicated substance could contribute to this, or even be accepted.

We have learnt from our study of Numbers 28:7 and the other texts relating to it, that the Scriptures themselves endorse the fact that the word usually translated "strong drink" in the Old Testament (shekar, shakar, shecar), does not always refer to a strong alcoholic or intoxicating substance. We have also learnt from a study of this word, that "sweet drink" is an alternative rendering, depending on the context. Kitto's Cyclopedia sums this up:

> Shakar is a generic term, including palm-wine and other saccharine beverages, except those prepared from the vine.

Numbers 28:7 should therefore read:

> And the drink offering thereof shall be the fourth part of an hin for one lamb: in the holy place shalt thou cause the sweet drink (unfermented palm-wine) to be poured unto the Lord for a drink offering.

In the Bible God never approves of alcoholic beverages. Let us consider the following text:

> Do not drink wine nor strong drink, thou, nor thy sons with thee, when ye go into the tabernacle of the congregation, lest ye die: it shall be a statute for ever throughout your generations: And that ye may put difference between holy and unholy, and between unclean and clean. (Leviticus 10:9-11)

Notice how abstinence from alcohol is essential for being able to discriminate between clean and unclean, the text goes on to read:

> And Moses spake unto Aaron, and unto Eleazar and unto Ithamar, his sons that were left, Take the meat offering that remaineth of the offerings of the Lord made by fire, and eat it without leaven beside the altar: for it is most holy. (Leviticus 10:12)

Regarding the prohibition of leaven in all offerings by God in Leviticus 2:3-14, Professor Moses Stuart states:

> *The great mass of the Jews have ever understood this prohibition as extending to **fermented wine**, or strong drink, as well as to bread. The word is essentially the same which designates the fermentation of bread and that of liquors.*

Here we can see that leaven (fermented dough) was regarded as the same as vinuous fermentation; therefore fermented wine, strong drink, and leaven were all prohibited before the altar of the Lord "for it is most holy."

The next passage reads:

> *And thou shalt bestow that money for whatsoever thy soul lusteth after, for oxen, or for sheep, or for wine, or for strong drink, or for whatsoever thy soul desireth: and thou shalt eat there before the Lord thy God, and thou shalt rejoice, thou, and thine household.*
> (Deuteronomy 14:26)

Those proponents of moderation with respect to intoxicating beverages might suggest that this text sanctions and encourages the drinking of beer and alcoholic wine. To be fair, it appears to be so, but this is not the case. In examining this passage we will learn that the book of Deuteronomy furnishes us with a perfect example of the following:

(a) A correct understanding of the generic words which are used for "wine" and "strong drink" respectively.

(b) A proper application of the law of context.

(c) A complete understanding of God's view on the subject of drinking.

Now in returning to the text, we will see that the Bible itself conclusively refutes any suggestions whatsoever that this text endorses the use of alcoholic drinks.

We have already learnt in our studies that the words translated "wine" (yayin) and "strong drink" (shekar) here are generic, and may refer to fresh grape juice and a sweet pleasant drink which was unfermented. What kind of beverage is this verse referring to? Since it may be argued that this text can be interpreted according to one's own particular bias. The answer is very simple. Deuteronomy 29:6 explains:

> *Ye have not eaten bread, neither have ye drunk wine or strong drink: that ye might know that I am the Lord your God.*

Here this passage proves that the "wine" and "strong drink" in chapter 14:26, cannot be the same as that mentioned here! The inspired text later goes on to explain in no uncertain terms exactly what kind of wine the Jews did drink. It reads:

> *Butter of kine, and milk of sheep, with fat of lambs, and rams of the breed of Bashan, and goats, with the fat of kidneys of wheat; and thou didst drink the pure blood of the grape.* (Deuteronomy 32:14)

Here Moses names among the many blessings of the Lord, pure fresh grape juice, known as "the blood of the grape," which was highly esteemed. We will now take a look at some comments on this. Adam Clarke's Commentary states:

> *Red wine, or the pure juice of whatever colour, expressed from the grapes, without any adulteration or mixture with water: blood here is synonymous with juice. This intimates that their vines should be of the best kind, and their wine in abundance, and of the most delicious flavour.*

The Reverend B. Parsons also gives an interesting explanation:

> *Red was considered the best juice; pure, that which was unfermented and unmixed; thick that which had been boiled or spissated; or, rather, that the juice was very thick, saccharine, or sirupy. The text, therefore, means thou didst drink the purest, the sweetest, and the richest blood, or juice, of the grape.*

We thus learn from examination of these three passages (Deut 14:26; 29:6; 32:14) that the children of Israel in their wilderness wanderings were blessed with the most finest and nutritious delicacies from God. They did not eat bread as part of their regular diet, but were blessed with manna (Deut 8:3,16; 29:6). They did not drink intoxicating wine (Deut 29:6), but pure fresh grape juice (Deut 14:26; 32:14). Neither did they drink other strong intoxicating drinks (Deut 29:6), but drank the sweet, unfermented and pleasant juice of other fruits (Deut 14:26).

We also learn that God approved of unfermented drinks of health giving character, these were highly esteemed among the Jews. We also learn a vital and valuable lesson that the original words used for "wine" and "strong drink" may refer to an intoxicating substance as well as a non intoxicating one, and that these must be judged in context.

Most good scholars understand that the word usually translated "wine" (yayin) refers to unfermented as well as fermented wine. An example of this is The Bible Knowledge Commentary, which states the following concerning its use in Deuteronomy 14:26:

> *The Hebrew word for "wine" is yayin, which sometimes means an intoxicating beverage and other times means a nonintoxicating drink.*

Few however, realize that the same applies to "strong drink" (shekar). Its permissible use in Deut 14:26, and the statement later in 29:6, that the Jews *never* drank it or wine, is not a contradiction, but is a confirmation which declares without a shadow of a doubt that "strong drink" (shekar) and "wine" (yayin) referred to a fermented juice as well as an unfermented one, depending on the context.

Our opening text therefore (Deut 14:26), does not make any allowances for the drinking of alcoholic wine or other intoxicating substances such as beer, but rather the opposite, i.e. fresh grape and other fruit juices, as a correct understanding of the scriptural application of the law of context makes clear.

Before concluding our study on these texts, there is another important point that must be dealt with and understood for the

93

sake of the critics. This concerns the term "pure blood of the grape," used in Deuteronomy 32:14.

Objections may be raised against the unfermented nature of the wine (grape juice) because of the word translated "pure" in the King James or Authorized Version. The Hebrew word is chemer, which means to ferment, foam, or to be red, as in wine. Here is what certain authorities say concerning this word. Strong's Exhaustive Concordance:

> wine (as fermenting):-pure, red wine.

The Theological Wordbook of the Old Testament: "Wine."
Young's Analytical Concordance:
(1) "Fermented."
(2) "A thick, sticky syrup."
Dr. F.R. Lees' Biblical Commentary says that chemer:

> ...is a word descriptive of the foaming appearance of the juice of the grape newly expressed, or when undergoing fermentation.

Translations of the last clause of Deuteronomy 32:14, vary:

> and you drank wine of the blood of the grape.
> (Amplified Bible)

> and of the blood of the grape you drank wine.
> (Revised Standard Version)

> You drank the red blood of the grape.
> (New International Version)

> with the grapes' blood-you drank it foaming!
> (Moffatt Bible)

> And of the blood of the grape thou dost drink wine!
> (Young's Literal Translation)

We know that the latter part of this verse could not read, "and thou didst drink the fermented blood of the grape," or a fermented "fiery wine," as Keil and Delitzsch's Commentary states, since this would contradict the Scriptures that we have examined. Having already observed that this passage could not refer to intoxicating wine, it is still necessary to thoroughly answer any further objections by proving conclusively from the Scriptures themselves that the Hebrew word chemer (sometimes written hemer or khemer) when used in this text refers only to the pure, red, sweet, and unfermented juice (blood) of the grape. A clear outline of the reasons are as follows:

(a) Deuteronomy 29:6 expressly states that the Israelites did not drink wine or strong drink.

(b) The Septuagint (An early Greek translation of the Hebrew) which was the Bible of Christ, the Apostles and the early church basically translates the last clause of Deut 32:14 as, *and of the red blood of the grape you drank wine.* Here we receive a vital understanding of the early Christians understanding of the Hebrew word chemer, which judging by the translation refers to the redness of the grape juice which is an exaltation of its sweetness and fine quality. No idea of fermentation is conveyed by the translation whatsoever.

(c) Proverbs 23:31,32 states:

> *Look not thou upon the wine when it is red, when it giveth his colour in the cup, when it moveth itself aright. At the last it biteth like a serpent, and stingeth like an adder.*

The red wine spoken of here obviously cannot be the same as the red wine or, "blood of the grape" mentioned in Deut 32:14, which is hailed as a blessing from God. The bubbling or foaming process involved in the fermenting of the red and strong intoxicating wine described in Proverbs 23:31, is brought out more clearly by the Amplified Bible's rendering of the passage, which reads:

> *Do not look at wine when it is red, when it sparkles in the wineglass, when it goes down smoothly.*

Apart from the obvious context, note how the inspired writers in these two texts specifically make it plain that they

95

are referring to alcoholic and non-alcoholic wine respectively. Deut 32:14 describes the very red, fresh, sweet wine (grape juice) as the "blood of the grape."

(d) The Hebrew word translated "pure" (chemer), in Deut 32:14, is also used in Isaiah 27:2 (the only other place where it is used in the Bible), which reads:

In that day sing ye unto her, A vineyard of red wine.

The Hebrew word chemer, in this verse is translated into two words, "red wine." This obviously refers to fresh grape juice, because you cannot have a vineyard of alcoholic wine!

Some manuscripts instead of chemer, read chemed, which means pleasantness, beauty, or beloved. The use of this word is reflected in the Septuagint translation, which reads, "Beautiful vineyard." However, most manuscripts of the Hebrew use the word chemer, which in any case proves that wherever this Hebrew word is used in the Bible, no sense of fermentation is intended.

(e) The use of the term "blood of the grape," makes it absolutely clear that the juice is new and fresh as it is in the grape cluster. This is a principle employed by the inspired authors of the Bible to guard against any ambiguity. Thereby making it impossible (unless wilfully) for them to be misunderstood.

This technique was also used by Christ in the New Testament approximately 1400 years later, when He specifically describes unfermented wine as "the fruit of the vine" (Matthew 26:29; Mark 14:25; Luke 22:18).

The term "blood of the grape," always refers to fresh grape juice, as Genesis 49:11 makes plain:

Binding his foal unto the vine, and his ass's colt unto the choice vine; he washed his garments in wine, and his clothes in the blood of grapes.

Moses, the inspired writer of the Pentateuch (the first five books of the Law), when again referring to fresh grape juice in Deuteronomy 32:14, uses the same term as the inspired speaker in Genesis 49:11. The Reverent B. Parsons explains the use of the term "pure blood of the grape," used in Deuteronomy 32:14:

> *This word being used with the expressions "Dam Anabim, the blood of the grape," affords very strong evidence that the liquor drunk was not fermented; for a fermented liquor can never with any propriety be called "the pure blood of the grape."*

This explains why the Authorized or King James Version (abbreviated A.V or K.J.V) translators inserted the word "pure" to describe the "blood of the grape." This showed that they understood the juice to be unfermented or uncontaminated by alcohol.

Strong's Exhaustive Concordance explains that the reason why the Authorized Version used the word "pure," is because it is a multiplication which:

> *denotes a rendering in the A.V. that results from an idiom peculiar to the Hebrew.*

The "blood of the grape" also came to symbolize the blood of our Lord. This is reflected in Mark 14:24:

> *This is my blood of the new testament.*

That is, the fruit of the vine. Since the fruit of the vine refers to the pure unfermented juice of the grape, the KJV translators were justified in using the word "pure" to describe the "blood of the grape" in Deuteronomy 32:14, as this is certainly Biblically sound.

In concluding our study of these texts, it must be said that one has to admire the self-interpreting mechanism of Scripture. If in the area of drink one correctly applies the same principles, which constitutes this, as can be done in any other area of Biblical studies, the truth will be clearly understood as we have just demonstrated.

The next text reads:

> *And in this mountain shall the Lord of hosts make unto all people a feast of fat things, a feast of wines on the*

lees, of fat things full of marrow, of wines on the lees well refined. (Isaiah 25:6)

Some expositors point out that "wines on the lees" were wines that were left to stand for a long time after fermentation. The lees were the tiny particles of grape skin (dregs, sediment) which would eventually sink to the bottom of the container. It is also pointed out that "wines on the lees well refined," referred to the process of straining off the lees (sediment) after the wine was strong and fully fermented. If this line of interpretation is strictly followed, this passage could read:

> *And in this mountain shall the Lord of hosts make unto all people a feast of rich things, a feast of fermented wines, of fat things full of marrow, of wines well refined, strong and alcoholic.*

Obviously we have a problem here. In the light of God's Word such an interpretation is impossible. If expositors would sometimes consider the far reaching implications of some of their statements with prayer, caution, and Biblical scrutiny, then what they wrote would make more sense, and be more Biblically sound.

One cannot doubt that the facts mentioned above were practised, but the fact that the Lord uses such terms as a symbol of spiritual blessings is enough to tell us that this verse needs more than a superficial glance in order to correctly understand it.

It is a fact that fermented wines were left to stand on their lees as commentators such as Barnes, Clarke, Delitzsch, and others point out; but to assume that the above verse refers to this practice is another thing, as unfermented wines were also allowed to stand in this way. Also, the word translated "lees" in this verse (shemarim) can also refer to the preserving of wines. Young's Literal Translation of this verse explains:

> *And made hath Jehovah of Hosts, For all peoples in this mount, A banquet of fat things, a banquet of preserved things, Fat things full of marrow, preserved things refined.*

Just exactly how the wine was preserved one cannot be sure, but there is definitely a need for understanding the full scope of the words used in this text before attempting to interpret this passage. The Rev. B. Parsons explains:

Shemarim, is derived from shamar, to preserve, and the word literally means "preserves;" it sometimes refers to "lees," or "dregs," but this cannot be its meaning in Isaiah 25:6. There it signifies "preserved wine," or "preserves;" for no one can suppose that God would promise to make all people a feast of "refined lees," or "refined dregs." Indeed the idea of its being lees or dregs is contradicted by the assertion that it was well defecated or filtered. How this preserve was made, or in what manner the wine was preserved, we cannot say. The juice may have been kept in the same manner as Columella directs, or it may have been boiled down to a sirup, as we find was the case with most wines in Palestine. Its being "well refined or filtered" seems exactly to correspond with the words of Pliny. "Utilissimum vinum omnibus sacco viribus fractis;" "The very best wine is that which has had its strength broken by the filter." It is worthy of remark that the word zacac, used by the prophet, and rendered "well refined," is the same word as the Latin "saccus, a filter." and in Latin sacco has the same signification: and it is not a little remarkable that both the Roman naturalist and the Jewish prophet should have used the very same word to express the manner in which the very best wine was produced: Pliny says, "The best wine is that which has had its strength broken by the filter;" and Isaiah tells us, "In this mountain will the Lord God make unto all people a feast of fat things full of marrow, of preserved wines well refined or well filtered." Plutarch asserts that the most esteemed wines, and esteemed because because they would not intoxicate, were those which had been well refined or filtered: and Columella also directs that the filter should be used in making sweet or unfermented wines...; nor when he condescends to feast the nations, will give them wine which may be termed "saluberrimum" and "utilissimum:" most useful and most wholesome.

Leupold also explains that the wine has to be wholesome:

*If the wine is stressed first as being particularly good, that may be due to the fact that a feast is called a **mishteh**, "a drinking," but without any unwholesome connotation.*

This is merely a matter of common or Biblical sense! Alcoholic wines are not wholesome, they simply pollute and enfeeble the human system.

Those like Andre Bustanoby, who suggest that this text permit the drinking of alcoholic beverages, have simply not understood the text. On pages 53-56 of his book *The Wrath of Grapes,* Bustanoby uses Isaiah 25:6, to maintain his argument for the use of alcoholic or fermented wine. On page 53, Bustanoby comments on this text by stating:

Another passage that permits alcohol use is in Isaiah 25.

He quotes Delitzsch's Commentary on this passage which reads:

Shemarim mezukkakim are wines which have been left to stand upon their lees [dregs or sediment] after the first ferment is over, which have thus thoroughly fermented and which have been kept a long time (from shamar, to keep,) spec. to allow to ferment, and which then are filtered before the drinking..., hence the wine is both strong and clear.

Christians need not be alarmed by this commentary, for this reflects a liberal and narrow-minded application of the key words used. R.B. Grindrod gives us a more fuller explanation of the text and the words used, which is absolutely vital for a correct understanding of the text. He states:

Shemarim, from Shamar, to keep, to keep safe, to preserve. The word shemarim is used in the scripture to express the dregs or lees of wine whether unfermented or fermented. Biblical writers labour under the impression that this word when used in the Old Testament, has reference only to a liquor strongly intoxicating. This, however, is not the case. In Isaiah, allusion evidently is made to unfermented wine...This feast was to be celebrated on Mount Zion, and had reference to the establishment of Christ's kingdom. The blessings of the gospel are frequently represented in the scriptures under the image of a feast. How incongruous to suppose that one of the articles of this feast would consist of intoxicating wine, made yet more potent by being allowed to remain on its lees. Fatness, moreover, is a word applicable only to unfermented wine, which retains its original and natural qualities. In the original of this passage, there is no mention of wine. The words shemarim mezukkakim, mean "well preserved, or well strained." They may also be applied to honey and to other articles of a similar description. Some product of the vine, however, is probably meant. Bishop Lowth translates the words "fat things, " a "feast of delicacies," "of delicacies exquisitely rich." Eustathius speaks of wine as forming a portion of delicate food for infants; it could not, therefore, be possessed of stimulating or inebriating properties.

As mentioned previously, methods were known of preserving wine for a long time in its unfermented state. The fact is that new wine was also left to stand on its lees just the same as old wine as we have just learnt. The difference is that while the lees (dregs, skin particles) added to the strength of old wine (alcoholic), the lees in the new wine (unfermented) merely added to its sweetness and colour. Marshall's Bible handbook also brings out this point:

> *The dregs of wine (lees) were used to improve the flavor, colour, and strength of new wine. "Wines on the lees well*

refined" (Isa. 25:6) referred to a rich full-bodied wine -
a symbol of the blessings of the feast of the Lord.

Let us further consider the following:

> But on the new wine being allowed to stand, this princi-
> ple would subside by natural gravity; hence the ancients
> poured off the upper and luscious portion of the wine into
> another vessel, repeating the process as often as neces-
> sary, until they procured a clear, sweet wine which would
> keep. (Kitto, ii.955 Roman Antiquities)

Another confirmation that wine standing on its lees, did not
always refer to alcoholic or fermented wine, is scientifically
explained by Dr. William Patton:

> Chemical science teaches that the gluten may be so effec-
> tually separated from the juice by subsistence as to
> prevent fermentation. The gluten, being heavier than the
> juice, will settle to the bottom by its own weight if the
> mass can be kept from fermentation for a limited period.
> Chemistry tells us that, if the juice is kept at a tempera-
> ture below 45 degrees, it will not ferment. The juice being
> kept cool, the gluten will settle to the bottom, and the
> juice, thus deprived of the gluten, cannot ferment.

We have thus learnt from a thorough examination of the text
and the facts concerning wine that it is totally unjustified to
automatically assume that Isaiah 25:6 refers to the drinking of
alcoholic or intoxicating wine.

Most expositors agree that this verse refers to the commencement of the Messiah's Kingdom on Mount Zion in
Jerusalem. The Amplified Bible explains:

> And on this Mount [Zion] shall the Lord of hosts make
> for all peoples a feast of rich things [symbolical of His
> coronation festival inaugurating the reign of the Lord on
> earth, after the background of gloom, judgment and ter-
> ror], a feast of wines on the lees, of fat things full of
> marrow, of wines on the lees well refined.

Let us now observe that in the New Testament when Jesus, who was thoroughly consistent with the Old Testament, mentioned the symbolic wine of His Kingdom, it was always new wine (Matt 9:17; Mark 2:22; Luke 5:37,38). The wine He drank and is to drink in His Father's Kingdom is new wine of superior quality (the fruit of the vine, unfermented; Matt 26:29; Mark 14:25; Luke 22:18). Therefore it is Scriptural and logical that the wine mentioned in Isaiah 25:6, could only be new wine, sweet, harmless, natural, and unfermented.

We will now see again that it is an obvious fact that the type of wine referred to must be judged in context. In Psalms 75:8 it states:

> For in the hand of the Lord there is a cup, and the wine is red; it is full of mixture; and he poureth out of the same: but the dregs thereof, all the wicked of the earth shall wring them out, and drink them.

The important thing to note is that the Hebrew word translated "dregs" (shemarim) is the same word translated "lees" in Isaiah 25:6, but notice how the writer makes it clear that this time the wine is well fermented by explaining, *the wine is red; it is full of mixture*. The Amplified Bible states, *...the wine foams and is red*. This describes the change in colour and the gas bubble process of fermentation. Note that in Isaiah 25:6, this is not included because the writer intended us to understand that the wine was unfermented. Again, it is obvious, for the wine that the wicked are to drink cannot be the same kind of the wine that the Lord has specially reserved as a blessing for His people!

The last problem passage that we will examine in this section reads:

> Thou shalt not delay to offer the first of thy ripe fruits, and of thy liquors: the firstborn of thy sons shalt thou give unto me. (Exodus 22:29)

The word translated "liquors" here, does not refer to alcoholic beverages, but means a liquid or juice. The Amplified Bible clarifies this point:

You shall not delay to bring to Me from the fullness [of your harvested grain] and the outflow [of your grape juice and olive oil];... (Exodus 22:29a)

Here this verse gives further force to the idea that the wine that was to be offered to God in other passages, was grape juice, i.e. wines sweet and unfermented.

BIBLE TERMS WHICH DISTINGUISH GRAPE JUICE FROM ALCOHOLIC WINE

Apart from the original Hebrew and Greek words used in the Bible, there are certain terms that are used by the writers which makes it obvious that there were two types of wines used, i.e. fermented and unfermented. First of all we will examine the case of alcoholic or fermented wine:

Wine of astonishment. (Psalm 60:3)

The very fact that the writer uses the term "wine of astonishment" or "wine which makes one reel and be dazed," shows without a shadow of a doubt that there was wine which *did not* make one drunk, i.e. wine which was unfermented. Barnes explains the meaning of the word translated "astonishment" and the meaning of the passage:

> *It means properly reeling, drunkenness; and the idea here is, that it was as if he had given them a cup-that is, an intoxicating drink-which had caused them to reel as a drunken man...*

If there was only intoxicating wine used in Bible times as some suggest, the writer would have only been required to say, *thou hast given us wine.*

Wine which is red and full of mixture. (Psalm 75:8)

We have already looked at this verse earlier, so we will just look at an additional viewpoint from Barnes, which states:

> *The true idea in the expression is probably that it ferments; and the meaning may be that the wrath of God*

seems to boil like fermenting liquor. Mixed with spices, in order to increase its strength; or, as we should say, drugged. This was frequently done in order to increase the intoxicating quality of the wine.

Wine is a mocker. (Proverbs 20:1)

Here wine is described as a "mocker." Surely Jesus did not create between 120-180 gallons of a substance which His Bible describes as a "mocker"! The fact is, that it is alcoholic or intoxicating wine which is being described here, which makes it clear that the wine our Lord created could not have been alcoholic. Note that there is no room for so called moderation or "temperance," the very use of the terminology makes it clear that abstinence from alcoholic wine is meant.

Strong drink is raging. (Proverbs 20:1)

Although we are mainly concentrating on wine in this section because it was commonly drank, this statement makes it plain that all other strong and intoxicating drinks were forbidden.

Wine of fornication (or wine associated with fornication). (Rev 17:2; 18:3)

Here again in this text, is another example that makes plain the intoxicating nature of the wine concerned.

We will now look at terms which describe unfermented wine:

Wine that maketh glad the heart of man. (Psalm 104:15)

Here it is obvious that the wine referred to here was fresh unfermented grape juice. Since the passage states that it is God that graciously bestows it upon man as a blessing for his health. Unfortunately, there are those who would grossly misinterpret this passage by saying that the gladness mentioned in the text was the stupor that was derived from drunkenness. Such an interpretation is utter nonsense.

It is only a matter of common sense that the virtuous qualities mentioned above for health, happiness, and vigour is not derived from alcoholic wine. Such wine does not exhilarate the heart and brighten the countenance, but dullens the perception and damages health.

> *Wine which sustains.* (Genesis 27:37)
>
> *Wine which is blessed by God.* (Deuteronomy 7:13)
>
> *Good wine.* (John 2:10)

We have learnt a valuable lesson from the terminology employed in the various above texts that there were undoubtedly two kinds of wine in use in Bible times. Intoxicating (alcoholic) and non-intoxicating (non-alcoholic). Understanding these principles is an excellent method of determining the nature of the wine the Bible is speaking of in any particular given context.

INSPIRED WORDS FROM THE BOOK OF JOEL

The writer of the book of Joel gives us an interesting and inspired understanding of the nature of the wine being referred to, by his rendering of different Hebrew words to convey whether God approved or disapproved of its use. Whenever wine is spoken of as a blessing from God, the writer uses Hebrew words that only convey the meaning of sweet unfermented grape juice. When referring to wine in the negative or sinful sense he uses a word which frequently means intoxicating wine.

The Hebrew words which he uses are yayin, which means wine in its fermented or unfermented state, and the words asis and tirosh, which *always* means sweet unfermented grape juice. We will now look at the passages that speak of wine unfavourably. Let us carefully observe the Hebrew words used:

> *Awake, ye drunkards, and weep; and howl, all ye drinkers of wine, (yayin) because of the new wine; (asis) for it is cut off from your mouth.* (Joel 1:5)

New wine had no intoxicating properties, as Jamieson, Fausset and Brown's Bible Commentary states:

wine...new wine-"New" or "fresh wine," in Hebrew, is the unfermented, therefore unintoxicating, sweet juice extracted by pressure from grapes or other fruit, as pomegranates.

New wine is only mentioned in the above text because the vintage from which *any* wine could be made would be cut off. F.A. Tatford states:

The devastation had been complete: every green thing had been devoured and the vines had suffered with all other plants. The intoxicated, sunk into inebriated slumber, were called upon to awake and to realise that the vintage had been ruined. The wine which stupefied them-a concoction of honey, raisins, dates and grapes-would no longer be available, since its ingredients had been destroyed. The sweet wine or must, made from the fresh juice of grapes, pomegranates or other fruits, could no longer be made: the fruit had perished. Pictorially, the prophet declared that the drink, which delighted these wine-bibbers, was cut off from their mouths.

The next passage reads:

And they have cast lots for my people; and have given a boy for an harlot, and sold a girl for wine, (yayin) that they might drink. (Joel 3:3)

The utter depravity of this passage speaks for itself, these winebibbers had such a low regard for human life that they sell a girl for wine!

The following passages on the subject of wine in the book of Joel, speaks of wine as a luxurious and precious commodity which was a blessing from God; but let us now note the change in the Hebrew words used (bracketed) to describe this:

The field is wasted, the land mourneth; for the corn is wasted: the new wine (tirosh) is dried up, the oil languisheth. (Joel 1:10)

Yea, the Lord will and say unto his people, Behold, I will send you corn, and wine, (tirosh) and oil, and ye shall be satisfied therewith... (Joel 2:19a)

And the floors shall be full of wheat, and the fats shall overflow with wine (tirosh) and oil. (Joel 2:24)

And it shall come to pass in that day, that the mountains shall drop new wine, (tirosh) and the hills shall flow with milk, and all the rivers of Judah shall flow with waters, and a fountain shall come forth of the house of the Lord, and shall water the valley of shittim. (Joel 3:18)

The wine (tirosh), often translated "new wine," mentioned in chapter 2:24 above, also included the fresh juice while it was still in the grape cluster. In the same way as the oil (olive oil) spoken of referred to the oil to be crushed out of the olives which were still in their natural state, as the passage clearly indicates. F.A. Tatford commenting on Joel 2:24, writes:

In consequence, the grain would fill the threshing floors, and the new wine and fresh oil (i.e. the grapes and olives to be crushed) would fill the vats to overflowing.

The Amplified Bible's rendering of the above Passages, brings out this truth more clearly:

The field is laid waste; the ground mourns, for the grain is destroyed, the new grape juice is dried up, the oil fails. (Joel 1:10, Amplified Bible)

Yes, the Lord answered and said to His people, Behold, I am sending you grain, and grape juice, and oil, and you shall be satisfied with them... (Joel 2:19a, Amplified Bible)

And the [threshing] floors shall be full of grain, and the vats shall overflow with grape juice and oil. (Joel 2:24, Amplified Bible)

And in that day, the mountains shall drip with fresh fruit juice, and the hills shall flow with milk, and all the brooks and river beds of Judah shall flow with water; and a fountain shall come forth from the house of the Lord and shall water the valley of Shittim. (Joel 3:18, Amplified Bible)

In this book we have learnt a precious lesson concerning God's view of wine and drinking, due to the inspired writer's careful and accurate rendering of the original Hebrew words, when speaking of wine.

Although the Hebrew word yayin meant anything pressed from the grape (translated "wine"), the fact that the writer always used this word in a negative sense, while contrasting it with the more specific Hebrew words (asis and tirosh, which only meant unfermented grape juice) when speaking of God's blessings, shows clearly that God condemns the abuse of the fruit of the vine, i.e. drinking it in its fermented or intoxicating state!

WINE IN THE SONG OF SOLOMON

In this book there are many references to wine, which speaks of it as a precious and virtuous commodity. This book furnishes us with good examples of how one must pay attention to context with respect to wine in the Bible. Throughout the Song of Solomon, the generic word for wine is used (yayin), and the context of the passages makes it clear that the wine is to be understood as being unfermented or non alcoholic. These passages read:

Let him kiss me with the kisses of his mouth: for his love is better than wine. (Song of Solomon 1:2)

Draw me, we will run after thee: the king hath brought me into his chambers: we will be glad and rejoice in thee, we will remember thy love more than wine: the upright love thee. (Song of Sol 1:4)

How fair is thy love, my sister, my spouse! how much better is thy love than wine! and the smell of thine ointments than all spices! (Song of Sol 4:10)

I am come into my garden, my sister, my spouse: I have gathered my myrrh with my spice; I have eaten my honeycomb with my honey; I have drunk my wine with my

109

milk: eat, O friends; drink, yea, drink abundantly, O beloved. (Song of Sol 5:1)

Here in the immediate above passage it is obvious that the wine spoken of is unalcoholic for would not a call to "drink abundantly" be an endorsement of drunkenness?! The Hebrew word translated "drink abundantly," is shakar, which in this case and a few others does not refer to drunkenness, but to drinking to satisfaction. Concerning the use of the word in this passage, Young's Analytical Concordance states, "To drink to satiety." The Theological Wordbook of the Old Testament states:

With very few exceptions shakar and its derivatives are used in a highly unfavourable and negative context. But the few passages where the root is used in an acceptable sense should be observed.

It goes on to quote some passages including the Song of Solomon 5:1, and concludes:

Thus of almost sixty uses of the root shakar, only five refer to something good and acceptable.

The Scriptural evidence then, clearly shows that the admonition to "drink abundantly" was therefore fitting, since the wine was good and acceptable, and thus unintoxicating!

The other passages that speak of wine in this book, read:

And the roof of thy mouth like the best wine for my beloved, that goeth down sweetly... (Song of Solomon 7:9)

...I would cause thee to drink of spiced wine of the juice of my pomegranate. (Song of Sol 8:2b)

It is amazing how throughout this book that love the greatest of all virtues, which has its ultimate origin in God, is compared with or likened to wine.

The book of the Song of Solomon is traditionally attributed to the wise king Solomon because of the many references to him (1:1,5; 3:7,9,11; 8:11). How do scholars then explain why Solomon in his other book, the book of Proverbs, continually condemns the very use of wine (yayin, Proverbs 20:1;

23:20,31) and praised its use in the Song of Solomon? The answer to this question is very simple. One wine was intoxicating, wild and inflaming; and the other was sweet, unintoxicating and health giving!

INSPIRED WORDS FROM
THE BOOK OF NUMBERS

The book of Numbers furnishes us with conclusive evidence that both fermented and unfermented juices were used in Bible times. In God's instructions to Moses concerning the conduct of the Nazarite, we read:

> *He shall separate himself from wine and strong drink, and shall drink no vinegar of wine, or vinegar of strong drink, neither shall he drink any liquor of grapes, nor eat moist grapes, or dried. All the days of his separation shall he eat nothing that is made of the vine tree, from the kernels even to the husk.* (Numbers 6:3,4)

The writer is here is very specific. In this text he describes every connotation in which the juice of the grape (Hebrew, yayin) and other fruit juices (translated "strong drink;" Hebrew, shekar) were commonly used. On close examination of this inspired text, we will see that it destroys the arguments of those one track minded individuals who insist that when the Bible refers to "wine" and "strong drink" respectively, it always speaks of a fermented beverage.

In verse 4 of the above text, the Nazarite is commanded to separate himself from "wine" (Hebrew, yayin) and "strong drink" (Hebrew, shekar). This is a clear reference to unfermented wine and the juice of other fruits, because the prohibition is then extended to "vinegar of wine" and "vinegar of strong drink." The Hebrew word translated "vinegar" in each case is chomets, which means *anything* fermented. Concerning this text, Today's Dictionary of the Bible states:

> *In Num. 6:3, "vinegar of wine" is more correctly "fermented wine."*

111

Clarke's Bible Commentary states:

> *chomets signifies fermented wine, and is probably used here to signify wine of a strong body, or any highly intoxicating liquor.*

What we learn from this text then, is that the Hebrew word usually translated "wine" (yayin) meant as Young's Analytical Concordance puts it, "What is pressed out, grape juice." This could be either fermented or unfermented. Equally, the Hebrew word shekar, usually translated "strong drink," referred to any beverage apart from the juice of the grape, which was either strong and intoxicating or sweet and unfermented. Thus when this word is being used in its unfermented sense, "sweet drink" is the proper translation.

An alternative translation of Numbers 6:3,4 could thus be rendered:

> *He shall separate himself from wine and sweet drink, and shall drink no fermented wine, or fermented sweet drink, neither shall he drink any newly pressed grape juice, nor eat fresh grapes, or dried raisins. All the days of his separation shall he eat nothing that is made of the vine tree, not even the seeds or the skins.*

This text clearly vindicates the arguments of those who maintain that the Hebrew words translated "wine" and "strong drink" in the Bible respectively are generic, and that whether they are to be understood in their fermented or unfermented sense must be judged by the context of the Bible passage.

CHAPTER 8

FERMENTATION –
A SYMBOL OF CORRUPTION

To the Jew all kinds of fermentation were symbols of corruption. Whether it was vinuous fermentation (from the vine) or leaven (sour dough in a high state of fermentation), all was regarded as corrupt and unclean. Unger's Bible Dictionary explains:

> *To the Hebrew mind, whatever was in a decayed state suggested the idea of uncleanness and corruption.*

The Hebrews developed this concept from God Himself, who was very strict concerning anything that was fermented when it came to certain offerings. Anything that was liable to ferment was to be excluded from the altar. Fausset's Bible Dictionary explains:

> *Honey was forbidden in meat offerings...It produces fermentation, which is a symbol of the working of corruption in the heart.*

Keil and Delitzsch's Old Testament commentary states:

> *Whilst leaven and honey were forbidden to be used...because of their producing fermentation and corruption...*

Let us further consider the following:

> *No meat offering, which ye shall bring unto the Lord, shall be made with leaven: for ye shall burn no leaven, nor any honey, in any offering of the Lord made by fire.* (Leviticus 2:11)

There are expositors who object to the fact that leaven was regarded in the same way as vinuous fermentation (fermented wine) on the grounds that leavened bread was allowed in certain offerings. Many misconceptions have also been derived from the fact that our Lord compares the Kingdom of heaven to the operation of leaven (Matthew 13:33; Luke 13:21). The spiritual significance of leaven in the Bible therefore deserves a full explanation.

The following passages show that leaven was permitted in certain offerings:

> *Besides the cakes, he shall offer for his offering leavened bread with the sacrifice of thanksgiving of his peace offerings.* (Leviticus 7:13)

Leaven was not excluded from the tithes and first-fruit offerings, which included all things:

> *And as soon as the commandment came abroad, the children of Israel brought in abundance the firstfruits of corn, wine, and oil, and honey, and of all the increase of the field; and the tithe of all things brought they abundantly.* (2 Chronicles 31:5)

Again, leaven was permitted in the pentecostal loaves:

> *Ye shall bring out of your habitations two wave loaves of two tenth deals: they shall be of fine flour; they shall be baken with leaven; they are the firstfruits unto the Lord.* (Leviticus 23:17)

Let the reader notice that leaven was permitted in some offerings because leavened bread was part of Israel's daily food, but it was *never* to be offered on the altar:

> *As an offering of first fruits you may offer leaven and honey to the Lord, but they shall not be burned on the altar for a sweet odor [to the Lord, for their aid to fermentation is symbolic of corruption in the human heart].* (Leviticus 2:12, Amplified Bible)

> *And Moses said to Aaron, and to Eleazar and Ithamar, his sons who were left, Take the cereal offering that remains of the offerings of the Lord made by fire, and eat*

it without leaven beside the altar, for it is most holy.
(Leviticus 10:12, Amplified Bible)

Why was leaven or anything else fermented prohibited before the altar? The answer is that the altar was the place where the blood sacrifice was to be offered for the sins of the people. This was a type of the incorruptible atoning blood of our Lord and Saviour Jesus Christ, which was to be offered for the sins of the whole world:

> *For the life of the flesh is in the blood: and I have given it to you upon the altar to make an atonement for your souls: for it is the blood that maketh an atonement for the soul.* (Leviticus 17:11)

Here we can see why the wine drank at the Lord's Supper had to be pure and unfermented, that is, the fruit of the vine. The symbol had to be perfect as the apostle Peter explains:

> *Forasmuch as ye know that ye were not redeemed with corruptible things, as silver and gold, from your vain conversation received by tradition from your fathers; But with the precious blood of Christ, as of a lamb without blemish and without spot.* (1 Peter 1:18,19)

Just as how Jesus' blood was incorruptible, so the wine that was to symbolize that blood naturally had to be uncorrupted, that is unfermented or uncontaminated from alcohol.

Leaven was to be excluded from the Passover which was a type of the Lord's Supper (Exodus 12:14-20; 23:15; 34:18; Deuteronomy 16:2-4). Although there are expositors that emphasise the point that the reason why the children of Israel ate unleavened bread while they were leaving Egypt was because they were in haste (Exodus 12:11). However, the real significance of the unleavened bread was that it was to be symbolic of Christ who perfectly fulfilled the Passover:

> *[In celebration of the passover in future years] seven days shall you eat unleavened bread; even the first day you shall put away leaven [symbolic of corruption] out*

115

of your houses; for whoever eats leavened bread from the first day until the seventh day, that person shall be cut off from Israel. (Exodus 12:15, Amplified Bible)

If we now look further at the New Testament we will see that our Lord understood very well the Old Testament facts concerning the symbolic meaning of leaven. Matthew 16:6, states:

Then Jesus said unto them, Take heed and beware of the leaven of the Pharisees and of the Sadducees.

In verse 11, Jesus states again:

How is it that ye do not understand that I spake it not to you concerning bread, that ye should beware of the leaven of the Pharisees and of the Sadducees?

In verse 12, the metaphor is understood:

Then understood they how that he bade them not beware of the leaven of bread, but of the doctrine of the Pharisees and of the Sadducees.

Here we see Jesus warning of the corrupt and fermented doctrine of the Pharisees and Sadducees.

In the light of these truths, many have misunderstood the words of Jesus in Matthew 13:33, when He said:

The kingdom of heaven is like unto leaven, which a woman took, and hid in three measures of meal, till the whole was leavened.

Jesus is not saying here that the Kingdom would eventually become totally corrupted, but that the gospel would spread in the same manner that leaven or yeast does, from within. J. Dwight Pentecost explains:

Christ, then, was not using yeast to teach that the kingdom will be corrupted, for He had already explained to Nicodemus that only those who are born again can enter the kingdom. And Christ explained in later parables that not only is it true that the saved are in the kingdom now but they will have their part in the messianic form of the king-

116

dom that is to come. Thus the emphasis is not on the nature of yeast that could represent evil but rather on the way that yeast works when it is once introduced into the mixture.

Jesus further reinforces this truth when He said:

The kingdom of God cometh not with obsevation: Neither shall they say, Lo here! or, lo there! for, behold, the kingdom of God is within you. (Luke 17:20b, 21)

We thus learn here that Christ's parable likening the Kingdom to the operation of leaven, does not change the fact that leaven or yeast and all other forms of fermentation is still regarded as representative of evil consistently throughout Scripture.

We will now turn our attention to what the apostle Paul has to say about this. In 1 Corinthians 5:6-8, we read:

Your glorying is not good. Know ye not that a little leaven leaveneth the whole lump? Purge out therefore the old leaven, that ye may be a new lump, as ye are unleavened. For even Christ our passover is sacrificed for us: Therefore let us keep the feast, not with old leaven, neither with the leaven of malice and wickedness; but with the unleavened bread of sincerity and truth.

Here the apostle is writing concerning the sin of one who was committing fornication by having his father's wife. The sinning one here is called the leaven of wickedness, they are commanded to expel him just as how the children of Israel were to purge out all leaven out of their houses during the Passover. The apostle Paul here clearly explains the symbolic meaning of the unleavened bread at the Passover, by saying Christ is our Passover. The NIV translation says, *For Christ, our Passover lamb, has been sacrificed.* The unleavened bread represents the sincerity and truth of our Lord Jesus Christ of whom we have become a part. Here we have a revelation of Jesus Christ's absolute holiness and perfection.

We thus learn from our studies that it was inconceivable that fermented or leavened like wine could be used at the Lord's Supper of which the Passover was a type. There is therefore no need whatsoever for any speculation concerning the nature of the

117

wine that our Lord drank; for the principles furnished by the Old Testament does not allow the use of fermented things.

This chapter has laid the foundations for a more in depth study of the Lord's Supper, which we will encounter in part 2.

We have seen that leaven was prohibited from the altar, God's most holy place of sacrifice; the priests also had to abstain from wine when ministering on penalty of death (Leviticus 10:9). Today we are under grace and should live up to our spiritual responsibilities as the apostle Peter states:

> *Ye also, as lively stones, are built upon a spiritual house, an holy priesthood, to offer up spiritual sacrifices, acceptable to God by Jesus Christ.* (1 Peter 2:5)

CHAPTER 9

THE AUTHORITY AND SUFFICIENCY OF SCRIPTURE

Remember the former things of old: for I am God, and there is none else; I am God, and there is none like me, Declaring the end from the beginning, and from ancient times the things that are not yet done, saying, My counsel shall stand, and I will do all my pleasure. (Isaiah 46:9,10)

Concerning the subject of drink and total abstinence, there are many good and well meaning people who unfortunately use rational and subjective reasons to encourage people to stop drinking, rather than the full force of Scripture. What one needs to realize is that if there is no Scriptural authority behind one's arguments then one is under no real obligation to submit, no matter how noble the argument may be, such we have to admit is merely human reasoning. Such a view relegates abstinence from alcohol to a mere option, and those who wish to drink can easily justify their action; but as our opening text states, God knew exactly what would happen in every age of human history.

His Word therefore is relevant in its capability to meet every problem in any era of human history. And with such a major problem as drink which has plagued man throughout his history, we can be sure that our intelligent God in His foresight, was and is, perfectly aware of this issue. He has therefore made specific provisions in His inspired Word to protect men from the destructive potential of alcohol, without the need for us to set our own judgments on what we think is right by arguing about how much alcohol we consider to be acceptable, the differences in the alcoholic content of the beverages in Bible times compared with today etc.

The purpose of this section is to help those who are sincerely trying to combat the evil of alcoholic drinks, but may not be sufficiently enlightened from a Biblical perspective. The author has considered it necessary to select some material for examination that highlights these problems. The aim is not to pull down the good work that people are doing to combat this evil, but to help all to be better equipped to meet the critics, and to show that one can be confident that the Bible *does* condemn the use of alcoholic drinks.

We will also deal with the arguments of those writers who claim that the Bible does not sufficiently enlighten us on this subject, thereby making it unsafe for us to dogmatize or advocate total abstinence.

We will now proceed in examining extracts from our first piece of material selected for reference. The first extract reads:

> *The Bible neither COMMENDS nor CONDEMNS the use of fermented fruit juice (wines) as a general principle. However, there are many references that help us in our thinking about this question.*

Genesis 9:20; Proverbs 20:1,23:29-35 were given but not quoted concerning the misuse of wine and strong drink respectively. We will be looking at the more important or relevant verses of these Scriptures in another chapter, but one thing we must note here is that Proverbs 23:29-35 is definitely a command to abstain from intoxicating wine. Let us look at this passage from the Amplified Bible:

> *Who has woe? Who has sorrow? Who has strife? Who has complaining? Who has wounds without cause? Who has redness and dimness of eyes?*

> *Those who tarry long at the wine, they who go to seek and try mixed wine.*

> *Do not look at wine when it is red, when it sparkles in the wineglass, when it goes down smoothly.*

> *At the last it bites like a serpent, and stings like an adder.*

120

[Under the influence of wine] your eyes will behold strange things [and loose women], and your mind will utter things turned the wrong way, untrue, incorrect and petulant.

Yes, you will be [as unsteady] as he who lies down in the midst of the sea, and [as open to disaster] as he who lies upon the top of a mast.

You will say, They struck me, but I was not hurt! They beat me [as with a hammer], but I did not feel it! When shall I awake? I will crave and seek more wine again [and escape reality].

The writer here merely explains the actions of what occurs in the case of one who is drunk, but still commands total abstinence in verse 31, *Do not look at wine.* The writer then concludes the chapter by showing what happens in the extreme case of drunkenness, of which would be impossible if the earlier command to abstain is followed. The line of thought begins from verse 20 of the same chapter from the command, *Be not among winebibbers* (wine-drinkers). Keil and Delitzsch's translation reads, *And be not among wine-drinkers.* Keil and Delitzsch's Old Testament Commentary goes on to state that the Septuagint (**LXX,** the early Greek translation) translates this clause as, *be no wine-bibber* (wine-drinker). And that while the word is incorrect, the sense is right. It reads:

The LXX. incorrectly as to the word, but not contrary to the sense, "be no wine-bibber..."

Matthew Henry's Bible Commentary also states, *Be not a wine-bibber.* So we can see that whether the clause is translated *be not a wine-drinker,* or *be not among wine-drinkers,* the meaning is the same, as the Septuagint translators understood it. That is, to totally abstain from intoxicating wine!

Similarly, Proverbs 20:1 can hardly be regarded as a statement which does not condemn the use of intoxicating wine and strong drink. It reads:

Wine is a mocker, strong drink is raging: and whosoever is deceived thereby is not wise.

121

Concerning this text, the Bible Knowledge Commentary explains this point:

> *Wine and beer are personified as people of degraded character: a mocker and a brawler. The idea is that wine mocks the one who drinks it and beer makes him aggressive...Intoxicating drinks can lead people astray, causing them to do foolish things.*

Now in returning to the material under examination, four other Scripture references were given for consideration regarding abstinence, relating to certain groups or individuals commanded to abstain from wine or strong drink (Hebrew, shekar), either for a period or for life. The passages given were Numbers 6:3; Jeremiah 35:6; Judges 13:4; Luke 1:15. unfortunately, these passages can in no way be cited for the case of abstinence from intoxicating drinks.

Numbers 6:3; Judges 13:4, and Luke 1:15 concerned the vow of the Nazarite which we examined earlier, who was to abstain from *everything* from the vine, including grapes. Jeremiah 35:6 however, concerned the commandments given to the Rechabites, specifying the way that they should live. This passage also is not a warning against wine or strong drink, for the rechabites were not even allowed to plant vineyards or live in permanent homes, but were to live nomadic lives. The passage with the addition of verse 7, states:

> *But they said, We will drink no wine: for Jonadab the son of Rechab our father commanded us, saying, Ye shall drink no wine, neither ye, nor your sons for ever: Neither shall ye build house, nor sow seed, nor plant vineyard, nor have any: but all your days ye shall dwell in tents; that ye may live many days in the land where ye be strangers.* (Jeremiah 35:6,7)

The first section of this leaflet concluded with this statement:

> *The Scriptures accept the use of wine or beer as part of the normal pattern of life in both the Old and New Testaments, recognising its dangers and condemning its abuse.*

This statement would surely mean that God approves of public bars, beer joints etc., and also social drinking as long as one did not get drunk. As we have observed throughout this book from examination of the Scriptures, the above quote is not strictly correct. Although the statement is well intentioned, it may prove more harmful than beneficial. While the drinking of intoxicants was the normal practice for sinners in the Old and New Testaments, it was certainly unacceptable for the people of God.

Under a next heading entitled *TODAY'S WORLD!*, it opened with this statement:

> *The world in which we now live is in many respects very different from the world of the Bible. This must affect our thinking on many issues, including the question of Drink, (which contains a narcotic drug-alcohol).*

It goes on to give us the following facts concerning alcohol:

> *Wine and strong drink in Bible days were the product of natural fermentation, a process which would have yeilded a maximum alcohol concentration of 14% (normally about 10-12%). Today many drinks are produced by distillation which may result in alcohol concentrations in the order of 60-70%. This means that a person drinking the same amount of a modern beverage may take in 2-7 times as much alcohol as his counterpart in Bible times.*

These facts may be interesting and helpful, but as we read in the case of Noah (Genesis 9:20,21), Lot (Genesis 19:30-36), and the warnings in Proverbs 20:1 and 23:29-35, excessive drunkenness was still possible and still a problem in Bible times.

The Theological Wordbook of the Old Testament in its exposition on alcohol, also brings out this point:

> *Wine was the most intoxicating drink known in ancient times. All the wine was light wine, i.e. not fortified with extra alcohol. Concentrated alcohol was only known in the Middle Ages when the arabs invented distillation ("alcohol" is an Arabic word) so what is now called liquor or strong drink (i.e. whiskey, gin, etc.) and the*

twenty percent fortified wines were unknown in Bible times. Beer was brewed by various methods, but its alcoholic content was light. The strength of natural wines is limited by two factors. The percentage of alcohol will be half of the percentage of sugar in the juice. And if the alcoholic content is much above 10 or 11 percent, the yeast cells are killed and fermentation ceases. Probably ancient wines were 7-10 per cent. Drunkenness therefore was of course an ancient curse, but alcoholism was not as common or as severe as it is today. And in an agricultural age, its effects were less deadly than now. Still, even then it had its dangers and Prov 20:1 and 23:29-35 are emphatic in their warnings.

The point to be taken note of here is that irrespective of the concentration or origin of the alcohol, its potential destructiveness from the viewpoint of the Scriptures makes it absolutely forbidden.

Albert Barnes' Commentary of the New Testament states the following concerning alcohol:

All intoxication is prohibited in the Scriptures-no matter by what means it is produced. There is, in fact, but one thing that produces intoxication. It is alcohol-the poisonous substance produced by fermentation. This substance is neither created or changed, increased nor diminished, by distillation. It exists in the cider, the beer, and the wine, after they are fermented, and the whole process of distillation consists in driving it in a concentrated form, and so that it may be preserved. But distilling does not make it, nor change it. Alcohol is precisely the same thing in the wine that it is in the brandy after it is distilled; in the cider or the beer that it is in the whiskey or the rum; and why is it right to become intoxicated on it in one form rather than in another? Since therefore there is danger of intoxication in the use of wine, as well as in the use of ardent spirits, why should we not abstain from one as well as the other? How can a man prove that it is right for him to drink alcohol in the form of wine, and that it is wrong for me to drink it in the form of brandy or rum?

We will now turn our attention to the section in this leaflet entitled, *THE PERSONAL CHALLENGE* and observe the opening statement which reads:

It is true that Scripture does not include a general command for abstinence. That is not to say that this concept was unknown in those days. Instances are recorded where God imposed such an instruction.

We have already observed from our study of the Bible on this subject, that there *are* in fact general commands to totally abstain from intoxicating drinks. If this were not the case, then all arguments concerning abstinence from intoxicating drinks would amount to nothing.

After presenting its arguments concerning drink, this is the major point posed in the closing section of the leaflet to those contemplating a decision in respect to alcoholic or intoxicating drinks:

In many areas of Christian life and action the Scriptures are explicit as to what our response should be. In other matters we have to come to our own decisions under the guidance of the Holy Spirit. Many Christians have been led by His promptings to take a personal stand of abstinence from alcoholic drinks. It is encouraging to see that the numbers taking such a stand are increasing.

This type of argument will always collapse under scrutiny, because the drink issue is not something that can be left to an individual's feelings. Also there are those who will state quite categorically, that they will feel that the Holy Spirit approves of them drinking intoxicating drinks, as long as they are "temperate." The Holy Scriptures are not open for debate or for rational and subjective opinions in the area of drink or any other drugs. Either the Bible is for these vices or it is against it.

125

The only conditions that permit any practices to be optional, is when the Bible specifically makes such an idea clear. This would include certain social customs and meats (foods) and drinks (not intoxicating), which will be covered more fully in another chapter.

The idea that individuals need to be led by the Holy Spirit in determining whether to abstain from alcoholic drinks or not, is unnecessary and unsafe. The same Holy Spirit that inspired the many passages that we have examined from the Bible which clearly upholds total abstinence, is the same Spirit who indwells and leads the true child of God, and we can be sure that His leading will not depart from the Word of God. Let us consider the following:

> *All scripture is given by inspiration of God, and is profitable for doctrine, for reproof, for correction, for instruction in righteousness: That the man of God may be perfect, throughly furnished unto all good works.* (2 Timothy 3:16,17)

The arguments lacking Scriptural force presented in the leaflet we have just examined concerning drinking and abstinence are not unique to it. These types of arguments are often the ones presented by many Christians when trying to deal with the drink problem. The reason why this leaflet was selected for examination is that most of these common arguments are conveniently gathered under one heading.

It is sincerely hoped that those reading this will be helped in making the abstinence truth more forceful in their lives from a Scriptural perspective. This will serve as greater ammunition when confronting the liberals and critics of the Bible. The information which we examined in this section were taken from a leaflet published by the UK Band of Hope (now Hope UK), an organisation which contributes greatly in helping many give up drinking and other drugs.

The next point that we will now examine in this area, are certain answers given by James M. Gray, in his book where he answers questions to Bible problems. These questions concerned the types of wines used in the Bible, the nature of the wine our Lord created at the marriage feast in Cana, and the type used at the Lord's Supper. In reply to the question whether the Bible teaches that there were two kinds of wines in use, fermented and unfermented, he states:

> The Bible itself does not positively settle the question, and hence men are inclined to settle it for themselves according to their early training, or prejudice, or their general judgment as to what it ought to be. It is, therefore, not safe ground on which to dogmatize.

In answer to this statement, the present author would like to stress again that the Bible *does* indeed positively settle the question as we have determined very clearly from thoroughly investigating it. An honest and open-minded approach will always bring one to the truth irrespective of any prejudices.

There are those who may regard this truth as insignificant, but to understand the fact that there were two kinds of wines described in the Bible (both fermented and unfermented), is a key to understanding the nature of God and the Bible itself. In reply to the questions regarding the nature of the wine Jesus created at the marriage feast in Cana, the wine used at the Lord's Supper, and the subject of the saloon, Gray goes on to state:

> I have always thought it was intoxicating wine Jesus made at the feast in Cana because the context seems to compel that view. As to the institution of the Lord's Supper, however, the case is different, because it is not called wine, but `the fruit of the vine.' This phrase may mean the expressed juice of the grape in an unfermented state as yet. There is some authority for saying that such was the character of the "wine" commonly used by the Jews at the Passover and if this be so, it goes far to establish the conclusion that such was the wine which Jesus used in instituting the supper at the close of that feast. The correspondent who asks these questions speaks of advocates of high license in his town who are

urging the alcoholic character of Bible wine as an argument in favor of the saloon. But surely there are enough arguments against the saloon to down it in the mind of every Christian, and right-thinking man, without touching this question at all.

Unfortunately, these uncertain and unsatisfactory answers are similar to the ones, which many Christians give when confronted with this challenge, which creates all kinds of problems. What we must realize is that these statements to the most part are contradictory. First of all, to suggest that our Lord created alcoholic wine at the marriage feast of Cana, and then in the next moment say that the saloon is wrong, is a gross contradiction. One is entitled to ask the question what is the difference between social drinking at a marriage feast and social drinking at a saloon? Or social drinking at home? As Albert Barnes stated, it is but one thing that causes intoxication and that is alcohol, the poisonous substance that is caused by fermentation. Whether it is 12% or 70% it is still dangerous because of its deceptive nature.

If one believes that Jesus created 120-180 gallons of good alcoholic wine as Gray suggests, to satisfy and bless the guests at a marriage feast because the so-called context compels it, then there is no argument in the World that can be drawn from the Bible to down the cause of the saloon or public bar. One can't have it both ways!

It is this kind of inconsistent reasoning and uncertain approach to Scriptural truths, which brings the exceedingly high reputation of our Lord and the Bible itself into disrepute, and also brings confusion to many young and sincere Christians.

Since as Gray's argument states, the idea of the saloon should be out in the mind of every Christian and right-thinking man, then should not the drinking of alcoholic wine as Proverbs 20:1 makes clear? Therefore from a Scriptural point of view, it is impossible that the context could compel the idea that Christ created alcoholic wine as we will clearly see in the chapter which deals more fully with this point. The main point we need to understand here, of which this whole chapter is based, is that God is perfectly capable of positively making clear His views towards drinking in His Word without the subjective reasoning of even Christian men!

We will now take a further look at some of the problems regarding the understanding of unfermented wine in the Bible. There is apparently uncertainty among various authorities and individuals in this area. A problem of which only the Bible can settle. Concerning the Hebrew word usually translated "new wine" (tirosh) from which we already understand from the Scriptures to mean sweet and unfermented wine; Jamieson, Fausset and Brown's Bible Commentary states:

> *new wine-from a Hebrew root implying that it takes possession of the brain, so that a man is not master of himself. So the Arabic term is from a root "to hold captive," It is already fermented, and so intoxicating...*

We have already seen from a thorough examination of the Scriptures that this statement is completely in error. The Collins Dictionary of the Bible gives a more precise definition, but is still not quite correct from a Scriptural standpoint. It reads:

> *Another word is tirosh, sometimes trans.`new wine' in the AV, and always so trans. in RV. This is really the fresh grape juice before it becomes wine.*

Here we can see that although the definition of new wine (tirosh) above is correct, the terminology given to this fresh unfermented juice of the grape is not precise because Biblically speaking it *was* still regarded as wine. The Collins Dictionary of the Bible goes on to put this erroneous aspect in no uncertain terms by making this bold statement, which reads:

> *There was no such thing as unfermented wine.*

Here we have before us then two differing views (which are held by other readers of the Bible on either side) from two authorities. One which regards "new wine" (tirosh) as alcoholic or intoxicating which is obviously incorrect, and the other while correctly holding that "new wine" (tirosh) is unfermented, states that it is not regarded as wine until it ferments.

The way to answer this problem is not just to say that there are views on either side and that one cannot be dogmatic about it, because with a subject as serious as this one, we must go to the Bible for the answer because somewhere there has got to be a misunderstanding. The reason why the former statement is totally in error, is that "new wine" (tirosh) is spoken of even while it is still in the grape cluster as Isaiah 65:8 makes plain:

> *Thus saith the Lord, as the new wine (tirosh) is found in the cluster, and one saith, Destroy it not; for a blessing is in it: so will I do for my servants sakes, that I may not destroy them all.*

It is absolutely clear from Scripture that "new wine" (tirosh) was not intoxicating, can anyone get drunk from eating grapes?!!

As to the point of whether "new wine" (tirosh, unfermented grape juice) was ever regarded as wine, the Hebrew word tirosh (new wine) is translated as "wine" (oinos) in the early Greek Old Testament (**LXX** or Septuagint). This is very important because this same Greek word is translated "wine" some 33 times in the New Testament. This shows clearly and conclusively that the sweet unfermented juice of the grape (tirosh) was regarded as wine equally well as the fermented solution, and the Bible settles that!

PART 2

WINE IN THE
NEW TESTAMENT

INTRODUCTION

We will now proceed in taking a thorough look at the references to wine drinking in the New Testament, both in its fermented and unfermented form. We will also look at the numerous instructions for total abstinence, whether they mention the word wine or not.

Today the problem is that people automatically assume that any references to wine in the Bible means the alcoholic type. This is simply not the case. Edersheim gives us a list of some of the wines used at meals in New Testament times:

> *To begin with: the wine was mixed with water, and, indeed, some thought that the benediction should not be pronounced till the water had been added to the wine. According to one statement, two parts, according to another, three parts, of water were added to the wine. Various vintages are mentioned: among them a red wine of Saron, and a black wine. Spiced wine was made with honey and pepper. Another mixture, chiefly used for invalids, consisted of old wine, water, and balsam; yet another was "wine of myrrh;" we also read of a wine in which capers had been soaked. To these we should add wine spiced, either with pepper, or with absinth; and what is described as vinegar, a cooling drink made either of grapes that had not ripened, or of the lees. Besides these, palm-wine was also in use. Of foreign drinks, we read of wine from Ammon, and from the province Asia, the latter a kind of "must" boiled down. Wine in ice came from the Lebanon; a certain kind of vinegar from Idumaea; beer from Media and Babylon; a barley-wine (zythos) from Egypt. Finally,*

we ought to mention Palestinian apple-cider, and the juice of other fruits.

We can thus see very clearly that there were a large variety of wines in use during New Testament times, both fermented and unfermented and that cannot be denied.

CHAPTER 1

CHRIST AND SCRIPTURE

the scripture cannot be broken. (Jesus Christ, John 10:35)

This is one of the most important principles that can be applied when correctly interpreting Scripture. Many fail to grasp this vital truth stated by our Lord, which would solve many a long dispute. When Jesus said, *the scripture cannot be broken,* He was simply saying that what was written in the Old Testament could not be set aside or cancelled. The Amplified Bible states, *the Scripture cannot be set aside or cancelled or broken or annulled.* We can thus see that Jesus regarded all of the Old Testament as inspired and authoritative. John W. Wenham, writing on the subject, states:

> To Christ the Old Testament was true, authoritative, inspired. To him the God of the Old Testament was the living God, and the teaching of the Old Testament was the teaching of the living God. To him, what Scripture said, God said.

This vital principle can now be applied with infallible forcefulness to the question, did Jesus create or drink fermented wine? Or whether He would have commanded total abstinence from intoxicating beverages. If God commanded total abstinence in the Old Testament, then Christ would certainly have upheld it in the New Testament. Brian H. Edwards explains:

> No one who has any knowledge of the Old Testament can doubt that Christ's thinking was full of its words and phrases. He used them all the time, indirectly or directly, and never did He give His approval to anything other than the words of the Old Testament.

In Proverbs 23:20, it states:

Be not among winebibbers; among riotous eaters of flesh.

Notice how the Scripture says do not even be among alcoholic wine drinkers, which is what is meant by the term "winebibber." The Moffatt Translation reads, *never sit down with tipsy men or among gluttons.* The Amplified Bible says, *Do not associate with wine bibbers; be not among gluttonous eaters of meat.* When Christ's enemies accused Him of these same forbidden vices in Matthew 11:19, and Luke 7:34; His reply *But wisdom is justified of her children,* was a perfect answer to show the folly and ignorance of His accusers. Since His life, relationship with the Father, and knowledge and compliance with the Old Testament, made this an impossible act.

If we now look further to Proverbs 23:31, we read:

Look not thou upon the wine when it is red, when it giveth his colour in the cup, when it moveth itself aright.

The Amplified Bible states:

Do not look at wine when it is red, when it sparkles in the wineglass, when it goes down smoothly.

The sparkling action describes the fermentation process, thus we can see that the command is to have nothing to do with fermented wine. These Scriptures settle the issue, and show that it was impossible for Jesus to make or drink alcoholic wine in any quantity, but could only have created and drank the pure juice of the grape. Notice the instructions in Proverbs were given by the wise king Solomon. Jesus said of Himself, *behold, a greater than Solomon is here.* (Luke 11:31)

In the Old Testament the prophets erred through wine and strong drink (Isaiah 28:7), the priests were commanded to abstain from strong wine (Leviticus 10:9), and likewise the kings (Proverbs 31:4). Christ came to fulfil the Scriptural role of the great Prophet (Acts 7:37), Priest (Hebrews 7-10), and King (Revelation 17:14), and therefore had to abstain. In Isaiah 9:6, Jesus is called the Prince of Peace, and in Proverbs 31:4 the princes were also commanded to abstain from strong drink.

135

Christ never deviated from Scripture, He continually stressed the importance of Scripture with phrases such as *Have ye not read?* Or *Ye have heard that it was said.* When He was tempted by the Devil He appealed to the authority of Scripture, and overcame him with the classic words, *it is written.* When a lawyer posed a question to Him concerning eternal life, He replied by saying:

> *What is written in the law? how readest thou?* (Luke 10:26)

When stressing the awesome importance of understanding prophecy, He again appealed to the reliability of Scripture by saying:

> *Whoso readeth, let him understand.* (Matthew 24:15)

Jesus was a diligent student of the Law, the Prophets, and the Psalms, and therefore would not have introduced something that was impure and forbidden by Scripture such as fermented wine.

Hear the words of Jesus:

> *O fools, and slow of heart to believe **all that the prophets have spoken.*** (Luke 24:25)

Verse 27 of the same chapter reads:

> *And beginning at Moses and all the prophets, he expounded unto them in all the scriptures the things concerning himself.*

Hear again the words of Jesus:

> *These are the words which I spake unto you, while I was yet with you, that all things must be fulfilled, **which were written in the law of Moses, and in the prophets, and in the psalms, concerning me.*** (Luke 24:44)

Luke then makes a point that many readers of the Bible need today:

> *Then opened he their understanding, that they might understand the scriptures.* (Luke 24:45)

Basically, many today need to open their hearts so that the One Whose Spirit inspired the writing of the sacred Scriptures, may enable them to understand it. To have a correct understanding of the Scriptures therefore, is to have a correct understanding of Christ. The Apostle Paul sums up this principle in 1 Corinthians 15:3,4:

> *For I delivered unto you first of all that which I also received, how that Christ died for our sins **according to the scriptures**; And that he was buried, and that he rose again the third day **according to the scriptures**.*

Yes, Jesus was an obedient Son in every aspect and never acted independently of His Father's will. Note again His words which declares His Father's confidence in Him:

> *When ye have lifted up the Son of man, then shall ye know that I am he, and that I do nothing of myself; but as my Father hath taught me, I speak these things. And he that sent me is with me: the Father hath not left me alone; **for I do always those things that please him.*** (John 8:28-29)

CHAPTER 2

JESUS AND WINE

The grape and its juice was very precious to the Jew and this our Lord was well aware of. Jesus often referred to wine and the vine in His teachings in a metaphorical sense to show various spiritual aspects of the New Kingdom. Jesus was acquainted with the vine and its juice in the following New Testament gospel passages:

(a) Speaking of the kind of fruit that is produced by a good and evil heart, Jesus metaphorically contrasts the good qualities of the grape over against the unfruitful and barren nature of the thorn or bramble bush. (Matt 7:16; Luke 7:44)

(b) Jesus refers to Himself as the True Vine, and again metaphorically likens the good fruit of the grape to the good fruit that should be produced by His disciples. (John 15:1-8)

(c) Jesus' statement that John the Baptist came *neither eating bread nor drinking wine,* and that He The Son of Man *is come eating and drinking.* (Matt 11:18,19; Luke 7:33,34)

(d) The digging of a winepress (vat) in the parable of the wicked husbandmen. (Matt 21:33; Mark 12:1)

(e) The parable of the wine and wineskins. (Matt 9:17; Mark 2:22; Luke 5:37-39)

(f) Jesus mentions wine in the parable of the Good Samaritan. (Luke 10:33,34)

(g) Jesus turned water into wine at the marriage feast in Cana of Galilee. (John 2:1-11)

(h) Jesus institutes the Lord's Supper. (Matt 26:26-30; Mark 14:22-36; Luke 22:17-22)

(i) Wine was offered to Jesus on the cross. (Mark 15:23)

(j) Vinegar (sour wine) was offered to Jesus on the cross (Matt 27:34,48; Mark 15:36; Luke 23:36; John 19:29,30)

(k) Jesus warned against drunkenness, although He does not mention wine. (Matt 24:49; Luke 12:45; 21:34)

We have now set before us all the passages in the gospels where Christ mentions or is involved with wine or the fruit of the vine, and the situations surrounding them. We will now look at the more important passages more closely.

JESUS AND JOHN THE BAPTIST

In Luke 7:33-35, Jesus said:

> *For John the Baptist came neither eating bread nor drinking wine; and ye say, He hath a devil.*

> *The Son of man is come eating and drinking; and ye say, Behold a gluttonous man, and a winebibber, a friend of publicans and sinners!*

> *But wisdom is justified of all her children.*

The first part of this passage we will deal with is the case regarding John the Baptist's abstinence. Some in their zeal for the abstinence cause have incorrectly used this as a case for total abstinence from strong and intoxicating drinks, and have ran into deep problems when faced with explaining Jesus' statement that He had come eating and drinking.

The point is that John the Baptist's case is **not** one that can be used for the cause of total abstinence. On announcing John's birth the angel said:

> *For he shall be great in the sight of the Lord, and shall drink neither wine nor strong drink; and he shall be filled with the Holy Ghost, even from his mother's womb.* (Luke 1:15)

This was a statement declaring that John would adopt a life long Nazarite vow, which would mean he had to abstain from *everything* from the vine, whether it was grapes, grape juice or

139

fermented wine. As was stated earlier in another chapter, this corresponds to the command given by God to Moses in Numbers chapter six verses one to four, which reads:

> *And the Lord spake unto Moses, saying, Speak unto the children of Israel, and say unto them, When either man or woman shall separate themselves to vow a vow of a Nazarite, to separate themselves unto the Lord: He shall separate himself from wine and strong drink, and drink no vinegar of wine, or vinegar of strong drink, neither shall he drink any liquor of grapes, nor eat moist grapes or dried. All the days of his separation shall he eat nothing that is made of the vine tree, from the kernels even to the husk.*

Although Jesus was a Nazarene because He was brought up there, He was not a Nazarite, in that He had not taken this vow. This is why He was free to eat and drink the fruit of the vine, hence Christ's statement that He had come eating and drinking. This answers the question of those who pose the argument that the term "drinking" as Jesus used it, was being used in the same sense as we understand it today. In that He was saying that He was a drinker of alcoholic, fermented, or intoxicating beverages.

The Greek language also refutes this suggestion, because a different word is always used to distinguish a drinker of intoxicating beverages from a drinker of something pure such as water or milk. The word Jesus uses to describe His drinking is pino, the ordinary word for drink. This is different from the word His enemies use to describe His alleged drinking, as we shall see.

Christ's enemies called Him a winebibber (a wine drinker), the original word is oinopotes; from oinos, wine and potes, a drinker. When the word oinos (wine) is used in Scripture it means wine in its fermented or unfermented state; but when it is compounded with potes to produce oinopotes, a wine drinker, it always means a drinker of alcoholic wine.

In our opening text Jesus refutes the false accusations of His enemies by saying, "But wisdom is justified of all her children." The amplified Bible states:

Yet wisdom is vindicated [shown to be true and divine] by all her children [that is, by their life, character and deeds]. (Luke 7:35)

The original word translated "justified" is dikaioo, which primarily means, "to be deemed to be right." Jesus therefore was saying that the accusations aimed at Him by His enemies that He was a glutton and a wine drinker were false. And that He would be vindicated or shown to be right by the lives of His children or disciples.

Christ's statement was correct because as we read earlier in Acts 2:13, His disciples were accused of being drunk with new wine (sweet grape juice). This however was not a literal accusation but mockery. This was because it was known that the disciples of Christ did not drink intoxicating wine.

We can thus see clearly from the Scriptures, that Christ, who is the personification of Wisdom, was not a winedrinker, and He all but states it word for word!

THE PARABLE OF THE WINE AND WINESKINS

This parable is recorded in Matthew 9:16, Mark 2:22, and Luke 5:37-39, but we will deal with the passage which gives us the most information. The passage is from Luke and reads:

And no man putteth new wine into old bottles; else the new wine will burst the bottles, and be spilled, and the bottles shall perish. But new wine must be put into new bottles; and both are preserved. No man also having drunk old wine straightway desireth new: for he saith, The old is better. (Luke 5:37-39)

The primary lesson that Jesus was teaching was that legalism and grace could not be mixed. The Pharisees had to change their system completely to receive His message. J.Dwight Pentecost explains:

The parables clearly indicate that Christ did not come to reform an old worn out system but to introduce something new...Rather, what He was introducing had to be

141

entirely separated from the old. The incident closed with Christ's words that if men would taste His wine, that is, if they would accept what He was offering them, they would not want the old. However, the Pharisees, having tasted the old, were satisfied with it; they had no desire for what He was offering them.

Some scholars have sought to explain the analogy of the new wine and old bottles, by suggesting that old bottles would lose their elasticity and would not contain the wine once it had fermented. New bottles being elastic would expand enough to contain the gas bubble process of fermentation. Hence narrowing the interpretation of the parable solely to the practice of keeping and drinking fermented wine; but we will see quite clearly from the context of the parable, that this was *not* the sense in which Christ was applying it.

To automatically take this view is a rather narrow-minded approach, because sweet unfermented wine was also kept in wineskins. This also does injustice to the parable, as we will see. In actual fact, the context of the parable provides a strong argument for the preservation and use of unfermented wine.

It is obvious from the parable that the new wine contained in the bottles was unfermented, for if the wine had already fermented no significant change in the wine could have taken place to cause the bottles to burst. If the intention was to have fermented wine, then the wine would have been allowed to ferment significantly enough before sealing the bottles. Thus eliminating the problem of bursting the skins.

Therefore in the light of the text, the intention must have been to keep the new wine (unfermented grape juice) in the bottles from fermenting, thus ensuring that the bottles would not burst. Concerning this, The Rev.B. Parsons states:

> *The art required was to keep the new wine from fermenting, not to keep the bottles from bursting.*

This brings us to the point of explaining the dilemma of the old bottles. Parsons explains the following:

142

*The difference between the new bottles and the old con-
sisted not in the relative proportion of their strength; but
arose solely from the fact that the new bottles had in them
no fermentable matter.*

Let us consider this. If new wine was poured into old bottles
the particles of yeast on the old wineskins would cause the wine
to ferment thus bursting the wineskins, "A little leaven (fermentation) leaveneth the whole lump." (Galatians 5:9) The aim
therefore was to keep the wine sweet and unfermented hence the
new bottles. This goes perfectly with Christ's parable, because
His teaching had to remain uncorrupted (unfermented). Dr.
William Patton explains the following:

> *The new bottles, or skins, being clean and perfectly free
> from all ferment, were essential for preserving the fresh
> unfermented juice, not that their strength might resist the
> force of fermentation, but, being clean and free from fer-
> menting matter, and closely tied and sealed, so as to
> exclude the air, the wine would be preserved in the same
> state in which it was when put into the skins.*

He goes on to add:

> *Columella, who lived in the days of the Apostles, in his
> receipe for keeping the wine "always sweet," expressly
> directs that the newest must, be put in a "new amphora,"
> or jar.*

This agrees with Parson's explanation, which states:

> *The vessel they required was not one that could bear fer-
> mentation without breaking, but one which would
> effectually preserve the wines from fermenting; and,
> therefore, the text alludes to the custom of preserving
> wines from fermentation, which both Pliny and
> Columella inform us was common at that very period
> when the Saviour uttered these words.*

Jesus could not have been likening His teaching of the
Kingdom of grace to eventual fermentation, since this is funda-

mentally a decay process. Christ's teaching must remain uncorrupted or uncontaminated. If Christ's teaching was put into old bottles (legalistic tradition) it would eventually ferment, that is, be perverted, thus causing utter confusion.

We have seen that Jesus in no way condones the use of intoxicating wine but rather the opposite. He presents new wine in a figurative sense to show the virtue of grace, in contrast to old wine, which represented the hopelessness of legalistic tradition. Like the new wine He speaks of in His parable, His teaching must not be changed (ferment), but must remain in its original form. Note Christ's words, *But new wine must be put into new bottles; and* ***both are preserved.***

WINE AT THE MARRIAGE FEAST IN CANA (SECTION 1)

And the third day there was a marriage in Cana of Galilee; and the mother of Jesus was there: And both Jesus was called, and his disciples to the marriage. And when they wanted wine, the mother of Jesus saith unto him, They have no wine. Jesus saith unto her, Woman, what have I to do with thee? mine hour is not yet come. His mother saith unto the servants, Whatsoever he saith unto you, do it. And there were set there six waterpots of stone, after the the manner of the purifying of the Jews, containing two or three firkins apiece. Jesus saith unto them, Fill the waterpots with water. And they filled them up to the brim. And he saith unto them, Draw out now, and bear unto the governor of the feast. And they bear it. When the ruler of the feast had tasted the water that was made wine, and knew not whence it was: (but the servants which drew the water knew;) the governor of the feast called the bridegroom, And saith unto him, Every man at the beginning doth set forth good wine; and when men have well drunk, then that which is worse: but thou hast kept the good wine until now. This beginning of miracles did Jesus in Cana of Galilee, and manifested forth his glory; and his disciples believed on him. (John 2:1-11)

This passage of Scripture has been misunderstood by many scholars and commentators of the Bible. Proponents of the moderation cause have used this passage to justify the use of alcoholic beverages. Automatically assuming that the wine Jesus created was alcoholic. Some commentators have sought to explain this difficulty by suggesting that in order to prevent drunkenness, not all the water in the pots was turned into wine, but only that which was drawn off. Our Lord does not need such theories as this for His defence. The answer is much simpler and less inventive. The wine simply was not alcoholic, as will be seen from viewing the Scriptures in the right context.

First off all, there is no justification whatsoever for suggesting that not all the water was turned into wine as the Scripture clearly indicates. If only that which was drawn off was made wine, then there would have been no need to fill all the pots. Christ always gives good things in abundance, He said, *I am come that they might have life, and that they might have it more abundantly.* (John 10:10b) In Ephesians 3:20, it states, *Now unto him that is able to do exceeding abundantly above all that we ask or think...* We only have to read of the twelve baskets of fragments that were left over after the feeding of the five thousand, to see that it is in our Lord's nature and character to provide plentifully for His people (Matt 14:13-21; Mark 6:30-44; Luke 9:10-17; John 6:1-14). J.Dwight Pentecost states:

> *He did not deny that He was the Messiah and that as Messiah He will provide abundantly for those in His kingdom. He also did not deny the prophetic concept that wine is a sign of joy in Messiah's kingdom.*

This first miracle was a sign of Christ's mighty power as Lord and Creator, and also of what would be experienced in His future Kingdom. Each pot would have contained approximately between 20-30 gallons of water. Therefore Christ transformed between 120-180 gallons of water into fresh new, unalcoholic, health giving wine! Contrary to the views of many, unfermented wine or grape juice was not an uncommon thing in Christ's time. Shepard says:

> *Jesus made real wine out of water. But there was a great difference between the Palestinian wine of that time and the alcoholic mixtures which today go under the name of wine. Their simple vintage was taken with three parts of water and would correspond more or less to our grape juice. It would be worse than blasphemy to suppose, because Jesus made wine, that He justifies the drinking usages of modern society with its bars, strong drinks, and resulting evils.*

In verse 10, the term "well drunk" as we looked at earlier does not necessarily mean intoxication, but can mean "drunk freely," or drunk sufficiently." The Amplified Bible's translation brings out this point, it states, "drunk freely." So therefore the governor of the feast was not saying that it was a common practice for people to get so drunk that they would not be able to discriminate between good and bad wine. But rather that when they had drunken sufficiently, they would not be too fussy about the quality of the latter wine.

The remark by the governor of the feast in which he says, "thou hast kept the good wine until now" deserves a full explanation, as many automatically assume that the best wine must have been the most alcoholic. The problem with some is as Jesus said, *Ye judge after the flesh.* (John 8:15) In understanding the nature of the wine we should again take heed to our Lord's words, *Judge not according to the appearance, but judge righteous judgement.* (John 7:24) The Rev. Dr. William Patton quotes The Rev. Dr. Jacobus' comments on the wine our Lord created, which states:

> *This wine was not that fermented liquor which passes now under that name. All who know of the wines then used will understand rather the unfermented juice of the grape. The present wines of Jerusalem and Lebanon, as we tasted them, were commonly boiled and sweet, without intoxicat-*

ing qualities, such as we here get in liquors called wines. The boiling prevents the fermentation. Those were esteemed the best wines which were least strong.

He also quotes Dr. S.M. Isaacs, an eminent Jewish rabbi as saying:

In the Holy Land they do not commonly use fermented wines. The best wines are preserved sweet and unfermented.

We also find agreement with this in Professor Moses Stuart's writings, which state:

Facts show that ancients not only preserved their wine unfermented, but regarded it as of a higher flavor and finer quality than fermented wine."

Dr. Adam Clarke's comment on the term "good wine," reads:

That which our Lord now made being perfectly pure, and highly nutritive.

This is a clear reference to pure, fresh, unfermented grape juice. Albert Barnes' in-depth comments on this point here are worthy of consideration:

We should not be deceived by the phrase "good wine." We use the phrase to denote that it is good in its strength, and its power to intoxicate. But no such sense is to be attached to the word here. Pliny, Plutarch, and Horace describe wine as good, or mention that as the best wine which was harmless, or innocent...It should not be assumed, therefore, that the "good wine" was stronger than the other. It is rather to be presumed that it was milder. That would be the best wine certainly. The wine referred to here was doubtless such as was commonly drunk in Palestine. That was the pure juice of the grape. It was not brandied wine; nor drugged wine; nor wine compounded of various substances such as we drink in this land. The common wine drunk in Palestine was that which was the simple juice of the grape. We use the word wine now to denote the kind of liquid which passes under

that name in this country-always fermented, and always
containing a considerable portion of alcohol-not only the
alcohol produced by fermentation, but added to keep it
or make it stronger. But we have no right to take that
sense of the word, and go with it to the interpretation of
the Scriptures. We should endeavour to get into the exact
circumstances of those times; ascertain precisely what
idea the word would convey to those who used it then;
and apply that sense to the word in the interpretation of
the Bible. And there is not the slightest evidence that the
word so used would have conveyed any idea but that of
the pure juice of the grape;...

We can thus see from mature consideration of the facts that
the good or best wine was not alcoholic at all,...*for that which is*
highly esteemed among men is abomination in the sight of God.
(Luke 16:15)

Again when we examine the Scriptures, we see that there are
certain principles that make it clear that the wine Jesus created
could not have been alcoholic as we shall see. Genesis 1:31, states:

And God saw every thing that he had made, and, behold,
it was very good.

We see here that every thing that God created was absolutely
perfect. Genesis 2:1-3, states:

Thus the heavens and the earth were finished, and all the
host of them. And on the seventh day God ended his work
which he had made; and he rested on the seventh day from
all his work which he had made. And God blessed the sev-
enth day, and sanctified it: because that in it he had rested
from all his work which God created and made.

The above is a categoric statement which makes it clear that
on the seventh day of creation God ceased from creating. In other
words, the Scripture declares that since creation ended on the
seventh day, everything that God created was finally accomplished, and after that nothing new could be created.

Concerning this text, Dr. Henry M. Morris states:

148

After describing the events and sequence of creation during the six days, the writer strongly emphasizes that the work of creation thereupon stopped.

Alcohol was not a part of God's original creation, which is now complete. Jesus would have violated the Scriptures and His own creative laws if He had restarted this process again by creating alcoholic wine, a substance which was foreign to His original handiwork. Dr. Henry Monroe, medical lecturer, states:

Alcohol is nowhere to be found in any product of nature, was never created by God, but is essentially an artificial thing prepared by man through the destructive process of fermentation.

One of the great themes of the Bible is Christ's perfect unity with the Father and joint participation in everything that was created:

All things were made by him; and without him was not any thing made that was made. (John 1:3)

For by him were all things created, that are in heaven, and that are in earth, visible and invisible, whether they be thrones, or dominions, or principalities, or powers: all things were created by him, and for him. (Colossians 1:16)

Jesus Himself stated that the miracles He performed were only possible because of His unity with God the Father:

Verily, verily, I say unto you, The Son can do nothing of himself, but what he seeth the Father do: for what things soever he doeth, these also doeth the Son likewise. (John 5:19)

Scripture is also clear that God, or His actions are unchangeable:

Every good gift and every perfect gift is from above, and cometh down from the Father of lights, with whom is no variableness, neither shadow of turning. (James 1:17)

We can thus see that because of Jesus' consistency with Scripture, it is abundantly clear that the wine that He created could not have been alcoholic. The wine had to be perfectly fresh and not rotten; just as in any other thing that God creates. It was not fermented wine diluted with water to the so-called "right" proportion as some imagine, but the pure juice of the grape. That which Jesus as Lord of creation produces yearly in the grape cluster which grows on the vine. Dr. R.A. Torrey correctly writes:

> *The wine provided for the marriage festivities at Cana failed. A cloud was about to fall over the joy of what is properly a festive occasion. Jesus came to the rescue. He provided wine, but there is not a hint that the wine He made was intoxicating. It was fresh-made wine. New-made wine is never intoxicating. It is not intoxicating until sometime after the process of fermentation has set in. Fermentation is a process of decay. There is not a hint that our Lord produced alcohol, which is a product of decay or death. He produced a living wine uncontaminated by fermentation.*

The same way that our Lord changed the water into wine, is the same way the vine He created drinks in the rain and transmutes it into good wine in the grape cluster. Both are miracles. One done instantly and the other performed yearly through the providence of nature:

> *For the soil which has drunk the rain that repeatedly falls upon it, and produces vegetation useful to those for whose benefit it is cultivated, partakes of a blessing from God.* (Hebrews 6:7, Amplified Bible)

Let us further consider that if the wine Jesus made were alcoholic, He would be tempting men to become drunken. In Luke 21:34, Jesus Himself warns against drunkenness. James 1:13, states:

> *Let no man say when he is tempted, I am tempted of God: for God cannot be tempted with evil, neither tempteth he any man.*

If we turn again to the book of Genesis, we read:

150

> *And out of the ground made the Lord God to grow every*
> *tree that is pleasant to the sight, and good for food.*
> (Genesis 2:9b)

Again we see that the reason why God created fruit including that of the vine, was for man's health. Alcohol is not a food but a poison. The Bible speaks loudly, plainly, and authoritatively that the wine our Lord created could only be pure and harmless,...*as unto a faithful creator.* (1 Peter 4:19)

The wine Christ provided at Cana was a preview of the literal heavenly wine that the saints are to drink:

> *I say to you, I shall not drink again of this fruit of the vine*
> *until that day when I drink it with you new and of supe-*
> *rior quality in my Father's kingdom.* (Matthew 26:29,
> Amplified Bible)

Concerning this, Trench states:

> *...a turning of the water of earth into the wine of heaven.*

Even though from a natural standpoint the wine created by Jesus was non-alcoholic grape juice, it was a very special and perfect blend from the Hand of the divine Creator Himself.

Opinions varied as to exactly which was the best wine. Vines varied in quality (the grapes of Hebron were considered the finest), but the Master put everyone straight. And anyone who drank the delightful substance knew instantly that this was the *best*, because they had not tasted anything so good. Note again the words of the governor, *thou hast kept the good wine until now.*

JESUS' FIRST MIRACLE-FURTHER ARGUMENTS (SECTION 2)

The purpose of the first section was to keep the material simple, and to a point devotional in style. The aim therefore of this section, is to answer some of the more technical arguments or objections posed by those who do not accept that the wine that our Lord provided through His first miracle in Cana of Galilee, was indeed grape juice.

The first objection we will answer is from M.R. Vincent's Word Studies in the New Testament. His argument primarily concerns the words of the governor of the feast in John 2:10, which states:

> *Every man at the beginning doth set forth good wine; and when men have well drunk, then that which is worse: but thou hast kept the good wine until now.*

His objection is to how the word translated "well drunk" is interpreted by some to mean not necessarily drunkenness or intoxication. Vincent states the following:

> *The ruler of the feast means that when the palates of the guests have become less sensitive through indulgence, an inferior quality of wine is offered. In every instance of its use in the New Testament the word means intoxication. The attempt of the advocates of the unfermented-wine theory to deny or weaken this sense by citing the well-watered garden (Isa.58:11; Jer.31:12) scarcely requires comment.*

First of all, before commenting on the arguments in this statement, it must be stated that irrespective of whether the word should be translated to mean drunkenness or not in this passage. It does not make an ounce of difference to the fact that the wine Jesus created must have been sweet, non-alcoholic grape juice. The ruler of the feast was merely referring to a common practice, and not to the actual actions of the guests at the marriage feast where our Lord performed this miracle. Adam Clarke explains this point:

> *It is not intimated, even in the most indirect manner, that these guests were at all intoxicated. The words are not spoken of the persons at the wedding at all: the governor of the feast only states that such was the common custom at feasts of this nature; without intimating that any such custom prevailed there.*

Alford, an eminent Greek scholar, in his exposition of the Greek New Testament, also refutes Vincent's remarks. He writes:

152

We may be sure that the Lord would not have sanctioned, nor ministered to, actual drunkenness. Only those who can conceive this, will find any difficulty here; and they will find difficulties everywhere.-The account of the practice referred to is, that the palates of men become after a while dull, and cannot distinguish between good and bad wine.

Albert Barnes also agrees with this. Regarding this point and the word translated "well drunk," in our text, he states:

This word does not of necessity mean that they were intoxicated, though it is usually employed in that that sense. It may mean when they have drunk sufficient; or to satiety; or so much as to produce hilarity, and to destroy the keenness of their taste, so that they could not readily distinguish the good from that which was worse. But this cannot be adduced in favour of drunkenness, even if it means to be intoxicated. For, 1st. It is not said of those who were present at that feast, but of what generally occurred. For any thing that appears at that feast, all were perfectly temperate and sober... Further, the word translated "well drunk" cannot be shown to mean intoxication. But it may mean when they had drunk as much as they judged proper, or as they desired, then the other was presented. It is clear that neither our Saviour, nor the sacred writer, nor the speaker here, express any approbation of intemperance, nor is there the least evidence that anything of the kind occurred here. It is not proof that we approve of intemperance, when we mention, as this man did, what occurs usually among men at feasts.

Also, concerning this point, Hendriksen's Commentary states:

So he called the bridegroom and said to him, Everybody serves (lit.: sets on the table) the good wine first, and when men have drunk freely (not necessarily: have become drunk), they serve the wine of inferior quality; but you have kept the good wine until now.

Here we can see very clearly that other scholars agree that the word translated "well drunk"(methuo), in John 2:10, does not necessarily refer to drunkenness in this case, as Vincent insists. Adam Clarke further states the following concerning this word:

> *The original word bears a widely different meaning from that which the objection forces upon it. The verbs...signify not only to inebriate, but to take wine, to drink wine, to drink enough: and in this sense the verb is evidently used in the Septuagint...And the prophet Isaiah, chap.lviii.11, speaking of the abundant blessings of the godly, compares them to a watered garden...by which is certainly understood, not a garden drowned with water, but one sufficiently saturated with it, not having one drop too much, nor too little.*

Clarke here thoroughly explains the usage's of this word, and is also one of those who cites the case of the well watered garden in Isaiah 58:11, not to justify the so called "unfermented-wine theory," as Vincent erroneously suggests; but because of the usage's of this word in the Septuagint (the early Greek Old Testament, Gen 43:34; Hag 1:6). The understanding that this word does not only refer to drunkenness but also to drinking freely is therefore perfectly valid. This valid understanding of the word is also borne out by many Bible translations, some of which read:

> *drunk freely* (R.V)
> *drunk freely* (R.S.V)
> *drunk freely* (Amp. Bib)
> *drunk freely* (N.A.S.B)
> *drunk freely* (Young's lit. trans.)

After examining the evidence it is obvious that the translation "drunk freely" is justified, not because of a few who are trying to uphold the so called "unfermented-wine theory." But because of the Biblical force behind it, which enough Bible scholars and translations make clear. Therefore Jesus' miracle in John 2:1-11 does not make allowances for the use of alcoholic or intoxicating beverages.

Those like Vincent who obviously try to justify the use of alcoholic drinks, by suggesting that Jesus sanctioned the practice of social drinking, by being present at what would have become a drunken brawl, and that He even went to the extent of creating lots more fermented wine. Which would have certainly made things worse, forget that the passage does *not* say that Christ created fermented wine. Neither does it say as we learnt earlier, that these guests were drunk. And even if they were drunk before Christ arrived, we can be absolutely sure that He did not create an alcoholic substance just because "they wanted wine," as R.A. Torrey explains:

> *Even if some of the guests were already drunken, or had drunk freely (see v.10, RV) of wine that may have been intoxicating, there would be no harm, but good, in substituting an unintoxicating wine for the intoxicating drink which they had been taking. Our Lord, as far as the story goes at least, did not make intoxicating liquor for anybody to drink, but simply saved a festive occasion from disaster by providing a pure, wholesome, unintoxicating drink. By turning the water into a wholesome wine, He showed His creative power and manifested His glory.*

Having said this, it is clear from Scripture that the guests were not drunk. It is also extremely unlikely that the wine that had run out was intoxicating, because Christ Himself warned:

> *But if that evil servant shall say in his heart, My lord delayeth his coming; And shall begin to smite his fellowservants, and to **eat and drink with the drunken**; The lord of that servant shall come in a day when he looketh not for him, and in an hour that he is not aware of, And shall cut him asunder, and appoint him his portion with the hypocrites: there shall be weeping and gnashing of teeth.* (Matthew 24:48-51)

Proverbs 23:20, also states:

> *Be not among winebibbers...* (Alcoholic wine drinkers, see also Part 2, Chapter 1)

It is clear therefore from Scripture that our Lord did not approve of drinking. Neither would He appear to sanction it by being present with drinkers or drunkards, let alone creating an alcoholic and intoxicating substance. The arguments therefore of those who try to use Christ's first miracle as an excuse for drinking, completely collapses under the sheer weight of Scripture!

Let us now turn our attention to another of Vincent's statements concerning the so called "unfermented-wine theory." The present author would like to make it clear that the drinking of unfermented or non-alcoholic wine is not a theory, but a Biblical and present day fact. At the time of writing, the author has two bottles of highly recommended unfermented red grape juice in his fridge. This is what is written on the front of one of the bottles:

> RED GRAPE JUICE pure natural juice made from choice quality grapes no colour or preservative added

Another bottle reads:

> SPARKLING RED GRAPE JUICE DRINK
> ALCOHOL-FREE
> NO ARTIFICIAL COLOUR OR SWEETENER

The names of the producers are in the bibliography at the back of the book for those who are interested!

Let us again take a closer look at the historical evidence that supports the Biblical arguments for the use of unfermented wine. When we examined this subject earlier in another chapter, many reliable authorities were quoted which substantiated the Biblical arguments, but for the sake of pressing this truth home, we will look at some more. Smith's Bible Dictionary states:

> As to the subsequent treatment of the wine, we have but little information. Sometimes it was preserved in its unfermented state, and drunk as must...It is very likely that new wine was preserved in the state of must by placing it in jars or bottles, and burying it in the earth.

The Zondervan Pictorial Bible Dictionary states:

Wine was also widely used, both in the form of new wine, called must, and fermented wine. "

Speaking of the Hebrew word tirosh, which means sweet unfermented grape juice, often translated "new wine." The Theological Wordbook of the Old Testament states:

...apparently the fresh juice from the vineyard, never by itself associated with intoxication.

We will now take a closer look at the Bible to prove that the word "wine" (Greek, oinos) used in John Chapter 2, did not only mean fermented wine, but also unfermented.

THE TESTIMONY OF THE SEPTUAGINT (LXX)

We referred to the Septuagint earlier, but for those who are unfamiliar with the meaning, the Septuagint is the early Greek translation of the Hebrew Old Testament (generally agreed by scholars to be completed by about 180 B.C). It is apparently the Bible that Christ, the Apostles, and the early church used. Geisler and Nix's General Introduction to the Bible states:

Furthermore, the Septuagint was the Bible of Jesus and the apostles. Most New Testament quotations are taken from it directly, even when it differs from the Masoretic text. (Hebrew Text)

Even though there is evidence that both the Hebrew text (Masoretic text) and the Septuagint (**LXX**) were used by the apostles, an understanding of the Septuagint is of vital importance in determining the thought of the early Christians on various issues. Which naturally includes drinking, the point which concerns us here (See also Part 1, Chapter 9, *The Authority and Sufficiency of Scripture,* for key discussion on the Septuagint's rendering of Proverbs 23:20).

Before we examine any texts from the Bible, we will take a further look at how some authorities make clear the importance of the Septuagint. In a symposium entitled, *How Reliable Is the Old Testament Text?*, R. Laird Harris, states the following important facts:

The fact is that if we discard our Hebrew Bibles, the Septuagint, though sounding strange in places, would be a very satisfactory copy of the Old Testament. Indeed, for the first three centuries of the Christian Church, when most Christians spoke Greek fluently, the Septuagint was used almost exclusively.

The Zondervan Pictorial Bible Dictionary makes it clear how important this is in terms of understanding the Old Testament (OT):

It is a valuable witness to the understanding of the OT in pre-Christian days.

William Barclay explains how the Septuagint greatly influenced the writers of the New Testament (NT). He states:

The Septuagint is of the greatest importance because it was the Bible of the Christian Church before the NT came to be written. Very often when the NT writers quote the OT it is the Septuagint which they use, and not the original Hebrew. The language of the Septuagint therefore became entwined in Christian thought.

Brian H. Edwards, also writes:

The Septuagint can guide our translators where the Hebrew text is particularly hard...In addition we must not forget that the New Testament writers often used the Septuagint in preference to the Hebrew text.

He further states this important point:

It is important to realise that nowhere does a New Testament writer contradict either the Greek Septuagint or the Hebrew Massoretic Text, though he may add to or interpret the one or the other.

In order to determine therefore, whether the Greek word oinos (wine) used in John chapter 2, also conveyed the idea of sweet unfermented grape juice, as well as intoxicating wine. We can check if the Hebrew word tirosh, which means unfermented grape juice (often translated "new wine" which we noted above earlier) is ever translated oinos (wine) in the Septuagint. If this proves to be the case, this puts it beyond a shadow of a doubt that the Greek word oinos (wine) which is used to refer to the wine our Lord created at the marriage feast in Cana, and which is also used throughout the New Testament, was undoubtedly understood to mean non alcoholic grape juice, as well as alcoholic wine. Young's Analytical Concordance defines the meaning of this word oinos (wine) as, "Wine, grape juice."

For the sake of brevity and easy reference, we will not quote the full Old Testament verses, but only how the relevant or respective words are translated. The passages selected for comparison, read:

Old Testament (AV)		Hebrew	Septuagint(Greek OT)
Genesis 27:28	"wine"	tirosh	oinos
Genesis 27:37	"wine"	tirosh	oinos
Num 18:12	"wine"	tirosh	oinos
Deut 7:13	"wine"	tirosh	oinos
Deut 11:14	"wine"	tirosh	oinos
Deut 12:17	"wine"	tirosh	oinos
Deut 14:23	"wine"	tirosh	oinos
Deut 18:4	"wine"	tirosh	oinos
Deut 28:51	"wine"	tirosh	oinos
Deut 33:28	"wine"	tirosh	oinos
Neh 10:39	"new wine"	tirosh	oinos
Neh 13:5	"new wine"	tirosh	oinos
Neh 13:12	"new wine"	tirosh	oinos
Prov 3:10	"new wine"	tirosh	oinos
Joel 1:10	"new wine"	tirosh	oinos
Mic 6:15	"sweet wine"	tirosh	oinos
Hag 1:11	"new wine"	tirosh	oinos
Zec 9:17	"new wine"	tirosh	oinos
Isa 24:7	"new wine"	tirosh	oinos
Hos 9:2	"new wine"	tirosh	oinos

Let us note carefully how the Septuagint translates the Hebrew word tirosh, which means unfermented grape juice, as oinos (wine). Here we have complete proof from the Septuagint that the word translated "wine" (oinos) most of the times in the New Testament, could refer to grape juice equally as much as fermented or alcoholic wine, and no liberal scholar can deny that!

John, a disciple of Christ, and a reader of the Septuagint, understood this meaning. He therefore takes it for granted when writing his gospel narrative that the readers knowing the reputation of Christ would obviously understand that the wine He created was unfermented grape juice.

After our fairly extensive examination of the events surrounding Jesus' first miracle of turning water into wine at the marriage feast in Cana of Galilee, it would be appropriate to summarize our conclusions with:

10 REASONS WHY THE WINE JESUS MADE COULD NOT HAVE BEEN ALCOHOLIC

(1) The vast quantity created (between 120-180 gallons).

This amount of intoxicating wine would have turned the wedding feast into a drunken brawl. Scholars who try to overcome this by suggesting that not all the water was turned into wine, but only that which was drawn off, only complicate things. For did not Christ know all things? He would know exactly how many people might drink one cup. Why then did He not have the attendants fill only one pot? Or even two pots etc.? No, the miracle was divine wisdom and providence in action. Christ's abundant wisdom and providence made it obvious that such an amount could not have been intoxicating, thereby protecting His flawless reputation.

(2) Christ's sinlessness and moral perfection.

Jesus Himself said in John 8:46:

Which of you convinceth me of sin?

In other words, no one was able to convict or find Him guilty of the slightest sin. Thus He declares His sinlessness and moral perfection. Those scholars, who talk about

Christ's impeccability (perfection) and almost in the same breath declare that He was a drinker and advocate of alcoholic wine, are totally in error. Concerning Christ's character, Hendriksen states:

> *Today's radical theologian is inconsistent when on the one hand he loudly proclaims the moral perfection of Jesus; yet on the other hand rejects his majestic claims! If Jesus is sinless, his claims should be accepted. Any other course is positively wicked.*

Although this statement refers to rejecting Jesus as God, declaring that He was a drinker and that He made intoxicating wine is not far from this dangerous stance.

Even Jesus' enemies realized that drinking was sin and call Him a winebibber (wine drinker, Matt 11:19; Luke 7:34), and what is even more amazing, people who profess to be Christians accuse Him of the same thing!

Many sinners, some of whom have been misinformed by Christians on this issue, also realize that drinking is sin and object to Jesus' claims on those grounds. R.A. Torrey explains this point:

> *A stock objection against the Bible, and not only against the Bible but against Jesus Christ Himself, is found in the story of Jesus turning the water into wine at the marriage festival at Cana of Galilee as recorded in John 2:1-11.*

Unfortunately, this kind of view only comes from those who do not really understand who Jesus is. An even sadder point is that many Christians do more to hinder unbelievers from coming to Christ by misrepresenting His character when it comes to the drink issue.

We will now look at some New Testament Scripture passages, which reaffirm Jesus' sinlessness and perfection, in the light of which makes it inconceivable that our Lord could have drank or created alcoholic beverages. These read:

And ye know that he was manifested to take away our sins; and in him is no sin. (1 John 3:5)

Who did no sin, neither was guile found in his mouth. (1 Peter 2:22)

For he hath made him to be sin for us, who knew no sin... (2 Corinthians 5:21)

For such an high priest became us, who is holy, harmless, undefiled, separate from sinners... (Hebrews 7:26)

In the light of these Biblical facts, it is plain that those who suggest that Jesus drank or created alcoholic wine have a very dim conception of His holiness indeed.

(3) Man's sinfulness.

John 2:24,25 states:

But Jesus did not commit himself unto them, because he knew all men, And needed not that any should testify of man: for he knew what was in man.

Jesus also stated:

...men loved darkness rather than light, because their deeds were evil. (John 3:19)

These passages alone tell us that Jesus would not have bowed to the sinful desires of men by creating intoxicating wine. As the Scripture states, Jesus knew what was in man, that is, He knew their sinful hearts and evil desires. They indeed loved darkness rather than light.

Those commentators of the Bible therefore, who state such arguments such as "temperance" is one of the qualities mentioned under the fruit of the Spirit. Or that the guests at the wedding feast, which Christ attended in Cana of Galilee, were a select and holy band of people, who would therefore not drink too much, is not a valid reason for explaining away why Christ would have created intoxicating wine. Since all were sinners.

Such an act of making alcoholic wine would not have produced faith in Him as the glorious Son of God. Instead it

162

would have merely identified Him as another sinful man with the usual desires for finding pleasure in evil things.

(4) Temptation.

In Matthew 6:13, Jesus states:

And lead us not into temptation, but deliver us from evil.

Christ would not therefore have tempted men to become drunkards, which would mean exclusion from the Kingdom of God in which He Himself proclaimed.

(5) Christ would have approved of social drinking.

Pubs, bars etc., would therefore be the accepted thing amongst Christians if the wine Christ made was alcoholic as some insist. Christ could also be held responsible to a large extent for the problem of alcoholism today, as the Encyclopaedia Britannica points out:

First in the realm of health, the most serious and detrimental effect is alcoholism. Although drinking itself is hardly ever regarded as the sufficient cause of alcoholism, this disease could not arise without the use of alcohol.

(6) It was and is in the nature of Christ to do good.

The Apostle Peter stated in Acts 10:38:

How God anointed Jesus of Nazareth with the Holy Ghost and with power: who went about doing good...

Albert Barnes explains this principle in the light of Jesus' first miracle:

Jesus delighted to do good. In the very beginning of his ministry he worked a miracle to show his benevolence. This was the appropriate commencement of a life in which he was to go about doing good. He seized every opportunity of doing it; and at a marriage feast, as well as among the sick and poor, he showed the character which he always sustained-that of a benefactor of mankind. An argument cannot be drawn from this

163

instance in favour of intemperate drinking. There is no evidence that any who were present on that occasion drank too freely. Nor can an argument be drawn from this case in favour even of drinking wine, such as we have. The common wine of Judea was the pure juice of the grape, without any mixture of alcohol, and was harmless. It was the common drink of the people, and it did not tend to produce intoxication.

Again after consideration of these facts, it is inconceivable from a Biblical perspective, to suggest that our Lord would have created an alcoholic substance which is not good but harmful to the body. Also, Jesus the great Physician and Creator of our bodies, who knows all things, designed our bodies to reject alcohol (in any quantity) because of its destructive potential. He therefore would not have bestowed upon men something which He in is infinite knowledge, purposely designed our complex bodies to reject. The Encyclopaedia Britannica bears this out:

The body begins to dispose of alcohol immediately after it is absorbed.

This scientific fact is borne out by the Spirit inspired writer of 1 Samuel 25:37, when referring to Nabal's **complete** recovery from drunkenness. It reads:

But it came to pass in the morning, when the wine was gone out of Nabal, and his wife had told him these things, that his heart died within him, and he became as a stone.

Again after consideration of the facts, can we accuse our Lord and Creator of ignorance?

(7) **Christ Himself warned against drunkenness and of drinking, and drinking with drunkards.**
(Matthew 24:45-51; Luke 12:45-46)

(8) **Christ Himself denied that He was wine drinker (winebibber).**

When accused of this vice, Jesus stated, *But wisdom is justified of her children.* (Matt 11:18,19; Luke 7:33,34) A paraphrase of this statement would read:

> *I am not a glutton neither am I a wine drinker, or a lover of the evil deeds of tax collectors and sinners, and this fact will be justly declared by those who are my true children.*

Today, those who are His true children will follow His example *...that we might be partakers of his holiness.* (Hebrews 12:10b)

(9) The Old Testament condemned drinking as well as drunkenness (Prov 20:1; 23:31-35).

Since Christ was well versed in the Old Testament and did not contradict its teachings, the truth of His abstinence from alcoholic wine is firmly established.

(10) He would have violated His own laws of creation.

Speaking of Christ, Colossians 1:16, states:

> *For by him were all things created, that are in heaven, and that are in earth, visible and invisible, whether they be thrones, or dominions, or principalities, or powers: all things were created by him, and for him.*

Jesus as Lord and creator, made all things perfect as Genesis 1:31 plainly states:

> *And God saw every thing that he had made, and, behold, it was very good.*

Alcohol is developed by fermentation, a product of decay and death. It therefore could not have been created by our Lord, whose actions were totally consistent with the nature of God and Holy Scripture. The wine He created could only be the fruit of the vine, which was not rotten and dead as is the case with fermented wine, but wholesome and fresh. Just like all the other fruits He produces on the trees yearly through His providence, which reflects His love for man.

165

It is sincerely hoped that after consideration of the facts that we have examined, that we grasp the seriousness of any allegations which may suggest that Jesus drank or made intoxicating or alcoholic wine.

It is also hoped that that any doubts that the reader may have had in this area has been answered, as we have thoroughly looked at this subject from a Scriptural perspective.

Irrespective of any difficulties which may remain, there are still no excuses which can be drawn from Jesus' first miracle to justify the use of alcoholic drinks. However, there are always those who do not want to understand the clear teachings of the Bible on this subject, and will not accept any truth which commands total abstinence from strong drinks, irrespective of how clear and Biblical it may be. We will therefore conclude this section with a wise quote from Albert Barnes' Bible Commentary, which states:

> *No man should adduce this instance in favour of drinking wine, unless he can prove that the wine made in the "water-pots" of Cana was just like the wine he proposes to drink. The Saviour's example may be always pleaded JUST AS IT WAS-but it is a matter of obvious and simple justice that we should find out exactly what the example was before we plead it.*

THE LORD'S SUPPER
Matthew 26:26-29; Mark 14:22-25; Luke 22:15-20

This sacred ordinance was instituted by Christ as a memorial of His sacrificial death:

> *And as they were eating, Jesus took bread, and blessed it, and brake it, and gave it to the disciples, and said, Take, eat; this is my body. And he took the cup, and gave thanks, and gave it to them, saying, Drink ye all of it; For this is my blood of the new testament, which is shed for many for the remission of sins. But I say unto you, I will not drink henceforth of this fruit of the vine, until that day*

166

when I drink it new with you in my Father's kingdom.
(Matthew 26:26-29)

J. Dwight Pentecost, writing on the Lord's Supper, states:

Bread and wine were significant parts of the Passover meal. Bread was used throughout the Old Testament as a symbol of God's provision for His People. Wine was used throughout the Old Testament as a symbol of the joy that would be the experience of those in Messiah's kingdom...It came as no surprise to the disciples that Christ used bread in the observance of the meal and that He passed the cup from which all drank. But now Christ departed from the normal use of these elements at the Passover Feast. He gave a new significance to the bread and wine.

That new significance was His Body and Blood, which He was to give for the life of the world. This had to be *perfectly* fulfilled according to the Scriptural principles laid down in the feast of the Passover, which was a type of the Lord's Supper.

Although in the Old Testament accounts of the Passover nothing is mentioned concerning wine, we know that Jesus' attachment of something new and special to this traditional practice had to be Scripturally based.

When we examine the Old Testament references of the Passover, we learn that it was impossible that the wine used by Jesus at the Lord's Supper could have been fermented or alcoholic. The events of the Passover are mainly covered in Exodus chapter 12-13, so we will only quote the texts that are relevant to our study. Concerning the feast of the Passover, we read:

Seven days thou shalt eat unleavened bread, and in the seventh day shall be a feast to the lord. Unleavened bread shall be eaten seven days; and there shall no leavened bread be seen with thee, neither shall there be leaven seen with thee in all thy quarters. (Exodus 13:6,7)

This text is very interesting and important, because the translation does not fully bring out the meaning of the text. The Hebrew word translated "leavened" in verse 7, (written chomits, chamets, hamets, or khahmatz in the Hebrew) conveys the idea of fermentation. Young's Analytical Concordance renders this word, "Anything leavened or fermented." Young's Literal Translation of the above text reads:

> *Seven days thou dost eat unleavened things, and in the seventh day is a feast to Jehovah; unleavened things are eaten the seven days, and any thing fermented is not seen with thee; yea, leaven is not seen with thee in all thy border.* (Exodus 13:6,7)

Today's Dictionary of the Bible, also gives an excellent translation of Exodus 13:7:

> *In Ex. 13:7, the proper rendering would be, "Unfermented things [Heb. matstsoth] shall be consumed during the seven days; and there shall not be seen with thee fermented things [hamets], and there shall not be seen with thee leavened mass [seor] in all thy borders."*

The punishment for disobeying this commandment was severe:

> *And this day hath become to you a memorial, and ye have kept it a feast to Jehovah to your generations;-a statute age-during: ye keep it a feast. Seven days ye eat unleavened things; only-in the first day ye cause leaven to cease out of your houses; for any one eating anything fermented from the first day till the seventh day, even that person hath been cut off from Israel.* (Exodus 12:14,15, Young's Literal Translation)

What we learn here is that not only was leavened bread prohibited at the Passover, but any other thing, which was fermented. Since God permitted no fermented things at the Passover, the wine drank at that feast could not have been alcoholic. In respect to the command that in all offerings to God, no leaven was permitted among the Jews, and to the Hebrew word often translated "leaven" (chomits, chamets, hamets, or khahmatz), Professor Moses Stuart states:

> *The great mass of the Jews have ever understood this prohibition as extending to fermented wine, or strong drink, as well as bread. The word is essentially the same which designates the fermentation of bread and that of liquors.*

The Jews did indeed understand very well this fact, as the Rev. B. Parsons explains:

> *As for the wine drunk at the Passover, we have the best proof that it was not fermented. The word Chomits, in Hebrew, signifies "leaven," "vinegar," and every kind of fermentation. It refers alike to the panary, the vinous, and the acetous fermentation, and where it stands for an evil doer, designated "vir corruptus," or a corrupt man, stands for the putrefactive fermentation. Now, the Jews at the Passover were commanded to have no leaven in their houses; and they, from that day to this, understood the term to refer just as much to fermented liquors as to fermented bread, and therefore at the Passover were exceedingly careful that no fermented wines should be among them.*

If we now turn our attention to looking more fully at the symbols attached to the Lord's Supper, we will gain a greater understanding of the purpose of the Passover, and also of the holiness and purity of our Lord and Saviour Jesus Christ, the Spotless Lamb of God.

The Passover lamb was a type of Christ, which Jesus perfected by giving His body and shedding His innocent blood for the sins of the world. In the Passover account we read of the instructions concerning the lamb. Let us take note of the most significant requirement regarding it:

> *Your lamb shall be **without blemish,** a male of the first year: ye shall take it out from the sheep, or from the*

169

goats: And ye shall keep it up until the fourteenth day of the same month: and the whole assembly of the congregation of Israel shall kill it in the evening. And they shall take of the blood, and strike it on the two side posts and on the upper door post of the houses, wherein they shall eat it. And they shall eat the flesh in that night, roast with fire, and unleavened bread; and with bitter herbs they shall eat it. (Exodus 12:5-8)

Jesus Christ therefore was the Lamb without blemish:

The next day John seeth Jesus coming unto him, and saith, Behold the Lamb of God, which taketh away the sin of the world. (John 1:29)

The unleavened bread was a symbol of Christ's body which did not under go corruption:

For thou wilt not leave my soul in hell; neither wilt thou suffer thine Holy One to see corruption. (Psalms 16:10)

This truth is also repeated by the apostle Peter in Acts 2:27,31 and the apostle Paul in Acts 13:34-36.

The wine was a symbol of Christ's life giving blood which cleanses from sin:

For the life of the flesh is in the blood: and I have given it to you upon the altar to make an atonement for your souls: for it is the blood that maketh an atonement for the soul. (Leviticus 17:11)

But if we walk in the light, as he is in the light, we have fellowship one with another, and the blood of Jesus Christ his Son cleanseth us from all sin. (1 John 1:7)

In the book of Corinthians, the apostle Paul links the symbolic meaning of the Passover to Christ:

Your glorying is not good. Know ye not that a little leaven leaveneth the whole lump? Purge out therefore the old leaven, that ye may be a new lump, as ye are unleavened. For even Christ our passover is sacrificed for us: Therefore let us keep the feast, not with old

leaven, neither with the leaven of malice or wickedness;
but with the unleavened bread of sincerity and truth. (1
Corinthians 5:6-8)

This text is loaded with symbolic truths. The command to the Jews in the Old Testament to remove all leaven or fermented things from their houses was symbolic of evil, which the believer should remove from his life. Also, eating the unleavened bread and drinking the unfermented wine represented the absolute sinlessness and purity of Jesus Christ. The apostle Paul makes it clear that every thing about the Passover found its total fulfilment in Christ, by stating that Christ is our Passover.

Concerning the unleavened bread that the children of Israel were to eat with the roasted lamb on the Passover night, as recorded in Exodus 12:8, Keil and Delitzsch's Old Testament Commentary explains the significance:

> *They were to eat...**pure loaves**, not fermented with*
> *leaven; for leaven, which sets the dough in fermentation,*
> *and so produces impurity, was a natural symbol of moral*
> *corruption, and was excluded from the sacrifices there-*
> *fore as defiling.*

Just as the bread had to be unleavened (free from fermentation or corruption), so did the wine have to be unfermented (free from contamination), in order to correctly fit the Biblical picture or symbol of the memorial of the Spotless Son of God.

Concerning this, Wilhelm Gesenius, who was professor of Theology at the University of Halle (1786-1842), and an expert in the Hebrew language and customs, wrote:

> *leaven applied to the wine as really to the bread.*

The Rev. B. Parsons again explains how the Jews prepared their wine for the Passover. He states:

> *At the present day, the Jews are especially careful in*
> *preparing their wine for the Passover, and make it by*
> *pouring water upon dried grapes or raisins, much in the*
> *same manner that Columella prescribes for making the*

171

wine which the Romans called "Passum," and which, Polybius says, females were allowed to drink because it would not intoxicate, and was used to quench thirst.

When Jesus instituted the Lord's Supper, He merely gave a new meaning to the Passover:

And he said unto them, With desire I have desired to eat this passover with you before I suffer: For I say unto you, I will not any more eat thereof, until it be fulfilled in the kingdom of God. And he took the cup, and gave thanks, and said, Take this, and divide it among yourselves: For I say unto you, I will not drink of the fruit of the vine, until the kingdom of God shall come. (Luke 22:15-18)

Jesus did not depart from the Old Testament principles of this ordinance, and therefore did not use alcoholic wine. R.B. Grindrod explains:

It was in fact, the feast of the Passover that our Lord and his disciples were then in the act of celebrating; and Jesus knowing that this Jewish ceremony having in its typical and only real use, accomplished in the shedding of his own blood, took this opportunity of instituting his own eucharistical festival in its stead; and it is certain, we have no account of any other kind of wine being introduced, than what was usually drunk at the celebration of the Passover.

Patton quotes the Rev. A.P. Peabody, D.D., writing on the Lord's Supper, as stating:

The writer has satisfied himself, by careful research, that in our Saviour's time the Jews, at least the high ritualists among them, extended the prohibition of leaven to the principle of fermentation in every form; and that it was customary, at the Passover festival, for the master of the household to press the contents of 'the cup' from clusters of grapes preserved for this special purpose.

172

The principle of pressing the grapes into the cup is also noted by Josephus, Jewish historian (cf Jos. Antiq. ii. 5,2); and is also noted in the Bible, way back in the Old Testament:

> *And in the vine were three branches: and it was as though it budded, and her blossoms shot forth; and the clusters thereof brought forth ripe grapes: And Pharaoh's cup was in my hand: and I took the grapes, and pressed them into Pharaoh's cup, and I gave the cup into Pharaoh's hand.* (Genesis 40:10,11)

Adam Clarke's Bible Commentary on this text reads:

> *From this we find that wine anciently was the mere expressed juice of the grape, without fermentation. The saky, or cup-bearer, took the bunch, pressed the juice into the cup, and instantly delivered it into the hands of his master. This was anciently the yayin of the Hebrews, the oinos of the Greeks, and the mustum of the ancient Latins.*

This proves without doubt that fresh grape juice (the fruit of the vine) was drank as well as the fermented type, from the earliest times. Dr. William Patton quotes Dr. S.M. Isaacs, an eminent Jewish rabbi, as repeatedly and emphatically saying:

> *The Jews do not, in their feasts for sacred purposes, including the marriage feast, ever use any kind of fermented drinks. In their oblations and libations, both private and public, they employ the fruit of the vine-that is, fresh grapes-unfermented grape-juice, and raisins, as the symbol of benediction. Fermentation is to them always a symbol of corruption, as in nature and science it is itself decay, rottenness.*

Jesus, when referring to the wine or fruit of the vine, in His institution of the Lord's Supper, said:

> *For this is my blood of the new testament (covenant), which is shed for many for the remission of sins.* (Matthew 26:28)

What Jesus was actually saying was "this is my life":

> *For the life of the flesh is in the blood: and I have given it to you upon the altar to make an atonement for your souls: for it is the blood that maketh an atonement for the soul.* (Leviticus 2:11)

Here we can see that just as the blood was life giving, so must the wine used at the Lord's Supper be health giving, to make the perfect symbol. Symbolically, the wine could not have been alcoholic or fermented, a rotten substance which is destructive to the body, which is a perfect picture of death. The apostle Peter was well aware of the important significance of the blood of Christ, when he wrote:

> *Forasmuch as ye know that ye were not redeemed with corruptible things, as silver and gold, from your vain conversation received by tradition from your fathers; But with the precious blood of Christ, as of a lamb without blemish and without spot.* (1 Peter 1:18,19)

How could the precious blood of Christ which the inspired apostle states was not "corruptible," be symbolized by alcoholic wine, a substance which itself is the embodiment of rottonness and corruption?!

When we read the Old Testament, we see how God is meticulous and exact regarding His instructions relating to symbols of whose substance and meaning are later revealed in the New Testament. How foolish then it is to suggest that the precious blood of Christ which was shed on the cross for the remission of sins. The blood which the writer of Hebrews in chapter 9:12, speaking of Christ says, *but by his own blood he entered in once into the holy place, having obtained eternal redemption for us.* The blood which the saints overcame the Devil by, along with the word of their testimony (Revelation 12:11), be eternally symbolized by a wine whose character does not properly represent the exceedingly high virtue and blessedness of that blood. The symbol of Christ's blood had to be the fruit of the vine, that is, pure fresh grape juice, which did not under go fermentation (corruption). This indeed was a perfect symbol of our Lord's life giving blood.

Let us note carefully how in Matthew 26:29, Jesus when referring to the contents of the cup, uses the term "fruit of the vine" so that there could not be an hint of doubt that He was referring to an unfermented juice. The word Jesus uses for "fruit" in this verse is very specific. The original Greek word is genema, which means to "to be born," or "to beget," and "to be produced." It comes from the root word ginomai, meaning, "to come into being." Thus when Jesus here mentioned the fruit of the vine, He was referring to that, which was produced by the vine in its natural state, that is, pure grape juice.

Vine's Expository Dictionary, says of this word:

as the produce of the earth, e.g., the vine.

Robinson's Lexicon of the New Testament:

what is born or produced, i.e...spoken of trees, etc. fruit produce, Matt. 26:29. Mark 14:25. Luke 22:18.

Thayer's Lexicon of the New Testament:

that which has been begotten or born;...the fruits of the earth, products of agriculture.

Concerning the full term "fruit of the vine," Today's Dictionary of the Bible states:

The fruit of the vine, "vintage fruit" (Heb. tirosh); grapes, whether moist or dried.

Here we see very clearly that when Jesus referred to the fruit of the vine, He meant exactly that; i.e a juice whose constituents was essentially the same as that of the grape. That is, an unfermented juice. Grindrod explains:

One general practice was to preserve the juice of the grape...In this state it was variously termed, must, new wine, or fruit of the vine. The latter appellation was appropriate, because thus preserved, it possessed all the essential properties of the grape.

So we can see very clearly that in partaking of The Lord's Supper, the correct emblem of our Lord's blood that must be used, according to the Scriptures and the example of Jesus, is unfermented grape juice. Regarding this, the Rev. Parsons states:

> *Hence those Christians who use unfermented wine at the Lord's table, have the countenance of history, and the example of the blessed Redeemer in support of this practice, and certainly partake of drink which much more resembling ancient wines than port, sherry, or tent, or any other liquor polluted with alcohol.*

Those Christians who use fermented wine at the Lord's Supper, whether they are aware of it or not, are spoiling the beautiful symbolic picture of Christ's holiness that God has intended them to see through this ordinance, and should cease from doing such on the authority of Scripture. Adam Clarke forcefully condemns this unscriptural practice by stating:

> *This is a most wicked and awful perversion of our Lord's ordinance. The matters made use by Jesus Christ on this solemn occasion, were unleavened bread, and the produce of the vine, i.e. pure wine. To depart in the least from his institution, while it is in our power to follow it literally, would be extremely culpable.*

If we look again at Jesus' words in Matthew 26:29, we learn something very interesting:

> *But I say unto you, I will not drink henceforth of this fruit of the vine, until that day when I drink it new with you in my Father's kingdom.*

Vincent's comments on this text states:

> *In our Lord's expression, "**drink it new,**" the idea of quality is dominant. All the elements of festivity in the heavenly kingdom will be of a new and higher quality.*

The translation from the Amplified Bible of Matthew 26:29, states:

*I say to you, I shall not drink again of this fruit of the vine
until that day when I drink it with you new and of superior quality in My Father's kingdom.*

Why superior quality? it may be asked. The answer is
because the wine will not be man made, but will be the same
kind as that produced by Christ at the marriage feast in Cana
of Galilee, in John chapter 2. Some say that this is only figurative and not literal, but there is no evidence in the Bible to
suggest this.

After Christ's glorious resurrection, He ate and drank real
food:

*And when he had thus spoken, he shewed them his hands
and his feet. And while they yet believed not for joy, and
wondered, he said unto them, Have ye here any meat?
And they gave him a piece of a broiled fish, and of an
honeycomb. And he took it, and did eat before them.*
(Luke 24:40-43)

1 John 3:2 reads:

*Beloved, now are we the sons of God, and it doth not yet
appear what we shall be: but we know that, when he shall
appear, we shall be like him; for we shall see him as he is.*

The glorified bodies of the saints will be like Jesus' and we
will eat and drink literal food. This superior wine will no doubt be
present at the marriage supper of the Lamb recorded in Revelation
19:7-9. There is no doubt that the saints will have the fruit of the
vine with them throughout all eternity as a memorial of Christ's
precious redeeming blood. This cannot be an alcoholic beverage
because the corruption which the earth was subjected to because of
man's sin will be removed. The following passages make this clear:

*For the creation (nature) was subjected to frailty-to futil-
ity, condemned to frustration-not because of some
intentional fault on its part, but by the will of Him who
subjected it. That nature (creation) itself will be set free
from its bondage to decay and corruption [and gain an*

entrance] into the glorious freedom of God's children. (Romans 8:20,21, Amplified Bible)

Unlike the fruit of the vine which was the produce of God's original creation which He described as "very good" (Gen 1:31). Fermented wine which has caused so much suffering to man will be removed from God's new creation for ever, ...*for the former things are passed away* (Rev 21:4). That is, sorrow, pain, death, and decay etc.; because God said, *Behold, I make all things new.* (Rev 21:5)

Scripture is again very consistent with its symbols. In the Bible fruit usually refers to something of virtuous quality. We have the fruit of the womb (Luke 1:42), the fruit of the loins (Acts 2:30), the fruit of the Spirit (Galatians 5:22), the fruit of the lips (Hebrews 13:15), the fruit of righteousness (James 3:18), the fruit of the earth (James 5:7), the fruits of the tree of life (Revelation 22:2), and in Matthew 26:29; Mark 14:25; Luke 22:18, the fruit of the vine!

WINE AT CHRIST'S CRUCIFIXION

And they gave him to drink wine mingled with myrrh: but he received it not. (Mark 15:23)

They gave him vinegar to drink mingled with gall: and when he had tasted thereof, he would not drink. (Matt 27:34)

After this, Jesus knowing that all things were now accomplished, that the scripture might be fulfilled, saith, I thirst. Now there was set a vessel full of vinegar: and they filled a sponge with vinegar, and put it to his mouth. When Jesus therefore had received the vinegar, he said, It is finished: and he bowed his head, and gave up the ghost. (John 19:28-30)

Here we have before us the necessary information relating to the offering of wine to Jesus at His crucifixion. In the first two accounts above, there appears to be a conflict. Mark states that Jesus was given wine mingled with myrrh, while Matthew states that it was vinegar mingled with gall.

Some believe that this refers to two different incidents, while others understand it to be two different descriptions of the same incident, because vinegar was merely sour wine, and gall described anything bitter, without actually specifying what it was.

Although the real reason for Jesus initially refusing the sour wine or vinegar was because it was drugged and hence designed to alleviate His suffering, the Scripture also makes it very clear that our Lord found the drinking of such substances as repulsive. The Messianic reference in Psalms 69:21 reads:

> *They gave me also gall for my meat; and in my thirst they gave me vinegar to drink.*

Luke 23:36 states:

> *And the soldiers also mocked him, coming to him, and offering him vinegar.*

Here we can see from this unique and important account, how the Roman soldiers, knowing the character of our Lord, sought to compound His humiliation through further ridicule, by coming and offering Him vinegar (sour wine). This was their common drink, of which they knew Jesus hated. Later however, just before Jesus gave up his spirit, He thirsted and was given vinegar to drink, which He received. Thus we can hear Jesus agonisingly crying through Psalms 69:21, ...*in my thirst they gave me vinegar to drink.*

It was no doubt the will of the Father that the Spotless Son of God, in His dying agony, should drink the bitter drink of sinners, just as how spiritually He drank the bitter cup of sin which every sinner deserved.

CHAPTER 3

THE PROBLEM IN THE CORINTHIAN CHURCH

The passages of Scripture that we are about to examine will show us how a holy God requires total obedience to the specific instructions, which He reveals to men through Holy Scripture. There are some Christians today who drink intoxicating wine at the Lord's Supper, and there are those who believe that it does not matter. What they fail to realize is that it *does* matter, and that it is the responsibility of Christians to search the Scriptures for the truth, lest they bring the displeasure of God upon themselves.

The Lord's Supper had to be carried out exactly as instructed by our Lord and anything less in any degree would bring God's disapproval. 1 Corinthians 10:14-22, is the central point of the apostle Paul's reproof to the church in Corinth for contaminating the Lord's Supper with idol feasts. In verse 16, he states:

> *The cup of blessing which we bless, is it not the communion of the blood of Christ? The bread which we break, is it not the communion of the body of Christ?*

The apostle Paul was reminding them that the traditional cup of blessing which was drank at the Jewish Passover feast (the third cup in which thanks giving was offered over, the fourth according to Edersheim), now had a special and sacred significance. That is, it represented the blood of Christ which was shed for the remission of sins. The unleavened bread, which was broken, now represented the body of Christ, which was broken in the act of paying the penalty for sin.

180

The Corinthians were perverting this extremely sacred ordinance. Not only was the food and drink being sacrificed to idols or demons, but also the Corinthians were drinking intoxicating wine, as can be seen in the later Scriptures. In verse 21, the apostle Paul goes on to state:

> *Ye cannot drink the cup of the Lord, and the cup of devils: Ye cannot be partakers of the Lord's table, and the table of devils.*

Although this text refers to the spiritual aspect of the cup of the Lord, and the cup of devils respectively, the contents of the cup determined these overtones. Patton explains:

> *The contrast between the tables and the cups is apostolic and instructive. Their table and the cup they used were the devil's. The proper table and the proper cup were the Lord's. If their cup contained that which was intoxicating, it was, as Paul declares, the devil's cup; but the cup which contained that which was the opposite, and was not intoxicating, was, as the apostle teaches, the Lord's cup, the cup of blessing.*

It is indeed a fact that the libations poured out to demons or idols were of an intoxicating nature. Concerning this, Albert Barnes states:

> *In the feasts in honour of the gods, wine was poured out as a libation, or drank by the worshippers;...The custom of drinking toasts at feasts and celebrations arose from this practice of pouring out wine, or drinking in honour of the heathen Gods; and is a practice that partakes still of the nature of heathenism. It was one of the abominations of heathenism to suppose that their gods would be pleased with the intoxicating draught.*

It is thus clear that amongst other things, this what the Corinthians were involved in. This was in sharp contrast to the unfermented wine that was drank at the Passover and hence at the Lord's Supper. Edersheim states:

> *The Paschal Supper itself commenced by the head of `the company' taking the first cup of wine in his hand, and `giving thanks' over it in these words: `Blessed art thou, Jehovah our God, who hast created the fruit of the vine!'*

As was clearly stated in the previous chapter, the term "fruit of the vine," naturally referred to the pure unfermented juice of the grape. The Zondervan Pictorial Bible Dictionary explains:

> *At the Last Supper Jesus spoke of the "fruit of the vine" (Matt. 26:29), as in the Passover liturgy; it may be studied avoidance of the term wine, indicating that the drink was unfermented, as the bread was unleavened.*

Some argue that in the Talmud the rabbis drank fermented wine. This fact cannot be denied, but let us not forget our Lord's constant reproval of the rabbis for breaking the laws of God. In Mark 7:13, Jesus said:

> *Making the word of God of none effect through your tradition, which ye have delivered: and many such like things do ye.*

It is by no means being suggested that the sole reason for the apostle Paul's reproval of the Corinthians in this case was because they were drinking intoxicating wine. However, the point that we must understand, is that while there are not many today that might be as extreme as the Corinthians in profaning the Lord's Supper, there are many that are guilty in this particular area.

There are those who claim that there is nothing wrong with drinking fermented wine at the Lord's table, and there are those who state that the Bible is not clear regarding this issue, therefore it is really insignificant. But with something as awesome and sacred as the Lord's Supper, it is hardly likely that God after specifically making clear that the bread which symbolizes the body of our Lord should be unleavened, should leave us in the dark concerning the symbolic meaning of the blood of which He by the Holy Ghost said:

182

> *And almost all things are by the law purged with blood; and without shedding of blood is no remission.* (Hebrews 9:22)

In 1 Corinthians 11:17-34, the apostle Paul further instructs the Corinthians after their blatant abuse of the Lord's Supper. He further goes on to state the judgment that would fall upon those who ate and drank unworthily, but earlier in verse 21, he states:

> *For in eating every one taketh before other his own supper: and one is hungry, and another is drunken.*

There are those who state that some of the Corinthians were not necessarily drunk because the word translated "drunk" can refer to someone who has drunken to the full, although this is not the usual sense of the word. It is unlikely however, that this was the sense in which Paul was using it, and that there were some who were in fact drunk. Albert Barnes explains:

> *The word here used (methuo) means properly to become inebriated, or intoxicated; and there is no reason for understanding it here in any other sense. There can be no doubt that the apostle meant to say, that they ate and drank to excess; and that their professed celebration of the Lord's supper became a mere revel.*

What also must be borne in mind, is that earlier in 1 Corinthians 10:21, the Corinthians were clearly indulging in what Paul calls "the cup of devils," which as we saw involved the drinking and offering of intoxicating wine to an heathen deity. After which it was customary to parade through the streets in an half-drunken revel in honour of such an idol. Again in 1 Corinthians 5:11, they are commanded to separate themselves from anyone calling himself a brother who amongst other things, was a drunkard. In 1 Corinthians 6:9-11, the Corinthians are again warned that they should not be deceived into thinking that those who committed the most heinous sins which included drunkenness, would inherit the Kingdom of God. It is clear then that the Corinthians were no strangers to drunkenness, for in 1 Corinthians 6:11, Paul says, "And such were some of you." Thus we can see that there were those who had clearly not given up this evil practice, and were involved in integrating this heathen practice into Christianity. So the weight of Scriptural evidence argues in favour of the fact that some of the Corinthians were indeed drunk at the Lord's table.

The apostle then goes on to explain the correct procedure which he received from the Lord personally:

> *For I received of the Lord that which also I delivered unto you, That the Lord Jesus the same night in which he was betrayed took bread: And when he had given thanks, he brake it, and said, Take, eat: this is my body, which is broken for you: this do in remembrance of me. After the same manner also he took the cup, when he had supped, saying, This cup is the new testament in my blood: this do ye, as oft as ye drink it, in remembrance of me. For as often as ye eat this bread, and drink this cup, ye do shew the Lord's death till he come. Wherefore whosoever shall eat this bread, and drink this cup of the Lord, unworthily, shall be guilty of the body and blood of the Lord. But let a man examine himself, and so let him eat of that bread, and drink of that cup. For he that eateth and drinketh unworthily, eateth and drinketh damnation to himself, not discerning the Lord's body.* (1 Corinthians 11:23-29)

These verses are often read today before taking the Lord's Supper, with the sole emphasis on the individual searching themselves before partaking. The Bible Knowledge Commentary states:

> *Nowadays when this passage is read before participation in the Lord's Supper, it is usually intended to produce soul-searching introspection and silent confession to Christ so that no one will sin against the spiritual presence of the Lord by irreverent observance.*

In actual fact, there is more to what the inspired apostle is saying than this. While it is true that one should search their hearts and make sure that they approach the Lord's table in a reverential manner, the Lord also wants us to understand completely what this sacred ordinance represents. The Corinthian situation supplies us with an example of what happens to those who deliberately disregard the symbolic meaning of the Lord's Supper. Concerning the apostle's warning in verse 27, stating that whoever takes the supper in an unworthy manner "shall be guilty of the body and blood of the Lord," Barnes quotes Bloomfield as stating:

> *He shall be guilty respecting the body, i.e. guilty of profaning the symbols of the body and blood of Christ, and consequently shall be amenable to the punishment due to such an abuse of the highest means of grace.*

When we look further to Paul's statement in verse 29, that whoever eats and drinks in an unworthy manner, eats and drinks damnation on themselves. Because they were "not discerning the Lord's body," we learn something very interesting. The original word translated "discerning" is diakrino, which means to separate or discriminate. Therefore Paul was saying that before one partakes, they should first examine themselves and then also ensure that they realize that what they eat and drink symbolizes the body and blood of the Lord. Anyone who does not do this, "eateth and drinketh damnation" on themselves because they are unable to discriminate or determine the significance of the Lord's body. There are some scholars who try to water down this statement by suggesting the use of this word here only refers to the discrimination between the Lord's Supper and common meals. The context of the passage however, does not make such a restriction. Regarding the use of the word in this text (diakrino), Vincent's Word Studies in the New Testament states:

> *...the discrimination between the Lord's body and common food may naturally be contemplated; but further, such discernment of the peculiar significance and sacredness of the Lord's body as shall make him shrink from profanation and shall stimulate him to penitence and faith.*

Vine's Expository Dictionary also states:

> ...and in 1 Cor. 11:29, with reference to partaking of the
> bread and the cup of the Lord's Supper unworthily, by not
> discerning or discriminating what they represent.

The Amplified Bible's translation of 1 Corinthians 11:29,
reads:

> For any one who eats and drinks without discriminating
> and recognizing with due appreciation that [it is
> Christ's] body, eats and drinks a sentence-a verdict of
> judgment-upon himself.

Here we can see, contrary to what many like to accept, that God
clearly desires those who would partake of the Lord's Supper to
understand *fully* its sacred significance so that they can carry it out
exactly as Christ intended. This is not an unreasonable expectation,
but is a requirement that is perfectly consistent with the demands of
the Law. Jesus made this principle clear when He stated:

> And thou shalt love the Lord thy God with all thy heart,
> and with all thy soul, and with all thy mind, and with all
> thy strength: this is the first commandment. (Mark 12:30)

It is a sad thing today that many Christians adopt a frivolous
and indifferent attitude towards truth. They forget that God expects
us to use our minds as well as are hearts in our pursuit of spiritual
things. There are also those who think that because we are no
longer under the severe conditions of the Old Testament Law, that
they can offer anything to God and He is obliged to accept it. They
forget that the price of grace as far as God is concerned, is
extremely costly. Even though we don't seem to realize it, the
penalties for deliberately abusing this gift of grace is even more
severe than that of those under the Old Covenant. This principle is
outlined by the writer of the epistle to the Hebrews, when he states:

> For if the word spoken by angels was stedfast, and **every**
> transgression and disobedience received a just recom-
> pence of reward; How shall we escape if we neglect so

great salvation; which at the first began to be spoken by the Lord...? (Hebrews 2:2)

The writer of Hebrews again echoes this principle, by stating that the consequences will be serious for those who despised the sanctity and priceless virtue of Christ's blood:

> *He that despised Moses' law died without mercy under two or three witnesses: Of how much sorer punishment, suppose ye, shall he be thought worthy, who hath trodden under foot the Son of God, and hath counted the blood of the covenant, wherewith he was sanctified, an unholy thing, and hath done despite unto the Spirit of grace.* (Hebrews 10:28,29)

It must be clearly understood that these passages are not being taken out of context to fit the wine issue. It is true that the epistle to the Hebrews was written to those who were reverting back to the Levitical priesthood and hence were rejecting Christ's once for all sacrifice. However, the same *principles* with respect to drinking certainly apply here. Hebrews 2:2, states, that **every transgression and disobedience** *received a just recompence of reward.* So those who drink an intoxicating substance at the Lord's table when our Saviour specifically states that it should be "the fruit of the vine," have committed an act which clearly constitutes blatant and wilful disobedience. This will be justly rewarded in an even stricter fashion than which was experienced under the old order.

A mature consideration of Dr. Adam Clarke's comments on this are again appropriate here. He states:

> *This is a most wicked and awful perversion of our Lord's ordinance. The matters made use by Jesus Christ on this solemn occasion, were unleavened bread, and the produce of the vine, i.e. pure wine. To depart in the least from this institution, while it is in our power to follow it literally, would be extremely culpable.*

This is a sobering thought (sobering is ironic) for those who drink alcoholic wine or eat anything other than unleavened bread at the Lord's Supper. If anyone made Himself clear it was Jesus, and when He said "fruit of the vine," He meant exactly that.

What we have learnt is that amongst other things, the Corinthians had missed the whole purpose of the meaning of the Lord's Supper. The sin was not just in eating and drinking to excess, or in displaying an uncharitable spirit, but also of being wilfully ignorant of its symbolic meaning as the apostle Paul makes clear.

Those such as Bustanoby who in his book entitled, *The Wrath of Grapes,* cynically and sarcastically state that it was the attitude of the Corinthians and not their food and drink that was the problem. And that if the apostle Paul had wanted to castigate them for something as serious as drinking fermented wine, he would have ended by telling them to stop such an act and go back to drinking grape juice, are totally in error. First of all, it is obvious that the Corinthians were not eating unleavened bread at their feast, as they should have been. Because they were treating the supper as a common meal; but the apostle Paul doesn't tell them to stop eating their common food and go back to eating unleavened bread!

What he does is to remind them of the symbolic meaning of the wine and bread respectively. That is why Paul is careful to mention in verse 24, that the Lord Jesus took bread and break it, and explained to His disciples that it symbolized His body. Paul then reminds them again in verse 25, that the cup represented the New Testament in Jesus' blood. Notice that Paul does not mention that the contents of the cup was wine, in the same way that he does not mention that the broken bread was unleavened. So the reference to the cup and bread was enough to convey the truths to the Corinthians regarding the nature of the bread and wine. This was merely a reminder to the Corinthians of something that he had already explained to them, of which they were already familiar with, but failed to carry out.

Also, another point which refutes any suggestion that the food and drink was not the problem in the above context, but merely the Corinthian's attitude, is Paul's statement near the end of chapter 11, which reads:

> And if any man hunger, let him eat at home; that ye come not together unto condemnation. (1 Corinthians 11:34b)

If the only bone of contention that Paul had with the Corinthian brethren over the Lord's table, concerned their attitude. Then it would mean that it would be right for them to eat their normal supper which they should eat at home in celebration of the Lord's Supper, as they were already doing, as long as their attitude was right! This of course would be utterly ridiculous.

As we come near to concluding our study of the Corinthian situation, the main point that must be noted is that God disapproves of the abuse of the Lord's Supper in any way. Although as the account makes clear, Paul did not write to state that the sole reason for the abuse of the Lord's Supper was the use of intoxicating wine. Obviously, because of the nature of this study, we are more concerned with what has become a common practice. That is, the abuse of this sacred ordinance by the use of alcoholic and intoxicating wine. Whether one wants to accept the fact that some of the Corinthians indulged in fermented wine at the Lord's table or not, from our study of the Scriptures we have learnt that this practice is wrong.

As we have seen from our studies, God is very severe concerning those who abuse the Lord's Supper. This is only natural when we consider the extremely sacred importance of this ordinance, of which words hardly begin to convey. When we read in the Old Testament about the various offerings, such as the sin offering, the trespass offering, the peace offering, the various drink offerings etc., and how God was strict and exact regarding all the articles used. And when we consider that these only dimly prefigured the sacrifice of the Saviour, we then understand that it is absolutely inconceivable that God would be silent and inexact in respect to the contents of the cup which was to represent the ransoming blood of our Lord.

Of all the multiple sacrifices, feasts, offerings etc., mentioned in the Old Testament, the Lord's Supper was the ultimate. The crowning culmination of all memorials. What folly it is for one to abuse it, how irreverent it is for one to take it thoughtlessly!

After consideration of these Scriptural truths, it is understandable therefore why after the Corinthians abuse of the Lord's Supper that the apostle Paul uses these strong words:

> *Wherefore whosoever shall eat this bread, and drink this cup of the Lord, unworthily, shall be guilty of the body and blood of the Lord...For he that eateth and drinketh unworthily, eateth and drinketh damnation to himself, not discerning the Lord's body.* (1 Cor 11:27,29)

Barnes' summary concerning the gravity of these injunctions is extremely relevant and worthy of much thought. He states:

> *To treat with irreverence and profaneness the bread which was an emblem of his broken body, was to treat with irreverence and profaneness the body itself; and in like manner the wine, the symbol of his blood. Those, therefore who treated the symbols of his body and blood with profaneness and contempt were **united in spirit** with those who put him to death. They evinced the same feelings towards the Lord Jesus that his murderers did. They treated with scorn, profaneness, and derision; and showed that with the same spirit they would have joined in the act of murdering the Son of God. They would evince their hostility to the Saviour himself as far as they could do, by showing contempt for the memorials of his body and blood.*

For those who think that this sounds too harsh, Scripture is clear regarding the fate of those, who after receiving instructions, disobey God's commandments:

> *And ye shall observe the feast of unleavened bread; for in this selfsame day I brought your armies out of the land of Egypt: therefore shall ye observe this day in your generations by an ordinance for ever. In the first month, on the fourteenth day of the month at even, ye shall eat unleav-*

ened bread, until the one and twentieth day of the month at even. Seven days shall there be no leaven found in your houses: for whosoever eateth that which is leavened, even that soul shall be cut off from the congregation of Israel, whether he be a stranger, or born in the land. (Exodus 12:17-19)

These severe God given injunctions were given concerning the Passover, which was perfected and fulfilled by Christ in the Lord's Supper. In the light of these truths, believers today should heed the following:

For if God spared not the natural branches, take heed lest he also spare not thee. (Romans 11:21)

CHAPTER 4

ABSTINENCE -
NOT "TEMPERANCE"

Many Christians today believe that they are permitted to drink alcoholic beverages as long as they are "temperate." They mention the fact that Paul told Timothy to take a little wine for his stomach's sake (1 Timothy 5:23). They also assume that Christ turned the water into alcoholic wine at the marriage feast in Cana of Galilee (John 2:1-11). They also state that the Bible only warns against drunkenness, and therefore does not command total abstinence. In actual fact as we have seen in our studies the Bible does teach abstinence. Let us remind ourselves of one of these passages:

> Look not thou upon the wine when it is red, when it giveth his colour in the cup, when it moveth itself aright. At the last it biteth like a serpent, and stingeth like an adder. (Proverbs 23:31-32)

This is a clear command to abstain from alcoholic wine. Notice that the Scripture says do not even look at wine when it ferments let alone drink it. This fact is obvious as the reddening effect and the "moveth itself aright," describes the change in colour and the gas bubble effect of fermentation. Virtue's New Treasury of Knowledge Encyclopaedia, Volume 1, explains:

> Wine, for example, is made from juice pressed from grapes. Yeasts from the grapes get into the juice and feed on the sugar it contains to produce alcohol and carbon dioxide gas which bubbles off.

The Amplified Translation brings out this point by stating:

192

Do not look at wine when it is red, when it sparkles in the wineglass, when it goes down smoothly.

This can be compared to Psalms 75:8 which reads:

For in the hand of the Lord is a cup [of His wrath], and the wine foams and is red... (Amplified Bible)

The writers of these verses are clearly pointing out by their descriptiveness, that the wine they are referring to is the alcoholic or fermented type which only sinful men partake of. This shows how repulsive it is in the eyes of God. There is no room here for so called "temperate" indulgence but simply abstinence. There couldn't be a clearer command to abstain than this.

The text then goes on to state in verse 32, the destructive potential of this deceptive substance, "It biteth like a serpent and stingeth like an adder." This is descriptive of Satan the arch deceiver (Rev 20:2), who in the garden deceived Eve into taking a bite of the fruit, which she gave to Adam, who ate and plunged mankind into sin, and suffering. To tamper with alcohol is to tamper with Satan!

In the light of Scripture, whether a person considers himself to be drunk or not he has sinned in that he has deliberately polluted himself. The Amplified Translation of 2 Corinthians 6:17 states:

...and touch not [any] unclean thing; then I will receive you kindly and treat you with favor.

In 1 Corinthians 6:19,20 we read:

What? know ye not that your body is the temple of the Holy Ghost which is in you, which ye have of God, and ye are not your own? For ye are bought with a price: therefore glorify God in your body, and in your spirit, which are God's.

1 John 5:17 also states:

All unrighteousness is sin...

Let us now look at some New Testament passages which some say permit "temperate" indulgence in alcohol:

The aged women likewise, that they be in behaviour as becometh holiness, not false accusers, not given to much wine, teachers of good things. (Titus 2:3)

Likewise must the deacons be grave, not doubletongued, not given to much wine, not greedy of filthy lucre. (1 Timothy 3:8)

Drink no longer water, but use a little wine for thy stomach's sake and thine often infirmities. (1 Timothy 5:23)

The Christian must be honest in facing these supposed "difficulties," realizing that irrespective of how things may seem, God's perfect and holy character and standard will always be untainted, *Let God be true, but every man a liar.* (Romans 3:3) Hebrews 11:6 states:

But without faith it is impossible to please him: for he that cometh to God must believe that he is, and that he is a rewarder of them that diligently seek him.

The Christian life is a life of faith, the believer knows (even though he does not see everything) that God is what He says He is. That is, He is holy, pure, unchangeable and perfect. It is hard therefore to understand how people who profess to have been transformed by the blood of Christ could even imagine that God would sanction the use (in any quantity) of such a deadly substance such as alcohol. Some even go as far as suggesting that Jesus Christ, God's perfect Son, turned water into alcoholic wine and that He drank alcoholic or intoxicating wine Himself. Drunkenness would have been the obvious result or at least encouraged, considering the vast quantity of water He changed into wine, approximately 120-180 gallons!

Considering God's holy character, there must be a perfectly good explanation for the above passages and any others that may pose any problems. God cannot contradict himself:

*Every good gift and every perfect gift is from above, and cometh down from the father of lights, **with whom is no variableness, neither shadow of turning.*** (James 1:17)

194

We will now examine 1 Timothy 3:8, and Titus 2:3, together because of their similarities. They read:

> *Likewise must the deacons be grave, not given to much wine, not greedy of filthy lucre.* (1 Tim 3:8)

> *The aged women likewise, that they be in behaviour as becometh holiness, not false accusers, not given to much wine, teachers of good things.* (Tit 2:3)

There are those who on reading these texts automatically assume that the wine mentioned is of the alcoholic type, hence allowing for moderation with respect to intoxicants, but this is not necessarily the case.

1 Timothy 3:8 and Titus 2:3, when referring to "much wine," does not in any way make allowances for so called "temperate" drinking. Even if one assumes that the wine spoken of is alcoholic. Barnes quotes Bloomfield on 1 Timothy 3:8, in explaining this point:

> *The word much is added here to what is said of the qualification of a bishop. It is not affirmed that it would be proper for the deacon, any more than the bishop, to indulge in the use of wine in small quantities, but it is affirmed that a man who is much given to the use of wine ought not, on any consideration, be a deacon. It may be remarked here, that this qualification was everywhere regarded as necessary for a minister of religion. Even the heathen priests, on entering a temple, did not drink wine.*

Adam Clarke in his exposition makes it clear that the text in no way makes room for drinking whatsoever, even if one assumes that the wine spoken of was of the alcoholic nature. He states:

> *Neither a drunkard, tippler, nor what is called a jovial companion. All this would be inconsistent with gravity.*

Now in returning to the alternative idea that the wine referred to in 1 Tim 3:8 and Tit 2:3 was not necessarily alcoholic, we will now focus our attention further on Titus 2:3 in explaining this point:

The aged women likewise, that they be in behaviour as becometh holiness, not false accusers, not given to much wine, not greedy of filthy lucre.

Let us first consider some of the problems that Paul was trying to correct in this epistle. The epistle was written to Titus who was ordained the first bishop of the church of the Cretians. At Crete one of the big problems they had was sensuous over indulgence and gluttony. In Titus 1:12, the Apostle Paul states:

One of themselves, even a prophet of their own said, The Cretians are alway liars, evil beasts, slow bellies. (Gluttonous)

Dr. William Patton explains the reasons for the Apostle Paul's instructions, regarding self-control in Titus Chapter 2:

...these, before their conversion, had been idolaters, and who, in the days of their ignorance, had given themselves up to voluptuous practices. (That is, sensuous pleasure seeking acts)

He goes on to quote Polybius in his 6th book (as quoted by Nott) as saying:

Among the Romans, the women were forbidden to drink (intoxicating) wine; they drink, however, what is called passum, made from raisins, which drink very much resembles AEgosthenian and Cretan gleukos (sweet wine), which men use for allaying excessive thirst.

He then quotes the Rev. W.H. Rule when speaking of this unfermented wine, as saying:

A larger quantity might be taken, and the eastern sot could enjoy himself longer over the cup, than if he were filled up with fermented wine, without being baffled by the senselessness of profound inebriation.

Dr. Patton sums up the passage by stating:

These voluptuous habits denoted such devotion to the enjoyment of luxury and pleasure, such an indulgence in

sensual gratification, as unfitted these women for a sta-
tion in the Christian church, and for the proper discharge
of the domestic duties particularly noticed in the text.

We can thus see that it is perfectly reasonable that Paul was warning against sensual indulgence with this sweet tasting mixture. This would be essentially the same as warning against gluttony. For those not fully convinced, there is even more information if one looks closely enough, to fully vindicate this idea.

In the preceding verse (Titus 2:2) it reads:

That the aged men be sober, grave, temperate, sound in
faith, in charity, in patience.

The word translated "sober" here is nephalios, which means to be free from the influence of intoxicants, especially wine. Concerning the meaning of this word, Robinson's Lexicon of the New Testament states:

sober, temperate, abstinet, espec. in respect to wine.

This word is used metaphorically in the New Testament; i.e., to be sober minded and circumspect, but here the literal also applies. Even when this word is used in its metaphorical sense, one is still commanded to abstain from alcohol in order to fulfil the metaphorical command. That is, to be sober minded, watchful and circumspect. This removes all excuses from those who would down the meaning of this word strictly to its metaphorical sense, so that they may be free to indulge in drink. In this verse the inspired Apostle includes the words "grave" and "temperate." The former means to be worthy of respect and the latter means to be self controlled. Thus this verse could read:

Teach the older men to abstain from intoxicants (in order
to be sober minded, watchful and circumspect), to be
worthy of respect, self controlled, sound in faith, in love,
in endurance.

Verse 3 would then continue:

Teach the older women to do the same, that they may also
be worthy of respect, not slanderers, not to be slaves to
much wine (sweet wine), but to teach that what is good.

Robert Young one of the great Bible scholars of the past, gives the literal translation for verses two and three of Titus chapter 2, with the most ablest and concise explanation:

> That, lit. 'aged (or elders, elderly) men to be not-drinking, reverent, sound minded, healthy in the faith, the love, the endurance.'

> Aged, or 'elderly women or elderesses..in staidness as is proper to priestesses, not devils (lit. 'thrusters through,') not having been in bondage to much wine, teachers of good (persons or things).'

Here we can see that it is obviously clear that the "much wine" mentioned here could not be alcoholic. Because Paul would not command total abstinence as the passage clearly shows, and in the next breath make allowances for so called moderate indulgence, this would not make sense.

There is also another important point here that must not be over looked. In the Greek New Testament, whenever there is a warning against drunkenness, the term "much wine" (oino pollo) is never used. The words used are methuo (Matt 24:49; 1 Thess 5:7), methusko (Eph 5:18; Luke 12:45), methusos (1 Cor 5:11), methe (Gal 5:21). These are the words always used for drunkenness in the Greek New Testament. Had the Apostle Paul been warning against the over use of alcoholic wine, it would seem reasonable that he would have used one of these words which he himself used every time he wrote about drunkenness elsewhere in the New Testament. The very fact that he employs the term "much wine," may have been to make it clear to the recipients that the wine he was referring to was the non alcoholic kind, and therefore does not endorse so-called "temperate" indulgence.

This explanation can also apply to our next Scripture passage under examination (1 Timothy 3:8), which reads:

> Likewise must the deacons be grave, not doubletongued, not given to much wine, not greedy of filthy lucre.

Although the subject here is identical to the previously explained verse, which makes it clear that the "much" wine"

198

referred to was not necessarily alcoholic. An even stronger case for total abstinence can be seen when this verse is looked at in context with the previous verses, which reads:

> *This is a true saying, If a man desire the office of a bishop, he desireth a good work. A bishop then must be blameless, the husband of one wife, vigilant, sober, of good behaviour, given to hospitality, apt to teach; Not given to wine, no striker, not greedy of filthy lucre; but patient, not a brawler, not coveteous; One that ruleth well his own house, having his children in subjection with all gravity; (For if a man know not how to rule his own house, how shall he take care of the church of God?) Not a novice, lest being lifted up with pride he fall into the condemnation of the devil. Moreover he must have a good report of them which are without; lest he fall into reproach and the snare of the devil. Likewise must the deacons be grave, not doubletongued, not given to much wine, not greedy of filthy lucre.* (1 Timothy 3:1-8)

Notice in verse 8, it says, "Likewise must the deacons be..." In other words the same standard that is required of a bishop, is the same standard that is required of the deacon. The Apostle Paul merely labels some additional qualifications. We will now see that the bishops were commanded to abstain from alcohol and likewise the deacons. Let us now look closer at the required qualifications of bishops and deacons. In verse 2 above, the word translated "vigilant" in the original Greek is nephalion, this is the same word translated "sober" in the passage we looked at earlier (Titus 2:2), which meant to abstain from intoxicants. Young gives us a literal and concise explanation of 1 Tim 3:2 (above):

> *lit. `the overseer, therefore, it behoves to be unlaid-hold-upon, husband of one woman (only), not drinking, sober-minded, seemly (in behaviour), a friend of strangers, apt to teach,'*

Here we have another clear command to abstain from intoxicants, and as we go further it gets stronger. In verse 3 it states,

"Not given to wine" which in itself obviously means abstinence. Let the reader now compare the commands "not given to wine" in verse 3, with the command "not given to much wine" in verse 8. Obviously the Bible does not contradict itself. This again makes it clear that there were two kinds of wine, alcoholic and non alcoholic respectively. One we must abstain from totally, and the other we must not be over indulgent in.

Let us now examine the words translated "not given to wine." The Greek is me paroinon; from me, (not) and para, (at, by, near, with) and oinos, wine. Thus we have the command not to be at or near intoxicating or alcoholic wine. Since we have already seen that the word translated "vigilant" meant to abstain, the construction of this inspired passage deserves a clearer explanation. Dr. Patton gives us a very interesting insight into the drink issue in 1 Timothy 3:2,3 (above):

> *Notice the careful steps of the progress. He must be neephalion, abstinent, sober in body, that he may be sophrona, sound in mind, that his influence may be unimpaired, meeparoinon, not with or near wine. We find in this passage no countenance for moderate use of intoxicating wine, but the reverse, the obligation to abstain totally.*

He goes on to explain the meaning of the term translated "not given to wine" (paroinos):

> *"The ancient paroinos was a man accustomed to attend drinking parties." Thus the Christian minister is not only to be personally sober, but also to withhold his presence and sanction from those assemblies where alcoholic drinks are used, endangering the sobriety of himself and others.*

Here we can see that the passage clearly condemns the use and association with alcoholic beverages. This is perfectly consistent with the command, "A bishop then must be blameless" (See also Titus 1:6,7). The word translated "blameless" here in verse 2, means "not laid hold on" i.e., free from reproach. The Amplified Bible states:

Now a bishop (superintendent, overseer) must give no grounds for accusation but must be above repoach...

Wuest explains:

That is, a bishop must be of such a spotless character that no one can lay hold upon anything in his life which would be of such a nature as to cast reproach upon the cause of the Lord Jesus. He presents to the world at large such a Christian life that he furnishes no grounds for accusation.

If we read further down the passage to 1 Timothy 3:10, it states again:

...then let them use the office of a deacon, being found blameless.

W.E. Vine explains the meaning:

It implies not merely acquittal, but the absence of even a charge or accusation against a person.

Now we can see even more clearly why the Christian minister is commanded to stay away from alcoholic drinks. This is in order to fully maintain his blameless reputation.

There are some however that will dispute the meaning of the translation of the command "not given to wine," some of which are reputable scholars. Admittedly there are problems in this area, but we will see that there are some Bible scholars who have been prejudiced on this subject. This is why most Bible translations have not clearly brought to light the full meaning of the inspired text in the abstinence case.

We will look more closely at Bible translations in another chapter. But first of all, it is only fair to look at the views of those scholars who oppose the abstinence cause and in the opinion of the author, take a liberal view which when examined in the light of the inspired text does not make sense.

Let us again take another unprejudiced examination of the above text (1 Tim 3:1-8) and let it speak for itself in bringing to light the true "hidden facts." First of all, the word translated "not given to wine" in verse 3 (paroinon), is translated in many cases to mean not a excessive drinker instead of its original meaning "not at wine." Some scholars have realized that this could not be possible in the light of the inspired text because the word translated "vigilant" in verse 2 (nephalios) is usually translated to mean "temperate" (which does not fully bring out the meaning). Surely Paul in the same verse would not say that overseers should drink moderately, and then repeat himself by going on to also say that they should not drink excessively!

We will now look at how some scholars have in the opinion of the author, liberally sought to overcome this "problem" due to their theological bias. We will also see that the word translated "not given to wine" means what it says, and demands the translation "not at wine." Young's Analytical Concordance correctly renders this word, "One alongside of wine." Vincent, in the view of the author takes a liberal view in translating this word. He states:

> *The verb paroinein to behave ill at wine, to treat with drunken violence, is found in Xenophon, Aeschines, Aristophanes, and Aristotle.*

He suggests the translation "not quarrelsome over wine." Wuest jumps on the band wagon by stating:

> *In our Timothy passage, the wine is fermented...Paul's meaning is that the bishop, in partaking of wine, which in the first century was a common beverage not having the associations with which it is identified today, must not drink it so freely that he becomes intoxicated and hence quarrelsome. While this injunction does not teach total abstinence in the case of intoxicating liquors, but rather temperance, yet the present day Christian should use such an injunction as 1 Corinthians 10:31 as a guide in the case of present day indulgence in intoxicating liquors.*

Unfortunately, it is this kind of liberal prejudice that brings the Word of God into disrepute. We will now look at various interpretations of this word. Alford is quoted as saying:

> *one in his cups, a man rendered petulant by much wine.*

202

Expositors says:

> *The word means 'violent temper,' not specially excited by over-indulgence in strong drink.*

Alfred Marshall literally translates the word as, "an excessive drinker." The Revised Version in the opinion of the author unjustifiably translates the command "not given to wine" as "not a brawler" (The foot note reads, "Or, not quarrelsome over wine"). What makes this translation (interpretation) so unsatisfactory, is that in the text (A.V) one of the command already reads, "not a brawler" (one who fights), and "no striker" (a reviler). Therefore to insert an idea already conveyed by the inspired text in the place of this clear warning against drink, limits the scope of Biblical truth, and does injustice to the inspired passage. Barnes' comments on the use of this word (paroinos) in 1 Timothy 3:3, is extremely fitting:

> *It means, properly, by wine; i.e., spoken of what takes place by or over wine, as revelry, drinking songs, &c. Then it denotes, as it does here, one who sits by wine; that is, who is in the habit of drinking it. It cannot be inferred, from the use of the word here, that wine was absolutely and entirely prohibited; for the word does not properly express that idea. It means that one who is in the habit of drinking wine, or who is accustomed to sit with those who indulge in it, should not be admitted to the ministry. The way in which the apostle mentions the subject here would lead us fairly to suppose that he did not mean to commend its use in any sense; that he regarded its use as dangerous, and that he would wish the ministers of religion to avoid it altogether.*

We can now sum up the various interpretations of the word as follows:

(a) One made quarrelsome as a result of wine.
(b) One who is generally quarrelsome or violent.
(c) One who is an excessive drinker, a drunkard.
(d) One who is at or near wine, a drinker.

Let us take a look again at the Scriptures which makes it perfectly clear that only one of these ideas was in the mind of the writer which is the most natural and obvious meaning of the word, that is not being at wine. This would naturally mean total abstinence. The Amplified Translation of verse 3, makes this clear. It reads:

> Not given to wine, not combative but gentle and considerate, not quarrelsome but forbearing and peaceable, and not a lover of money-insatiable for wealth and ready to obtain it by questionable means.

This is a good translation. Here we can see that the word translated "not given to wine," could hardly be translated "not quarrelsome over wine" or generally quarrelsome or violent, because Paul goes on to say just that, "not quarrelsome." To give the commandment that one should not be quarrelsome over wine, and then again go on to say that one should not be quarrelsome would be ridiculous. To translate it to mean not a drunkard or an excessive drinker is also contextually out of place as we learnt earlier, because the word translated "vigilant" (1 Tim 3:2) in the KJV literally means to abstain from intoxicants, especially wine.

To command total abstinence one moment and then in the next to say "don't drink too much" or "drink in moderation," would also be ridiculous. The inspired text contains a divinely built in self-protecting mechanism for those who try to tamper with its meaning! To change the meaning of the word and to break the flow of the text to suit a pre-conceived idea without even presenting the full scope of the word, is not only biased but is also unfair to the unenlightened reader. Strong's Concordance gives us the correct meaning and origin of the word translated "not given to wine" (paroinon), as used in the New Testament:

> Paroinos, from para and oinos; staying near wine, i.e. tippling (a toper):-given to wine.

Here even the most prejudiced reader will have to admit the overwhelming weight of Biblical evidence settles the argument.

The inspired Word commands total abstinence from intoxicating beverages.

The next text that we will examine is one, which many professed Christians use to justify the use of alcoholic beverages. In many cases it is lustful desire and wishful thinking which prevent people from intelligently looking at the situation, trusting God, and at least giving the Holy Scriptures the benefit of the "doubt." God's righteousness will always be vindicated. The passage reads:

> *Drink no longer water, but use a little wine for thy stomach's sake and thine often infirmities.* (1 Timothy 5:23)

Many automatically assume that the wine mentioned here was alcoholic, but in order to understand the verse we must know the circumstances of the day. Patton explains:

> *As there existed in the roman Empire, in which Timothy travelled, a variety of wines, differing from each other in character, we cannot decide, ex cathedra, that it was alcoholic wine that Paul recommended. Pliny, Columella, Philo, and others state that many of the wines of their day produced "headaches, dropsy, madnesss, and stomach complaints."*

Here we can see that when it comes to the Word of God we should not judge things by appearance, "but judge righteous judgment." (John 7:24) Unfortunately, this has not been the case with some Bible scholars. Take for instance Vincent's dubious and subjective opinion on this text:

> *The appearance at this point of this dietetic prescription, if it is nothing more, is sufficiently startling; which has led to some question whether the verse may not have been misplaced. If it belongs here, it can be explained only as a continuation of the thought in ver.22, to the effect that Timothy is to keep himself pure by not giving aid and comfort to the ascetics, and imperilling his own health by adopting their rules of abstinence. Observe that oinos here, as everywhere else, means wine, fermented and capable of intoxicating, and not a sweet*

syrup made by boiling down grape-juice, and styled by certain modern reformers "unfermented wine." Such a concoction would have tended rather to aggravate than to relieve Timothy's stomachic or other infirmities.

The errors in this statement clearly reflect the prejudices of a man who on writing was obviously a proponent of the "temperance" (drink but don't get drunk) idea. First of all, it must be said that Paul's warning to Timothy to "keep thyself pure," did not refer to the fact that Timothy was to keep himself pure from those who abstained from intoxicants. It was rather to the preceding command in verse 22, "neither be partaker of other men's sins." Concerning this statement, Albert Barnes correctly states:

This is evidently to be interpreted in connection with the injunction "lay hands suddenly on no man." The meaning, in this connection, is, that Timothy was not to become a participant in the sins of another by introducing him to the sacred office. He was not to invest one with a holy office who was a wicked man or a heretic, for this would be to sanction his wickedness and error.

This meaning is obvious. However, it shows us the extent that some scholars will go in taking liberties in their interpretation of the sacred text, by denouncing something which challenges their prejudices.

For an accomplished Bible scholar to say that Paul referred to the advice of those who abstained from alcohol as impure, and that Timothy on grounds of his health should keep himself pure from them, is not only unscriptural but also outrageous. Unfortunately, Jamieson, Fausset, and Brown's Bible Commentary also gives an erroneous view in this area. It states:

God hereby commands believers to use all due means for preserving health, and condemns by anticipation the human traditions which among various sects have denied the use of wine to the faithful.

These conclusions show a narrow minded misunderstanding of the word usually translated "wine" (oinos). This takes us back to Vincent's subjective statement that "wine" (oinos) only means wine fermented and capable of intoxication. This is only wishful thinking. Robert Young as we have seen earlier in his Analytical Concordance gives us the correct meaning of the word "wine" (oinos) as, "Wine, grape juice." Here we can see, which we learnt from our earlier studies, that "wine" (oinos) could also mean grape juice.

We know that it was not only fermented at all, but was anything pressed from the grape, which meant wine in its fermented or unfermented state. Therefore, the idea that there were believers who wrongly held to the teaching of total abstinence from intoxicants is completely alien to the text. Total abstinence from alcohol was something commanded by God as we saw earlier, and not something made up by some religious sect, neither was it traditional error perpetrated by ill led Christian ascetics (abstainers).

We will now examine Vincent's final statement regarding this text, which stated that, the wine that Timothy was instructed to drink had to be intoxicating. This is because as he puts it, a sweet syrup would have tended to make things worse rather than better. One wonders how such a categoric statement could be made, when neither he nor anyone else commenting on the text, could know the true nature of Timothy's infirmities. One thing we do know today, is that alcoholic wine is not good for the stomach. A paper published by the Teachers Advisory Council on alcohol and drug education in 1980, stated the following concerning the effects of alcohol on the stomach:

> *Alcohol can lead to inflammation of the stomach. This can be a factor in the formation of peptic ulcers and also slows down the rate at which they heal.*

Let us also consider again the testimony long ago of Dr. J.W. Beaumont, Lecturer on Materia Medica in Sheffield Medical School England, who stated:

> *Alcohoic liquors are not nutricious, they are not a tonic, they are not beneficial in any sense of the word.*

Peter Masters in his book, *Should Christians Drink?* States the following:

> ...*grapes contain a substance which is highly effective against stomach organisms, ...this substance is diminished and eventually destroyed by fermentation.*

Having seen that it is rather fermented wine that would have aggravated rather than relieve Timothy's infirmities, let us learn something from the ancient writer Athenaeus, who writes:

> *let him take sweet wine (glukus), either mixed with water or warmed, especially that called protropos, as being very good for the stomach.*

Pliny, the ancient writer also states that the best wine recommended for the sick was sweet and unfermented. Frank E. Gaebelein agrees with this when he states:

> *Apparently for medicinal purposes, Timothy is told not to restrict himself to drinking water...The word for wine (oinos) is sometimes used in LXX (The Septuagint) for "must," or unfermented grape juice.*

These facts clearly imply that Paul was merely prescribing grape juice because of Timothy's weaknesses, which was a well-known thing of the day. There is not a drop of evidence to suggest that the wine had to be fermented, but rather the opposite, that is, wine sweet and unfermented. Surely God's precious holy revelation deserves to be treated with more caution and reverence by those who seek to interpret it!

Young's Concise Bible translates 1 Timothy 5:23, as follows:

> *be no longer drinking water, but be using a little wine, because of thy stomach, and thy frequent want of strength.*

No medical doctor in his right mind on reading this would prescribe an alcoholic mixture as a remedy. At times it is easy to allow the situation around us to prejudice our minds. We are living in a sinful world, and we must not allow it to corrupt our conception of God's perfect holiness and knowledge revealed to us through the Holy Scriptures. With the testimony of history, medical science, the Holy Scriptures, and common sense all speaking clearly and emphatically. It is more than likely that the wine Paul recommended to Timothy was sweet, wholesome, and unfermented. Can we accuse the Holy Spirit of ignorance?

Why some may ask, was Timothy told only to take a little wine? Since it was unfermented and harmless. We have already covered this point earlier, but we will look at it again in order to fully answer this question. We saw earlier in 1 Timothy 3:8, and Titus 2:3, that the deacons and the aged women were commanded not to be slaves to much wine (possibly sweet wine, grape juice). This was due to the vices of the day. Lees and Burns' Commentary explains:

> *Excessive drinking, even of uninebriating drinks, was a vice prevalent in the days of St. Paul, and corresponded to gluttony, also common-the excessive use of food, but not of an intoxicating kind.*

This leads us to the conclusion that because of Paul's command earlier to abstain from intoxicating wine, and his warning not to over indulge in much sweet wine. Timothy being very careful about his reputation, took an extremely cautious stance and abstained from both alcoholic and non alcoholic wine. Paul writing here in 1 Tim 5:23, reminds him that it is perfectly acceptable to drink the type of wine which is good for his health regularly. Possibly with his water, as the NIV states:

> *Stop drinking only water, and use a little wine because of your stomach and your frequent illnesses.*

The Amplified Bible states:

> *Drink no longer water exclusively...*

Those who continue to insist that the wine was alcoholic, in order to justify drinking, are caught in their own trap. Because they are compelled to confess the obvious fact that Paul regarded all other drinking of intoxicants as totally unacceptable. As only a little fermented wine permitted just on health grounds, would mean total abstinence in all other cases.

There are those who suggest that the wine Paul prescribed may have been vinegar (sour wine). Today's Dictionary of the Bible states the following concerning vinegar, and this idea:

> *When mixed with water, an expedient which rendered the bacteria-and parasite-infested water safe to drink (possibly Paul's reason for the advice given to Timothy...)*

Whether one wants to admit that the wine that Paul prescribed to Timothy was grape juice or not, the inspired text still condemns all private and social drinking. It cannot be denied that the construction of the text removes all ambiguity and excuses for drinking.

Further proof (not the alcoholic type!) for the correct meaning of Paul's commandment "a bishop must be vigilant" (abstain, 1 Tim 3:2), and "Not given to wine" (not at or near wine, 1 Tim 3:2), becomes even more startling and obviously clear, because as our text shows Timothy was obviously an extremely strict abstainer from all alcoholic or intoxicating drinks. Albert Barnes explains this point:

> *Timothy was un-doubtedly in the habit of abstaining wholly from the use of wine. Paul knew this, and he did not reprove him for it. He manifestly favoured the general habit, and only asked him to depart in some small degree from it, in order that he might restore and preserve his health.*

The very fact that Paul carefully qualifies the reason for him prescribing wine to Timothy shows that Paul forbade the use of alcoholic wine. This proves that Timothy understood Paul's earlier instructions to mean total abstinence. It also proves that Timothy was not a regular "temperate" drinker of alcoholic wine, as some say Paul's writings endorse by incorrectly interpreting such passages as 1 Tim 3:3,8; Tit 1:7; 2:3. Since Paul referred to wine only for the use of preserving health, adds weight to the argument that unfermented wine was used in Paul and Timothy's day. And would suggest that Timothy understood that Paul was prescribing a sweet unfermented wine, which the ancient writer

Athenaeus informs us was good for the stomach. This automatically refutes any presumptuous thoughts such as Wuest makes in his commentary, that the wine that Paul was speaking of was naturally fermented.

Many Christians today, who proclaim the uniqueness and exceedingly high standard of holiness of the Bible over all other religions, grossly contradict themselves when they drink intoxicating drinks, and suggest that the Bible endorses it. There are other religions that realize the dangers of intoxicating drinks and condemn the use of it. Take for instance the Koran of the Muslim religion, which prohibits the use of intoxicating drinks. The text reads:

> *O you who believe, intoxicants and games of chance and (sacrificing to) stones set up and (dividing by) arrows are an uncleanness, the devil's work; so shun it that you may succeed.* (2:219)

Maulana Muhammad Ali's commentary on this text states:

> *This verse prohibits all intoxicants and games of chance; and besides, by classing them with sacrifices to stones set up for idols and dividing by arrows, subjects them to the prohibition of v.3. It is related that when this verse was revealed a crier proclaimed in the streets of Madinah that wine was prohibited, and in response to this every jar of wine in a Muslim house was emptied, so that wine flowed in the streets. Never in the history of the world was such a deep-rooted evil as drink so suddenly yet so completely eradicated.*

These wise and disciplined instructions are truths which many ministers, Bible commentators, and church goers, charge the Bible of being deficient of in the area of drink. The worlds greatest Book on morals they say, advocates the drinking of alcohol, and is ranked below other religions in this area. The folly of such hypocritical reasoning in the face of Scripture, is explained by Barnes:

> *The use of wine, and of strong drinks of all kinds, was absolutely prohibited to the Jewish ministers of every*

rank when they were about to engage in the service of God; lev.x.9. should it then be any more proper for a Christian minister to drink wine than for a Jewish or heathen priest? Shall a minister of the gospel be less holy than they? Shall he have a feebler sense of the purity of his vocation? Shall he be less careful lest he expose himself to the possibility of conducting the services of religion in an irreverent and silly manner? Shall he venture to approach the altar of God under the influence of intoxicating drinks, when a sense of propriety restrained the heathen priest, and a solemn statute of Jehovah restrained the Jewish priest from doing it?

It is very important that we realize that the Bible simply does not support the moderation or so-called "temperance" theory with respect to intoxicating drinks. Whenever the word is used in the New Testament it always means self-restraint. In Acts 24:25; Galatians 5:23; 2 Peter 1:16, the original word used is enkrateia, from kratos, meaning strength, and thus the full meaning of complete control and self discipline is heavily conveyed. There is a difference between abstinence from sin and "minor" indulgence in sin, "All unrighteousness is sin..." (1 John 5:17)

In actual fact, the moment one takes the first drop of an intoxicating drink, their judgment is impaired to a certain degree. His capacity of loving, reasoning, and worship is inhibited, if only slightly, and he therefore deliberately disobeys the greatest commandment in Scripture which comes from the lips of our Lord Himself:

AND THOU SHALT LOVE THE LORD THY GOD WITH ALL THY HEART, AND WITH ALL THY SOUL, AND WITH ALL THY MIND, AND WITH ALL THY STRENGTH... (Mark 12:30)

212

CHAPTER 5

ABSTINENCE ESSENTIAL FOR MORAL AND SPIRITUAL ALERTNESS

The greatest climax of the ages will be the return of our Lord Jesus Christ. Throughout the New Testament, we see that the inspired writers, through the Holy Spirit, admonish the necessity of total watchfulness for this event. We will also see that whenever these instructions are given, there is usually a warning against drunkenness, or a command to abstain from intoxicants. Whether the language is literal or metaphorical. The first passage that we will examine reads:

> *But of the times and the seasons, brethren, ye have no need that I write unto you.*
>
> *For yourselves know perfectly that the day of the Lord so cometh as a thief in the night.*
>
> *For when they shall say, Peace and safety; then sudden destruction cometh upon them, as travail upon a woman with child; and they shall not escape.*
>
> *But ye, brethren, are not in darkness, that that day should overtake you as a thief.*
>
> *Ye are all the children of light, and the children of the day: we are not of the night, nor of darkness.*
>
> *Therefore let us not sleep, as do others; but let us watch and be sober.*
>
> *For they that sleep sleep in the night; and they that be drunken are drunken in the night.*

But let us, who are of the day, be sober, putting on the breastplate of faith and love; and for an helmet, the hope of salvation.

For God hath not appointed us to wrath, but to obtain salvation by our Lord Jesus Christ. (1 Thessalonians 5:1-9)

The language of this passage is worth taking note of. The original Greek word for "sober" in verses six and eight is nepho. This word means to be free from the influence of intoxicants. This word is often used in the metaphorical sense, in association with watchfulness. Young gives us a literal translation of verse six:

`therefore, then, we may not sleep at all, as also the rest, but may we be wakeful and sober,' (lit. not drinking).*

Here we can see that the literal translation gives a clear command to abstain from alcohol, the language is merely used in a metaphorical sense to convey the idea of total alertness. The terminology perfectly illustrates the fact that one cannot be totally alert if one drinks. Commenting on the word nepho and the meaning of the text, Barnes states:

*It properly means, to be temperate or abstinent, especially in respect to wine...and then it is used in a more general sense, as meaning to be sober-minded, watchful, circumspect. In this passage there is an allusion to the fact that persons not only **sleep** in the night, but that they are frequently **drunken** in the night also. The idea is, that the Lord Jesus, when he comes, will find the wicked sunk not only in carnal security, but in sinful indulgences, and that those who are Christians ought not only to be awake and to watch as in the day-time, but to be temperate.*

In summing up this passage we can see that the apostle Paul through the Holy Spirit, had a specific reason for employing the language that he did. The best way that God could stress the need for spiritual alertness was to use the analogy of those who drink and get drunken. Here we can see with amazing clarity, that God in His wisdom regards indulgence in intoxicating beverages as being harmful to the thinking faculties, and therefore commands total abstinence.

We can thus see that the Bible's definition of "sober" does not permit moderate drinking, as is the common misunderstanding of the meaning of "temperate," but to be sober is to abstain totally from alcohol. Notice how the writer states that those who are of the day (those who are in spiritual light) should be sober (abstain), in contrast to those of the night (those in spiritual darkness), in order to be *totally* sensitive to God's Word. Patton states:

> *This sobriety is associated with putting on the Christian armor, and it is the call for vigilant wakefulness, having all the powers of mind and body in proper condition.*

We see therefore that Christians are commanded to be different from sinners and to abstain from alcohol. The Christian then should be alert and pay his attention to other things of greater importance, such as putting on the armour of God, "For God hath not appointed us to wrath, but to obtain salvation by our Lord Jesus Christ."

We will now look at other passages of Scripture where the word nepho is used. Although often used in its metaphorical sense, the total truth, which it conveys spiritually, is very important. W.E. Vine states:

> *NEPHO signifies to be free from the influence of intoxicants; in the N.T., metaphorically, it does not in itself imply watchfulness, but is used in association with it.*

Robinson's Lexicon of the New Testament states:

> *to be sober, temperate, abstinent, espec. in respect to wine.*

The next text we will look at reads:

> *Wherefore gird up the loins of your mind, be sober (nepho), and hope to the end for the grace that is to be brought unto you at the revelation of Jesus Christ.* (1 Peter 1:13)

Louis A. Barbieri commenting on this verse, correctly states:

> *The conversion of the individual through the regeneration of the Holy Spirit should be accompanied by a*

215

mental awakening and a new discipline of understanding. Peter urges the believer to "be sober," an expression commonly used to signify abstinence from wine. Peter uses the expression to speak of moral alertness and sobriety. The Christian should not live a life of self indulgence, but one of discipline and self-control, in full possession of his faculties.

Young's Concise Bible Translation beautifully brings out this point (key points highlighted by author):

*'have girded up for yourselves the loins of your full mind, **being not-drinking**, hope perfectly upon the grace of being borne to you in an uncovering of Jesus Christ.'*

In verse sixteen, the inspired apostle goes on to state why God demands such high standards:

Because it is written, Be ye holy; for I am holy.

The apostle Peter again uses the word nepho later on in the epistle:

But the end of all things is at hand: be ye therefore sober, (nepho) and watch unto prayer. (1 Peter 4:7)

Barbieri again states:

Sobriety of mind is a vital aspect of the believer's life, for it is indespensible to full prayerfulness. A Christian should keep himself awake and alert with complete control of his faculties so that he can give himself to prayer. Of all people, the Christian should not allow his mind to become confused or dazed by drink or drowsiness. The individual in complete control of his mind is able to have the proper perspective.

Here we can see the kind of life that God desires His people to live, that is a holy and separated life in anticipation of Christ's return. And that means total abstinence from all kinds of intoxicants.

Again we read in 1 Peter 5:8:

Be sober, be vigilant; because your adversary the devil, as a roaring lion, walketh about, seeking whom he may devour.

Young's Concise Bible Translation of this verse reads:

`be not-drinking, be wakeful, because the Devil (lit. thruster through), your opponent (in law), as a lion roaring for himself walks round about, seeking whom he may swallow down.'

Adam Clarke's comments on this text regarding the clause "seeking whom he may swallow down," reads:

Whom he may gulp down. *It is not every one that he can swallow down: those who are **sober and vigilant** are proof against him, these he MAY NOT swallow down; those who are **drunken** with the cares of this world, &c., and are **unwatchful**, these he MAY swallow down. There is a beauty in this verse, and a striking apposition between the first and last words, which I think have not been noticed: **Be sober, from nephate, from ne, not, and piein, to drink; do not drink, do not swallow down: and the word katapie, from kata, down, and piein, to drink.** If you swallow strong drink down, the devil will swallow you down. Hear this, ye drunkards, topers, tiplers, or by whatsoever name you are known in society, or among your fellow-sinners. Strong drink is not only the way to the devil, but the devil's way into you; and YE are such as the devil particularly MAY swallow down.*

In summing up these passages, it must be said that no one who honestly looks at them can really deny that a perfectly holy God demands a standard of holiness that commands total abstinence from alcohol, or anything of the kind. The Apostle Peter's writings are those of a man who well remembered the words of our Lord:

Be ye therefore perfect, even as your Father which is in heaven is perfect. (Matthew 5:48)

In 1 Corinthians 15:34, we read:

217

Awake to righteousness, and sin not; for some have not the knowledge of God: I speak this to your shame.

The original word translated "awake" is eknepho, this primarily means to return to soberness after being drunk, or to return to one's senses. The apostle Paul uses it here in a metaphorical sense when warning against false doctrine. Regarding the use of this word in this text, W.E. Vine states:

suggesting a return to soberness of mind from the stupor consequent upon the influence of evil doctrine.

One cannot imagine the apostle Paul advocating a "bit" of false doctrine through so called moderation. No, the analogy is perfect; false doctrine, like alcohol is evil, and we are commanded to abstain from both!

If we now turn to 2 Timothy 2:26, we read:

And that they may recover themselves out of the snare of the devil, who are taken captive by him at his will.

The word translated "recover" is ananepho, which again means to return to soberness from a state of drunkenness. Here again the word is being used in its metaphorical sense to stress the importance that total alertness and sensitivity to Gods Word is the only way to escape the devil's captive power.

The use of these words in the New Testament is no accident. The whole idea behind these words originated in the mind of God. The believer is to *abstain* from all forms of evil, as 1 Thessalonians 5:22 makes clear:

Abstain from all appearance of evil.

In actual fact the translation of this verse is slightly misleading, because the thought behind the text is that one should abstain from all forms of evil. The NIV states:

Avoid every kind of evil.

The Amplified Bible states:

Abstain from evil-shrink from it and keep aloof from it-in whatever form or whatever kind it may be.

218

The next set of Scriptures that we will look at, are the words of Jesus concerning His return, here we will see that Jesus warns against indulgence and drunkenness as a must for total alertness regarding this most crucial event. The first passage reads:

> *And take heed to yourselves, lest at any time your hearts be overcharged with surfeiting, and drunkenness, and cares of this life, and so that day come upon you unawares. For as a snare shall it come on all them that dwell on the face of the whole earth. Watch ye therefore, and pray always, that ye may be accounted worthy to escape all these things that shall come to pass, and to stand before the Son of man. (Luke 21:34-36)*

There are those who say that the disciples must have been in the habit of drinking intoxicating drinks because Jesus warned them against drunkenness, rather than drinking, but this is simply not the case. No such conclusion can be drawn from this statement whatsoever. We can see here how Jesus warns against drunkenness and the evils, which result from it, and shows how these things dullen the mind and heart, thereby preventing the individual from being sensitive to the events which will mark His coming.

Jesus again warns against indulging in strong drink which would prevent His servants from watching wisely, and being ready when he returns. The text reads:

> *Who then is a faithful and wise servant, whom his lord hath made ruler over his household, to give them meat in due season? Blessed is that servant, whom his lord when he cometh shall find so doing. Verily I say unto you, That he shall make him ruler over his goods. But and if that evil servant shall say in his heart, My lord delayeth his coming; And shall begin to smite his fellow servants, and to eat and drink with the drunken; The lord of that servant shall come in a day when he looketh not for him, and in an hour that he is not aware of, And shall cut him asunder, and appoint him his portion with the hypocrites: there shall be weeping and gnashing of teeth. (Matthew 24:45-51)*

Here we can see in this parable that the servant of Christ is not even to drink with the drunken lest it cost him his soul. This is yet another verse which reinforces Christ's knowledge of the Old Testament as this reflects Proverbs 23:20, "Be not among winebibbers" (wine drinkers). In the parallel passage to this, Jesus also states the sentence of the neglectful servant:

> *But and if that servant say in his heart, My lord delayeth his coming; and shall begin to beat the menservants and maidens, and to eat and drink, and to be drunken; The lord of that servant will come in a day when he looketh not for him, and at an hour when he is not aware, and will cut him in sunder, and will appoint him his portion with the unbelievers.* (Luke 12:45,46)

There is something very interesting and important to note concerning the construction of the words in this passage, which differs slightly from that of Matthew's account. When dealing with Luke's account, many Bible commentators merely refers the reader back to the parallel passage in Matthew 24:45-51, and do not bother or consider it important to deal with this point that we are about to examine.

Let the reader note here that the word translated "and to be drunken," is the verb methusko, which means to "become drunk" or to "grow drunk." Alfred Marshall's translation of the last clause of verse 45 reads, "both to eat and to drink and to become drunk." Here we can see that our Lord condemns the drinking of alcoholic drinks just as much as drunkenness, which is the culminating effect of continual drinking. Jesus here makes this point clear by saying that the servant who began to eat and drink (intoxicating drinks) and also became drunk would be punished. Let the reader understand here that eating in itself is obviously not sinful, but it is spoken against here because it is associated with drinking and drunkenness.

Our Lord here is very specific. Had He approved of drinking, He would only have warned against drunkenness, but the very fact that He states to "drink, **and to be** drunken," puts it beyond doubt that Jesus forbade both drinking and drunkenness alike.

There are those who may suggest that the drinking referred to here might not necessarily be of the alcohoic kind, and that Jesus only condemns it because it is associated with drunkenness just the same as eating. This might be a good argument, but the precise construction of the Greek makes this impossible, because the text simply states that the drunkenness was a direct result of starting the process of drinking. Since drunkenness therefore can only be caused by the use of intoxicating drinks, no one can deny the fact that Jesus spells out in no uncertain terms that drinking as well as drunkenness is evil.

CHAPTER 6

NEW TESTAMENT SCRIPTURAL PRINCIPLES FOR TOTAL ABSTINENCE

Many professed Christians today do not understand the true concept of Biblical holiness, they walk in the flesh and have not really experienced the Spirit filled life. Some ask the question is it wrong to drink? But they put the cart before the horse, the question should be is it right to gratify the lusts of the flesh? If they read the Bible they would see that drinking is one of the works of the flesh.

In this chapter we will look at a further list of Scripture passages, which shows the standard of holiness required of Christians. The reader will not find it written, "do not drink," but the principles laid down in the commandments are just as strong and obviously apply to the drink situation. These texts add further weight to the previous specific commands to abstain which we have looked at, thus showing that God's Word speaks clearly and emphatically on this subject. Comments will be given after certain passages for the purpose of greater emphasis. The passages are as follows:

> Having therefore these promises, dearly beloved, let us cleanse ourselves from all filthiness of the flesh and spirit, perfecting holiness in the fear of God. (2 Corinthians 7:1)

The Bible Knowledge Commentary states the following concerning this verse:

> These promises refer to God's assurances of His presence and fellowship to those who obey Him. This obedience requires purification, which here implies sep-

222

*aration **from everything that contaminates body and spirit** and from every person who pollutes the truth.*

Concerning the commandment that believers should cleanse themselves "from all filthiness of the flesh and spirit," Barnes states:

> *The noun here used...means to stain, defile, pollute, as a garment; and the word here used means **a soiling**, hence defilement, pollution, and refers to the defiling and corrupting influence of fleshly desires and carnal appetites. The filthiness of the flesh here denotes evidently the gross and corrupt appetites and passions of the body, including all such actions of all kinds as are inconsistent with the virtue and purity with which the body, regarded as the temple of the Holy Ghost, should be kept holy-all such passions and appetites as the Holy Spirit of God would not produce.*

Can anyone doubt that alcoholic beverages would be one of the things included here?

The next passage reads:

> *For the grace of God that bringeth salvation hath appeared to all men, Teaching us that, denying ungodliness and worldly lusts, we should live soberly, righteously, and godly, in this present world; Looking for that blessed hope, and the glorious appearing of the great God and our Saviour Jesus Christ; Who gave himself for us, that he might redeem us from all iniquity and purify unto himself a peculiar people, zealous of good works.* (Titus 2:11-14)

> *And every man that hath this hope in him purifieth himself, even as he is pure.* (1 John 3:3)

> *Because it is written, Be ye holy; for I am holy. (1 Peter 1:16)*

> *I beseech you therefore, brethren, by the mercies of God, that ye present your bodies a living sacrifice, holy, acceptable unto God, which is your reasonable service. And be not conformed to this world: but be ye trans-*

223

formed by the renewing of your mind, that ye may prove what is that good, and acceptable, and perfect, will of God. (Romans 12:1,2)

There is therefore now no condemnation to them which are in Christ Jesus, who walk not after the flesh, but after the Spirit. (Romans 8:1)

For they that are after the flesh do mind the things of the flesh; but they that are after the Spirit the things of the Spirit. For to be carnally minded is death; but to be spiritually minded is life and peace. Because the carnal mind is enmity against God: for it is not subject to the law of God, neither indeed can be. So then they that are in the flesh cannot please God. (Romans 8:5-8)

Therefore, brethren, we are debtors, not to the flesh, to live after the flesh. For if ye live after the flesh, ye shall die: but if ye through the Spirit do mortify the deeds of the body, ye shall live. (Romans 8:12,13)

This I say then, Walk in the Spirit, and ye shall not fulfil the lust of the flesh. (Galatians 5:16)

In whom also ye are circumcised with the circumcision made without hands, in putting off the body of the sins of the flesh by the circumcision of Christ. (Colossians 2:11)

Love not the world, neither the things that are in the world. If any man love the world, the love of the Father is not in him. For all that is in the world, the lust of the flesh, and the lust of the eyes, and the pride of life, is not of the Father, but is of the world. (1 John 2:15,16)

Dearly beloved, I beseech you as strangers and pilgrims, abstain from fleshly lusts, which war against the soul. (1 Peter 2:11)

No one in their right mind can deny that alcohol wars against the soul, it is one of Satan's most effective strategic weapons used against mankind whom he so much hates.

Again we read:

That ye put off concerning the former conversation the old man, which is corrupt according to the deceitful lusts. (Ephesians 4:22)

Alcohol is a deceitful lust. The drinker of alcoholic beverages is deceived by Satan into thinking that it is good for him, while it is destroying his body and soul. The believer is commanded to put off these things, which are characteristic of the corrupt nature of the old man.

The final text states:

Therefore if any man be in Christ, he is a new creature: old things are passed away; behold, all things are become new. (2 Corinthians 5:17)

CHAPTER 7

CHRISTIAN LIBERTY AND TOTAL ABSTINENCE

There are those who claim that those who advocate total abstinence from intoxicating drinks are legalists, who are imposing their unscriptural views on people's Christian liberty. Andre S. Bustanoby is one such person who dedicates virtually a whole book to this theory. In his book, *The Wrath of Grapes,* he is very critical of all those who promote the cause of total abstinence, including David Wilkerson's book, *Sipping Saints,* and others.

We have already thoroughly examined Scriptures that clearly command total abstinence from intoxicants, which automatically refute many of Mr. Bustanoby's arguments. It is very sad for someone claiming to promote the Christian cause to spend his time in what clearly appears to be championing the cause of drinking alcoholic beverages, and also labelling those who advocate total abstinence as hypocritical, ignorant legalistic prohibitionists!

In this chapter we will examine much of Mr. Bustanoby's arguments against total abstinence in an open minded, fair, and Biblical fashion. A principle which he himself failed to apply when dealing with this subject.

On page 26 of his book, he disapprovingly quotes a perfectly valid statement from David Wilkerson's book, *Sipping Saints,* which reads:

> *Were the ancients in the habit of preserving and using as such, free from fermentation, the juice of the grape? Beyond all doubt they were.*

Mr. Bustanoby's disagreement with this fact is clearly reflected throughout his book, his direct reply to the above statement reads:

Yet, in spite of this bold assurance, we must seriously doubt claims about the preservation of grape juice. Legalistic prohibitionists grossly misinterpret both the Bible and ancient historians, simply because they do not understand the chemistry of winemaking. If they did, they would not make the outrageous claims they pass for fact.

This is a very serious charge that has to be answered, but before replying in full, let us further consider the critical and compounding statements in Mr. Bustanoby's book concerning non-alcoholic or unfermented wine. Again on page 26, the opening page of his chapter entitled, *Dispelling Myths About Wine,* he opens with this statement:

The legalist, in pressing his case against fermented wine, contends that the wine consumed by believers in biblical times was not fermented wine as we know it today but grape juice.

On page 25, he also states:

Finally, the most critical question of all is whether believers in Old and New Testament times preserved grape juice in an unfermented state. To say that they did shows a serious misunderstanding of the chemistry of winemaking and leads to false interpretation of historical evidences. We will next consider the chemistry of winemaking and dispel some myths about wine.

On page 70, he states this concerning the preservation of grape juice, which is called "must":

Must cannot be kept from fermenting, even when immersed in water.

In order to expose the narrow minded approach of these statements in Bustanoby's book, it will be necessary to extensively quote ancient authorities, Bible commentators, and the Bible itself. Let the reader judge for him or herself concerning the reliability of these facts, and whether they have been correctly or incorrectly interpreted in the light of the Bible!

Chamber's Cyclopaedia, sixth edition (1750) states:

Sweet wine is that which has not yet fermented.

Rees' Cyclopaedia:

Sweet wine is that which has not yet worked or fermented.

Dr. Noah Webster's Dictionary:

Wine, the fermented juice of grapes. Must, Wine, pressed from the grape, but not fermented.

Professor Charles Anthon, LL.D., in his Dictionary of Greek and Roman Antiquities, article Vinum, states:

The sweet unfermented juice of the grape was termed gleukos.

Horace, born 65 BC, states:

There is no wine sweeter to drink than Lesbian; that it was like nectar, and more resembled ambrosia than wine; that it was perfectly harmless, and would not produce intoxication. - Anti-Bacchus, p. 220.

Dr. F.R. Lees, quotes Captain Treat as saying:

The unfermented wine is esteemed the most in the south of Italy, and wine is drunk mixed with water.

The New York Evangelist stated the following years ago:

...from authorities of the highest repute as exegists or personal observation, some of them adverse to the main question, by their unanimous concurrence, that the sweet wine, or unfermented juice of the grape, was of old a popular beverage in Palestine.

Strong's Exhaustive Concordance of the Bible, states the following concerning the Hebrew word tirosh (usually translated new wine):

from...the sense of expulsion; must or fresh grape-juice (as just squeezed out);...(rarely) fermented wine:-(new, sweet) wine.

Genesis 40:10,11 is very important in confirming these points. It reads:

And in the vine were three branches: and it was as though it budded, and her blossoms shot forth; and the clusters thereof brought forth ripe grapes: And Pharaoh's cup was in my hand: and I took the grapes, and pressed them into Pharaoh's cup, and I gave the cup into Pharaoh's hand.

Concerning this custom, Dr. Nott states the following:

Plutarch affirms that before the time of Psammetichus, who lived six hundred years before Christ, the Egyptians neither drank fermented wine nor offered it in sacrifice.

He also states, as the Bible confirms:

In remote antiquity, grapes were brought to the table, and the juice there expressed for immediate use.

These facts prove without a shadow of a doubt that unfermented wine was used in Bible times. The liberals might suggest that the drinking of freshly squeezed grape juice in Genesis 40:10,11, referred only to a dream and therefore cannot be taken seriously. But unfortunately for them as we have just noted, the custom outlined in the Biblical account of the dream is confirmed by ancient authorities. Even in Pompeii an exhumation revealed a statue of Bacchus the god of wine holding in his hands a cluster of grapes and squeezing the juice into a cup!

The most convincing point of all is that it was God who was the author of the dream, and therefore used a sensible and realistic custom, of which the butler and those of his day were well familiar with.

METHODS USED FOR PRESERVING GRAPE JUICE

Three methods of preventing all fermentation in grape juice are mentioned by Professor Donavan in the works of Anti-Bacchus:

229

(1) *Grape-juice will not ferment when the air is completely excluded.*

(2) *By boiling down the juice, or, in other words, evaporating the water, the substance becomes a syrup, which if very thick will not ferment.*

(3) *If the juice be filtered and deprived of its gluten, or ferment, the production of alcohol will be impossible.*

Dr. Ure, an eminent chemist, adds another method:

By those means which render the yeast inoperative, particularly by the oils that contain sulphur, as oil of mustard, as also by the sulphurous and sulphuric acids.

We will now look at numerous accounts of these methods from ancient authorities:

Smith, in his Greek and Roman Antiquities, states:

The sweet, unfermented juice of the grape was termed gleukos by the Greeks and mustum by the Romans-the latter word being properly an adjective signifying new or fresh." "A portion of the must was used at once, being drunk fresh," "When it was desired to preserve a quantity in the sweet state, an amphora was taken and coated with pitch within and without, it was filled with mustum lixivium, and corked so as to be perfectly air-tight. It was then immersed in a tank of cold fresh water, or buried in wet sand, and allowed to remain for six weeks or two months. The contents, after this process, was found to remain unchanged for a year, and hence the name, aeigleukos-that is, `semper mustum,' always sweet.

The care taken by the ancients in this preserving process, perfectly counteracts the scoffing statements on page 70, of Bustanoby's book, which reads:

...the idea of excluding air so the wine would be preserved in the same state in which it was put in those skins is also absurd. Air was not totally excluded. The skins were porous.

The ancients would have probably given Mr. Bustanoby little credit for such an observation, for it was for this very reason why the extra precaution was taken of coating the amphora with pitch!

Lees' Temperance Bible Commentary, quotes Baron Liebig in his writings on chemistry, as saying:

> *If a flask be filled with grape-juice and made air-tight, and kept for a few hours in boiling water, THE WINE does not now ferment.*

On the subject of boiling wine, he also says:

> *The property of organic substances to pass into a state of decay is annihilated in all cases by heating to the boiling point.*

Dr. William Patton explains this principle in respect to wine or grape juice:

> *The grape-juice boils at 212 degrees; but alcohol evaporates at 170 degrees, which is 42 degrees below the boiling point. So then, if any possible portion of alcohol was in the juice, this process would expel it. The obvious object of boiling the juice was to preserve it sweet and fit for use during the year.*

Another chemist, Herman Boerhave, is quoted by Dr. Nott as saying:

> *By boiling, the juice of the richest grapes loses all aptitude for fermentation, and may afterwards be preserved for years without undergoing any further change.*

Dr. Nott quotes Casper Neuman, MD, Professor of Chemistry, Berlin, 1759, as saying:

> *It is observable that when sweet juices are boiled down to a thick consistence, they not only do not ferment in that state, but are not easily brought into fermentation when diluted with as much water as they had lost in the evaporation, or even with the very individual water that exhaled from them.*

The Jews were well familiar with this custom, as Kitto informs us:

> *The Mishna states that the Jews were in the habit of using boiled wine.*

This custom was also adopted by Muslims (The Koran forbids the use of intoxicating wine, 2:219) and Christians alike. The Rev. Henry Homes, American missionary to Constantinople, in the Bibliotheca Sacra for May 1848. After careful observation, confirms this fact:

> *Simple grape-juice, without the addition of any earth to neutralize the acidity, is boiled from four to five hours...It ordinarily has not a particle of intoxicating quality, being used freely by both Mohammedans and Christians.*

We will now turn our attention to another method of preserving grape juice, which is that of filtering. Dr. William Patton explains the principle:

> *Gluten is indispensable to fermentation, whether vinous or acetous, as is sugar. It is a most insoluble body until it comes in contact with the oxygen of the atmosphere; but by frequent filtering of the newly-pressed juice, the gluten is separated from the juice, and thus fermentation prevented.*

He quotes Professor Donavan as saying:

> *if the juice be filtered and deprived of its gluten or ferment, the production of alcohol is impossible.*

Dr. F.R. Lees, quotes Captain Treat's observations from Italy in 1845:

> *From enquiries, I found that unfermented wines were esteemed the most. It was drunk mixed with water. Great pains were taken in the vintage season to have a good stock of it laid by. The grape-juice was filtered two or three times, and then bottled, some put in casks and buried in the earth-some kept in water (to prevent fermentation).*

After giving careful instructions for preparing the juice, Columella states the reason for filtering wine:

> ...strain the wine from its faeces, and pour it into a vessel. This wine will be sweet, firm or durable, and healthy to the body.

The last method of preserving grape juice we will look at is that of adding sulphur, known as fumigation. Dr. Lees quotes Miller's Gardener's Dictionary on wine, which reads:

> The way to preserve new wine, in the state of must, is to put it up in very strong but small casks, firmly closed on all sides, by which means it will be kept from fermenting. But if it should happen to fall into fermentation, the only way to stop it is by the fumes of sulphur.

Dr. Patton comments on this:

> Here we notice two important facts. The first is, that the exclusion of the air from the fresh juice will prevent fermentation. The second is, that, when fermentation has commenced, the fumes of sulphur will arrest it. How more certainly it will prevent fermentation if applied to the new wine.

After looking at the overwhelming weight of evidence from chemists, men of science, theologian's etc. It is abundantly obvious that the drinking of unfermented wine in Bible times was an established *fact*. Therefore, the allegations made by Andre Bustanoby in his book that, as he puts it, so called "Legalistic prohibitionists grossly misinterpret both the Bible and ancient historians." And that the claims that they make are outrageous, due to their ignorance of the chemistry of wine making, are totally unfounded. The allegations amount to nothing more than slander based on narrow minded prejudice!

After careful, honest, and fair examination of the facts. Let the reader note that it is the ancient writers *themselves* who clearly state that the wine that they were referring to or dealing with was in fact unfermented (unalcoholic) grape juice. The facts need no interpretation whatsoever.

The records show of the ancients, that they were intelligent men who thoroughly understood the chemistry of wine making. They used great care and skill in obtaining the finished product, and sensibly make their findings and intentions clear, as Dr. Patton observes:

> *We cannot imagine that Pliny, Columella, Varro, Cato, and others were either cooks or writers of cook-books, but were intelligent gentlemen moving in the best circles of society. So when they, with minute care, give the receipts for making sweet wine, which will remain so during the year, and the processes were such as to prevent fermentation, we are persuaded that these were esteemed in their day.*

Another point to be noted is that these men were not what Bustanoby calls, "Legalistic prohibitionists"!

We can now summarize this section by noting that in ancient or Bible times, unfermented grape juice was drank after it had been freshly squeezed from the grape cluster (Genesis 40:10,11). It was also preserved in its unfermented state by at least the four following methods:

(1) Putting the juice in an airtight container.
(2) By boiling the juice.
(3) By separating the gluten from the juice, either by filtering or subsistence.
(4) By fumigation (adding sulphur).

We thus learn from these facts, that it was just as foolish to say that there was no such thing as unfermented wine, as it is to say that there was no such thing as fermented wine.

The views therefore of David Wilkerson, Jack Van Impe and others, that the ancients drank and preserved unfermented wine is a perfectly valid fact. The argument then, as any reasonable person would observe, is not whether unfermented wine was drank in Bible times, but whether or not the *Bible* itself condemns the use of fermented or intoxicating beverages.

It is not the desire of the present author to clutter this chapter with all the arguments posed in Mr. Bustanoby's book, because many of them have been or will be shown to be in error in the light of the Bible and ancient history. But there are certain points however that must be thoroughly dealt with. The first point that we will examine is as follows:

WERE THE ANCIENTS TRYING TO PRESERVE UNFER-MENTED GRAPE JUICE, OR WERE THEY MERELY TRYING TO PREVENT ALCOHOLIC WINE FROM GOING SOUR OR TURNING TO VINEGAR?

According to Bustanoby, the principle of the ancients preserving unfermented grape juice is nothing but a myth. He insists that the various recipes given for keeping grape juice were merely to prevent fermented wine from spoiling. On page 22, of his book, he makes this bold and sweeping statement:

> *The recipes that come down from ancient historians do not tell us how to preserve grape juice. Rather, they tell us how to make wine and keep it from turning into vinegar.*

On page 27, of his book, Bustanoby gives *his* own definition of what he considers to be "wine." He states that "wine" is the juice of the grape after it has first fermented in open air, and then allowed to further ferment in a sealed container. On page 28, he goes on to state:

> *In legalistic literature there is a lot of talk about the use in Bible times of must, which people drank instead of wine-as though they were not drinking a fermented beverage. But must is the juice of the grape in aerobic ferment. Though must is not the finished product, aged wine, they were in fact drinking a fermented beverage.*

We have clearly seen from the variety of ancient authorities examined, which was not as Mr. Bustanoby puts it "legalistic literature," that the above statement is incorrect, as the ancient writers *themselves* make clear. It would seem appropriate in this context, to briefly quote from only two of these authorities again, to emphasize this point. Concerning the definition of the beverage "must," which Bustanoby claims was fermented, Webster's Bible Dictionary states:

Wine, pressed from the grape, but not fermented.

Smith's Greek and Roman Antiquities, states:

> *The sweet, unfermented juice of the grape was termed gleukos by the Greeks and mustum by the Romans-the latter word being properly an adjective signifying new or fresh.*

This is only a small part of an avalanche of conclusive evidence, in the face of which even Bustanoby himself has to admit that unfermented drinks were used. And that the words translated "wine" in the Bible, could also mean grape juice. On page 23, he states:

> *I agree that the word translated "wine" in the Bible at times may sometimes mean grape juice.*

On page 39, he goes on to make this admission:

> *There is no question that the ancients drank a variety of beverages, both fermented and unfermented.*

Unfortunately, these facts mean very little to a person who has already set their minds to think a certain way. Bustanoby's prejudice concerning the wine issue is made clear relatively early in his book, almost on his own admission. On page 22, he gives his opinion concerning it, which reads:

> *It comes down to interpretation of Scripture, which, we shall see, readily lends itself to the traditional interpretation of "wine" as a fermented beverage.*

This is exactly the point. Bustanoby's obsession with this viewpoint has led to numerous erroneous statements, based on his own subjective interpretation of Holy Scripture. Many of these statements cannot be conclusively substantiated by the Bible or ancient authorities.

We know that there were those who made alcoholic wines, who used methods of stopping them from turning into vinegar, largely due to the hot climate, but these people were intelligent enough to make this fact plain, in the same way we read of methods or recipes which categorically speak of the preservation of *unfermented* wine.

How Bustanoby could say that the grape juice (must) drank in Bible times had already undergone fermentation in open air (that is what is meant by the jargon "aerobic ferment"), is absolutely amazing. Considering the various methods we looked at of preparing wines and keeping them fresh and sweet. And also the fact that the wine (grape juice, must) was also drank after being freshly squeezed from the grape cluster (Genesis 40:10,11).

The burden of proof thus falls on Bustanoby to substantiate his bold statement that "they were in fact drinking a fermented beverage." To prove that the drinking of grape juice (must) in every situation or context in Bible times, had undergone fermentation, is impossible. Such irrational conjecture is clearly the figment of Mr. Bustanoby's own imagination, and what seems to be wishful thinking. Grapes are not alcoholic!

Bustanoby's continued reference to the fermenting of wine in sealed containers (a simplified explanation of the other term he uses, "anerobic ferment"), is totally irrelevant to this case. This process operated when the alcoholic wine makers purposely permitted the grape juice to begin the process of fermentation before bottling. After bottling it was then allowed to mature. This was a deliberate and calculated operation, which was wholly distinct from the process of preserving unfermented grape juice. As anyone visiting a wine cellar today would be told. The two processes must not be confused. Littleton, in his Latin Dictionary (1678) states:

Must, new wine, close shut up and not permitted to work.

Notice he doesn't say, "new wine, which is allowed to mature or finish fermenting." This is due to the fact that this is a reference to the bottling of freshly squeezed grape juice, and preventing the process of fermentation from working. Bustanoby suggests that this process is impossible. On page 70, he makes this clear by stating:

In the first place, it was impossible to keep airborne yeast out of the must when bottling. The idea that no fermenting matter went into the bottle is absurd.

In answer to this, we have to accept that since the ancient writers with great skill and precision, clearly state that must (grape juice) was unfermented. And because the methods they used for preserving grape juice are scientifically accurate, that they knew exactly what they were talking about. Also, the accounts of some of these writers or ancient wine makers, that grape juice was consumed in large quantities without causing impairment, is proof that the substance was indeed unfermented. Their methods were not crude and simplistic, as Bustanoby would have us believe.

We will now take a look at how science verifies the fact that the recipes given by ancient wine makers, for preserving wine or grape juice fresh, was indeed correct. And would ensure that the juice would *not* ferment, which is contrary to Bustanoby's subjective opinions.

On page 34, and 35, of his book, he quotes Pliny and Columella respectively. He states that their recipes produced a wine of low alcoholic content. Before we examine what the writers *themselves* say in their recipes, there is an important scientific fact that must be borne in mind. Dr. Ure explains:

> *By lowering the temperature to 45 degrees, it would not ferment. The juice being kept cool, the gluten will settle to the bottom, and the juice, thus deprived of the gluten, cannot ferment.*

With this important point in mind, let us now examine the relative facts (key points will be highlighted in bold by the author). On page 34, Bustanoby quotes Pliny (second century ad) who states:

> *Between the sirops and real wine is the liquor that the Greeks call aigleukos-this is our "permanent must [semper mustum]." **Care is needed for its production, as it must not be allowed to "boil [fervere]"**-that is the word they use to denote the passage of must into wine. Consequently, as soon as the must is taken from the vat and put into casks, **they plunge the casks in water till midwinter passes and regular cold weather sets in.***

238

On page 35, Bustanoby also quotes Columella (first century A.D) who states:

> *That must may remain always as sweet as though it were fresh,* do as follows. *Before the grape-skins are put under the press, take from the vat some of the freshest possible must and put it in a new wine-jar; then daub over and cover it carefully with pitch, that thus no water may be able to get in.* **Then sink the whole flagon in a pool of cold, fresh water** *so that no part of it is above the surface. Then after forty days take it out of the water. The must will then keep sweet for as much as a year.*

Let the reader note the remarkable fact that even though the writers do not state it in scientific terms, placing the containers with the pure juice in very cold water, made it impossible for fermentation to occur. The temperature obviously being below 45 degrees made fermentation inoperative. Note the great care taken to state that the water should be cold. The ancients were perfectly and scientifically accurate. The grape juice having undergone no fermentation would be fresh and sweet as when it went in, as Columella states.

Again, after honest and fair examination of the accounts of these ancient writers, let the reader note that it is *Bustanoby* himself who does the misinterpreting of the evidence, and not the so called "legalists." Note how Pliny states that before bottling, it should be ensured that the juice should not be allowed to ferment, that is, "boil [fervere]." On page 34, Bustanoby replies to this by stating:

> *...even though the juice was taken from the vat immediately...yeast and bacteria still contaminated the must.*

In reply to Columella's recipe for keeping must (wine, grape juice) as sweet as though it were fresh, Bustanoby on page 35, again refutes this by stating:

> *Keeping the must "as sweet as though it were fresh" is somewhat of an overstatement...*

239

Let the reader note again how he quotes ancient authorities and then refutes their claims, as though they did not know what they were talking about. All this he clearly does because the facts do not suit his biased and preconceived ideas. In his zeal to overthrow the so-called "false exegesis" of the "legalists," he is clearly found to be guilty of the very things he accuses others of doing!

Bustanoby's desire to deny all possibility of the drinking of unfermented wine in the Bible context is summed up in his closing remarks on these points. On page 35, he states:

> *One final observation should be made. Even if the Greeks and Romans did use this process, Italy was a water-rich country. In Palestine there were no convenient ponds. Palestine simply didn't have enough water to make wine processed this way available to the entire nation.*

In summing up this statement, and indeed Bustanoby's approach to the whole section, these points are to be noted:

(a) He denies that the wine was unfermented, which is contrary to the views of the ancient wine makers and drinkers, and the scientific principles applied in preserving unfermented grape juice. The best he can do is to state that the alcoholic content was low. This is designed to protect his view which we looked at earlier, that Scripture, *readily lends itself to the traditional interpretation of "wine" as a fermented beverage.*

(b) Even if he has to concede that unfermented wine was preserved and drank in Bible times, by saying it could not have been done on a large scale in Palestine, he covers himself and his "traditional interpretation."

INTERPRETATION OF SCRIPTURE

We will now turn our attention to answering another wild and slanderous allegation made by Mr. Bustanoby. Unfortunately, he seems to be infected with a disease which causes him to smear those who state that not all wine mentioned in the Bible was alcoholic, and those who believe that the Bible teaches total abstinence from alcoholic beverages, as "legalists." The gravity of such unfair generalisation is a slur on the reputation of good knowledgeable Christian Bible scholars and commentators, the inspired writers of the Bible, and God Himself!

On page 18, he makes this serious accusation:

> *Legalists, though well intentioned, are also dangerous. Just like the Scribes in Jesus' day, they bend Scripture to conform to their own traditions and prejudices...*

After reading Bustanoby's book, one is appalled by the hypocrisy of this statement. Seeing that he himself is guilty of bending Scripture to conform to his prejudices, and what he calls the "traditional interpretation." In the same way he misinterprets, modifies, and even ignores important facts from ancient writers, as we have we have observed. We will now take a look at some examples of this. Proverbs 20:1 reads:

> *Wine is a mocker, strong drink is raging: and whosoever is deceived thereby is not wise.*

On page 65, Bustanoby gives his interpretation of the passage. It reads:

> *Proverbs 20:1 tells us something else that is very enlightening. The person who unwisely surrenders himself completely to alcohol is said to be "not wise."*

He further comments on the text by stating:

> *Drunkenness is not only a sin against a holy God whose character is alien to drunkenness. Drunkenness is not smart!*

Let the reader carefully observe that there is absolutely *nothing* in the text of Proverbs 20:1, which refers to the degree of surrender to intoxicating drinks whatsoever! Also, *nothing* is said concerning drunkenness, moderation, or so called "temperance." The text simply personifies wine and beer as a mocker and a brawler. The Bible Knowledge Commentary gives the correct understanding, without tampering with the plain simple meaning of the text:

*The idea is that wine mocks the one who **drinks** it and beer makes him aggressive.*

The Rev. B. Parsons also explains this obvious fact:

*"Wine," says the wisest of men, "is a mocker, and strong drink is raging, tumultuous, confusing, or stupifying, and he that is deceived thereby is not wise." Here the Holy Ghost tells us that wine is a mocker, and that strong drink is raging or stupifying; and dare we say that the Spirit of truth wishes us to be "mocked," or that Author of peace, order, and spiritual life, commands us to use a draught which will make us rage, confound our intellects, and produce stupidity? Here it is **not** said **much** wine is a mocker, **much** strong drink is stupifying; but while the words "mocker and raging" point out the character of the drinks as intoxicating beverages, the plain implication of the text is, that we should avoid the deception by totally abstaining.*

Here we can see that the main thrust of the text is that of **abstinence,** which is the most natural and obvious meaning on reading it. The labelling of intoxicating drinks as dangerous in the text is clearly **unconditional.** The warning therefore, is against the **use** or **drinking** of these intoxicating beverages. Bustanoby's interpretation is distorted, subjective, and dangerous, and is totally alien to the text.

We will now examine Bustanoby's interpretation of Proverbs 31:4,5, which reads:

It is not for kings, O Lemuel, it is not for kings to drink wine; nor for princes strong drink: Lest they drink, and forget the law, and pervert the judgment of any of the afflicted.

Here we have before us, a clear command to **abstain** from intoxicating drinks. This is a beautifully inspired account, which shows that even the **drinking** of intoxicating beverages is enough to impair judgment. It is very strange indeed that Bustanoby cannot see this obvious fact, and reads into the text what is clearly not there! On examination, we will see that Bustanoby's interpretation of this passage is a somewhat dubious, subjective, and tongue in cheek approach. On page 49-50, he gives his interpretation of the passage:

> *The context argues for moderation. In verses 1 through 3 King Lemuel's mother warns him not to spend his strength on women-"those who ruin kings." She* **probably** *makes reference to the king's harem, a practice in which the king may lawfully indulge.* **But perhaps** *Lemuels's mother remembers how Solomon's harem led him astray (1 Kings 11:1-8).*

> *It does not sound as though Lemuel's mother is warning him to ignore women completely. It is simply a matter of not making the mistake Solomon made-allowing women to ruin him.* **If this observation is correct,** *then the context is introducing the theme of moderation, not abstinence.*

> *She then turns to the matter of alcohol. The warning is not about the use of alcohol. As with women, the warning is in the excessive interest in the perks that the king enjoyed-a harem and banquets.* **This seems to run parallel** *with the command in the Pastoral Epistles that elders and deacons are not to be "given to wine." Excessive interest, not use, is what is in view.*

After reading this disgraceful manipulation of divine truth. One can only wonder if he is commenting on the same passage in consideration!

Let the reader note how the interpretation is based on statements of uncertain guess work (these have been highlighted in bold print), which are so wildly inventive and erroneous, that they are hardly worth commenting on.

Let the reader again exercise their own God given reasoning, and empty their minds of Bustanoby's above nonsense commentary, and read the plain simple message of the Scripture again! A quote from Rev. B. Parsons on this passage is more than appropriate in summing up Bustanoby's hypocrisy, and others like him, who take such liberties with the inspired text. It reads:

> *In order to avoid the plain literal meaning of this text, the advocates of intoxicating liquors say, that the words, "It is not for kings to drink wine," &c. signify "It is not for kings to drink much wine, or drink wine to excess!!" Surely after taking such an obvious liberty as this with the Scriptures, our opponents will not charge us with wresting the word of God to suit our fancies. You might just as well say that the commandments, "Thou shalt not kill, thou shalt not steal," &c. do not mean "total abstinence" from murder and dishonesty, but only that you should slay and defraud with "moderation," as to affirm that the intimation to kings not to touch wine, and the command to all not to look at it, imply after all that you are to look, touch, and drink, and poison your health and souls, provided you will do it with "moderation!" We know who told our first parents not to touch the forbidden fruit, and we know also who told our mother not to heed the injunction, and we need not repeat the result of Eve's moderation. He who said of the tree of knowledge "Ye shall not eat of it, neither shall ye touch it," says "Look not upon the wine," "It is not for kings to drink wine,"&c.; and it would be the labour of years, and of volumes, to tell the fate of millions who have spurned the command, have looked, coveted, taken, tasted, drunk, died, and perished for ever.*

In refusing to submit to the fact that our text teaches total abstinence. And in realizing that most sensible people would not accept his inventive interpretation of the passage. Bustanoby seeks to uphold his moderation theory by misinterpreting the two subsequent verses of our text in Proverbs. They read:

> *Give strong drink unto him that is ready to perish, and wine unto those that be of heavy hearts. Let him drink,*

and forget his poverty, and remember his misery no more. (Proverbs 31:6,7)

On page 51, he states:

Let us say for sake of argument that a jury of scholars should declare that Proverbs 31:4-5 conclusively teaches that rulers must be total abstainers. That would be fine with me. It would be comforting to know that those who have their finger on the nuclear trigger are clearheaded men or women! But the rest of the proverb seems to leave the door open to the use of alcohol by the common man, particularly those who are distressed.

The first point to note on reading this statement, is that Proverbs 31:4-5 *does* conclusively state that rulers must be total abstainers from intoxicating drinks. Therefore there is no need for any debate on that score! Secondly, in stating that those who do not drink are clear-headed men and women, he admits that drinking impairs judgment, particularly in crucial areas. And what can be more significant than the management of spiritual things? Spiritual responsibilities are far more important than the nuclear trigger!

Since his book states that Jesus approved of fermented wine (page 68), he therefore indirectly accuses our Lord, the great Prophet, Priest and King, of not being a clear-headed man! He thus elevates the administration of secular affairs above spiritual things, which are of "a far more exceeding and eternal weight."

Now in returning to the exegesis of the passage. We will see that it makes no allowances for the use of alcohol to the common man. Apart from the prescribing of it to condemned criminals, which is the only case in which it was allowed. As we will see from examining the text. The statement, "Give strong drink unto him that is ready to perish, and wine unto those that be of heavy hearts," is not saying give wine to one class of people and strong drink to another. They are merely used synonymously to describe the same effect. Strong drink is used to reinforce the effect of wine, and in the same way the one that is ready to perish is said

245

to have a heavy heart, and later to have moral poverty. This is merely an expression of Hebrew parallelism, similar to that employed in Proverbs 20:1:

> *Wine is a mocker, strong drink is raging: and whosoever is deceived thereby is not wise.*

Bustanoby is inconsistent in his exposition, because this is a truth he himself knows, and explains on page 63, of his book, as follows:

> *The proverb goes on to say that beer (shekar) is a brawler. This does not mean that wine does one thing and beer does something else. This is an example of parallelism in Hebrew poetry. The idea of the first line is expanded on by the second.*

Note how here he correctly explains the Hebraism, but in Proverbs 31:6,7 he contradicts himself by suggesting that each line refers to a different case in which drinking is permitted. When one takes the view that the Bible supports drinking, such liberty is hardly surprising. Such hypocritical inconsistency in interpretation is the very same thing that Bustanoby accuses one of the so-called "legalistic prohibitionists" of being guilty of on page 56 of his book!

As stated previously, the use of wine and strong drink in Proverbs 31:6,7 refers only to the prescribing of it as a narcotic to condemned criminals. It doesn't even make room for so called medicinal use as some scholars think. Adam Clarke's Commentary on this text explains this, with no room for any other permissible circumstance. It states:

> *We have already seen, that inebriating drinks were mercifully given to condemned criminals, to render them less sensible of the torture they endured in dying. This is what was offered to our Lord; but he refused it.*

On page 51, Bustanoby continues his argument by stating:

> *It may be argued that the proverb is talking about the medicinal use of alcohol. But the proverb speaks of both*

246

"misery" and "povery." Poverty has to do with a broken spirit, not a sick body.

Having already established the fact that Proverbs 31:6,7 refers only to one and not two or three permissible conditions for the use of strong drinks, contrary to what Bustanoby would have us believe. Let the reader note that the text itself destroys his weak argument. Carefully note how Proverbs 31:7 states, "Let him drink, and forget his poverty." That is, the miserable and heavyhearted man who is condemned to death. That is why he remembers "his misery no more" (those translations such as the NIV who use the plural, by stating, "let them drink and forget their povery," do not alter the meaning, i.e. those condemned to death should drink and forget their poverty). "Poverty" is thus used metaphorically in this text to describe the moral condition of the condemned man and not his financial status.

Apart from the precise construction of the text, again through the law of context, the Bible makes it clear that Bustanoby's interpretation is impossible to accept. Proverbs 23:20,21 states:

Be not among winebibbers (winedrinkers); among riotous eaters of flesh: For the drunkard and the glutton shall come to poverty...

The inspired text would hardly prescribe a substance which itself names as a cause of poverty to be given to the poor!

This general area we have selected for examination, shows how Bustanoby is guilty of manipulating the plainest Scriptures to suit his own prejudices.

We will now take a further look at some examples of this from the perspective of selecting subjects. Some of the answers to these arguments will be found in the respective section of this book that deals with the subject. The reader would be advised to consult the relative or respective chapter for a more fuller treatment of the subject. The topics selected for examination are as follows:

THE ARGUMENT FOR MODERATION
AND "TEMPERANCE"

Bustanoby's approach to this subject amounts to nothing more than ignorance, as we shall see from examination of his frail arguments for moderate drinking. On page 84, he states the following:

> The use of alcohol is a "disputable matter" and therefore a matter of liberty (Rom. 14:1).

The Bible passage above (Romans 14:1), includes "wine" as a disputable matter and not alcohol! Even Bustanoby himself has to admit that the word translated "wine" can also mean grape juice (page 23). Therefore his argument that this passage endorses moderate drinking as a matter of Christian liberty, is based on his own speculation which is entirely without substance. He goes on to make this compounding statement:

> Paul, the great champion of liberty, understood this difference. His urging us to moderation and temperance is the kind of caution given us in the Old Testament. This warning is found in such statements as, "Every man that strives for mastery is temperate in all things..." (1 Cor. 9:25.KJV).

What Bustanoby fails to understand, is that the word translated "temperate" in 1 Corinthians 9:25, means exactly the opposite from what he claims. The original word enkrateuomai, includes total abstinence from all intoxicating drinks! *Never* does it refer to moderate indulgence. Young's Analytical Concordance renders it, "To be self restrained." Grindrod informs us that the Vulgate (the early Latin Translation) ...*renders the word in this case abstinet, the verbal of abstinence.* He continues:

> The same word, (enkrateuomai), is thus defined and illustrated by Parkhurst, in his Greek Lexicon, an authority of acknowledged standard excellence.

Which reads:

> (enkrateuetai), to contain, or restrain one's self with regard to sensual pleasures, to be temperate.

Parkhurst himself quotes an ancient writer (Epictetus) who includes the following in a recipe, which expands on this word:

> ...*you must abstain from wine...*

Grindrod's comments on this, reads:

> *These remarks of Epictetus are in accordance with the practice of the ancient Greeks, to which St. Paul evidently alluded, in the training of the athletae, at the Gymnasia or Palaestrae, academies established for that purpose at the public expense...They were enjoined continence and prohibited altogether the use of wine.*

Bustanoby continues his moderation argument by stating that Paul urges temperance and moderation in the following passages, Gal. 5:22-23; Phil. 4:5; Titus 1:7-8; Titus 2:2-3. We will now see that the words in these passages which are translated "temperance," "temperate," and "moderation" respectively, in no way includes moderate drinking in their definitions. The definition of the word (egkrateia) translated "temperance" in Galatians 5:23, and "temperate" in Titus 1:8, is given in Young's Analytical Concordance as, "Self restraint, continence." Concerning the word translated "moderation" in Philippians 4:5, Dr. William Patton gives an excellent explanation of its meaning and use in the text. He states:

> *Phil. iv. 5, "Let your moderation be known unto all men. The Lord is at hand." There is not the slightest evidence, either from the original word or the context, that this text has the remotest reference to moderate drinking. The Greek word epieikees occurs five times: thrice it is rendered gentle, once patient, and once moderation. In each case, reference is made to the state of the mind, and it might be properly translated, Let your moderation of mind be known unto all men. Robinson renders it meet, suitable, proper. The reason given for moderation is, "The Lord is at hand." How strange to say to the drinkers, Drink moderately, for the Lord is at hand!*

The final passage Bustanoby cites for moderate drinking is Titus 2:2, which reads:

> That the aged men be sober, grave, temperate, sound in faith, in charity, in patience.

The word translated "temperate" is rendered by Young in his Analytical Concordance as, "Sound minded, prudent." Another important point to note which further refutes Bustanoby's moderation theory, is that the second word preceding it in the text, translated "sober" (nephalios), means to totally abstain from intoxicating drinks. The Greek text of the Trinitarian Bible Society renders this word, "temperate."! Here we see that in the face of Scripture, Bustanoby's (and any other persons for that matter) arguments for moderate drinking completely collapses.

Bustanoby's ignorance in this area (whether wilful or not) is further revealed on page 84, as he continues his moderation argument, by stating the following:

> "Temperance" is a very good word and was used down to the twentieth century in its proper sense-moderation...It was not until the early twentieth century that "temperance" came to mean "total abstinence."

Biblically speaking, moderation is not the proper meaning of the word "temperance" at all. The word "temperance" meant total abstinence at the time of the first century!

What we must understand is that the early twentieth century meaning of the word "temperance" agrees with the Biblical definition. That is, total abstinence, and as Christians, that for us is the correct definition.

Someone obviously must have realized the error in its meaning. An error which Bustanoby is still clinging to. The "change" in the early twentieth century to the correct definition of total abstinence, was good, sensible, and Biblical.

UNSCRIPTURAL THEORIES ABOUT FERMENTED WINE

Bustanoby's tunnel vision view that "wine" in the Bible should be interpreted as a fermented beverage, and his obstinate stand against total abstinence from intoxicating beverages, conflicts with the inspired protective mechanism of Scripture. His insistence on maintaining what he calls the "traditional interpretation" has led him to inject certain theories into the Scriptural context in order to explain away certain difficult passages.

First of all, he makes a number of statements which are designed to show the futility of pressing a case from Scripture for total abstinence from alcoholic beverages. Since as he suggests, it was impossible for most people to get drunk because the wine that they drank was too weak. We will now examine these arguments in the light of Scripture. On page 22, he states the following:

> *The poor, who were in the majority, had to settle for a cheap, low-alcohol beverage. And there is evidence that the diluting of wine was common not only to the Greco-Roman world of the first century, but also among the Jews centuries before.*

On page 30, he further states:

> *I am convinced that one reason why alcohol abuse was not a major problem to the ancients is that truly good, high-alcohol wine was not in great supply and was thus expensive. There was a lot of poor-quality wine of low-alcohol content. And a lot of it never became true wine...*

When we read the Scriptures, these statements are simply incredible! The New Testament furnishes us with a number of references and warnings against drunkenness. In Matthew 24:49 and Luke 12:45; 21:34, Jesus warns His disciples about the dangers of drunkenness. Again in the epistles of Paul, there are numerous warnings against drunkenness in the following passages: Romans 13:13; 1 Corinthians 5:11; 6:10; 11:21; Galatians

5:21; Ephesians 5:18; and 1 Thessalonians 5:7. These brethren were certainly not rich, as James 2:5 makes clear:

> *Hearken, my beloved brethren, Hath not God chosen the poor of this world rich in faith, and heirs of the kingdom which he hath promised to them that love him?*

What we learn from the Scriptures is that drunkenness was not a problem that was confined to the rich. Indeed wine of high alcoholic content capable of producing drunkenness was available to the poor as the Scriptures themselves make absolutely clear. Also, the many references to drunkenness in the Old Testament add weight to this fact. Bustanoby's arguments therefore, are nothing more than sheer speculation.

We will now take a look at how Bustanoby tries to explain away Song of Solomon 5:1, which reads:

> *I am come into my garden, my sister, my spouse: I have gathered my myrrh with my spice; I have eaten my honeycomb with my honey; I have drunk my wine with my milk: eat, O friends; drink, yea, drink abundantly, O beloved.*

If one continues to insist that the Bible always speaks of wine as an alcoholic beverage he runs into serious difficulty, for he would have to admit that this text would sanction drunkenness. One of the ways Bustanoby seeks to get around this problem is stated on page 25. He states:

> *...there is evidence that relatively large quantities of fermented wine could be drunk because it was liberally diluted with water. This was a custom among the Jews in Old Testament times as well as among the Greeks and Romans in the first century. Wine drinking in those days was more a challenge to the bladder than to the equilibrium.*

Numerous Old Testament Scriptures such as Proverbs 23:20,21; 29-35, along with the other New Testament passages already mentioned concerning drunkenness, makes this statement absolutely nonsense. Also, the so-called "evidence" that the Jews in Old Testament times liberally diluted their wine with water is completely refuted by Scripture. We have already noted earlier in another chapter of our studies that the diluting of wine with water was unacceptable to the Jews, and regarded as worthless. This fact is made clear by Isaiah 1:21,22, which states the following concerning the judgment that would come upon the inhabitants of Jerusalem for her sinful ways:

> *How is the faithful city become a harlot! it was full of judgment; righteousness lodged in it; but now murderers. Thy silver is become dross, thy wine mixed with water.*

Another way in which Bustanoby seeks to explain away the admonition to "drink abundantly" of the wine in Song of Solomon 5:1, is stated again on page 25. It reads:

> *..there was an economic restraint on the use of intoxicating wine. Though God did indeed bless his people, good aged wine (three years old) was not commonly drunk. The common drink was a low-alcohol beverage made from the rinsing of the wine vat.*

This statement is truly amazing. What Mr. Bustanoby doesn't seem to realize is that the speaker in this text is the wealthy king Solomon! 1 Kings 9:26-28 is worth quoting here for emphasis:

> *And king Solomon made a navy of ships in Eziongeber, which is beside Eloth, on the shore of the Red sea, in the land of Edom. And Hiram sent in the navy his servants, shipmen that had knowledge of the sea, with the servants of Solomon. And they came to Ophir, and fetched from thence gold, four hundred and twenty talents, and brought it to king Solomon.*

Every year king Solomon received from Hiram this massive amount of gold in tribute. Weiss informs us that this totalled:

> *more than 90 million dollars (U.S) in value at the late-70's rate of 200 dollars-plus per troy ounce.*

He also had in abundance, silver, bronze, precious stones, spices, ivory, and cedar wood. This gives us a fabulous insight into the astronomical wealth of king Solomon. Surely in attempting to explain away this text, it cannot be suggested concerning him that there was an economic restraint on wine!

If as Bustanoby states, the poor had to settle for a cheap low alcohol beverage, the wealthy king Solomon would hardly have drank that! Also, again if as Bustanoby suggests, that the best and most expensive wine was aged wine of high alcoholic content, then surely this is what Solomon would have possessed! Hence this text (Song of Sol 5:1) would be one which would sanction drunkenness. There is no escaping or explaining away this fact, if one adopts Bustanoby's views concerning drink.

The present author has greatly emphasized this point because it demonstrates how the inspired Scriptures relegates Bustanoby's arguments to nothing more than wild conjecture. There was practically no economic restraint on the wine that king Solomon drank. The only kind of restraint on the use of intoxicating wine was a God fearing one!

We will now focus our attention on the text to determine its true meaning. The admonition to "drink abundantly" or "drink to satisfaction," is perfectly consistent with the New Testament accounts of Jesus' feeding of the five thousand. Mark 6:42 states:

And they did all eat, and were filled.

This example of God providing food in abundance is found elsewhere in Scripture. Leviticus 26:3-5 states:

If ye walk in my statutes, and keep my commandments, and do them; Then I will give you rain in due season, and the land shall yield her increase, and the trees of the field shall yield their fruit. And your threshing shall reach unto the vintage, and the vintage shall reach unto the sowing time: and ye shall eat your bread to the full, and dwell in your land safely.

It was thus therefore the will of God for people to eat and drink in abundance of the good things He has provided. This does not contradict the passages that condemn gluttony, which is a totally different thing. Gluttony refers to wasteful riotous indulgence, which the Bible usually associates with drinking or drunkenness (Deut 21:20; Prov 23:20,21; Matt 11:19; Luke 7:34).

The wine Solomon refers to in Song of Solomon 5:1, was obviously unfermented grape juice, of which one could drink abundantly and freely to one's satisfaction, without becoming drunk. It is fitting at this moment to quote an ironic statement by Bustanoby himself on page 26, which states:

> *It is therefore important, before we examine what the Bible has to say about wine, that we know something about its biochemistry. The same laws of chemistry that apply to winemaking today also applied to the ancients. Knowing what these principles are and how they were used will help us avoid false exegesis and some far-fetched ideas about the nature of wine in biblical times.*

Bustanoby's own words sum up his actions! In the light of Scripture, his ideas about wine in the Bible are indeed far-fetched. As for the false exegesis he tries to charge others with, it is blatantly evident from our examination of the Scriptures, that he himself is guilty of it. The Bible itself demonstrates that when one adopts a narrow-minded attitude that it always speaks of fermented wine, then far-fetched ideas and false exegesis are a natural outcome!

JESUS AND WINE

On page 68, Bustanoby claims that there is ample evidence in Scripture that Jesus approved of fermented (alcoholic) wine, he cites the following themes and New Testament passages as "evidence":

(1) Putting New Wine in Old Wineskins (Matt. 9:17; Mark. 2:22; Luke 5:36-39)

(2) Jesus Came Eating and Drinking (Matt. 11:19; Luke 7:33-34)

255

(3) *Turning Water into Wine (John 2:3-10)*

(4) *The Last Supper (Matt. 26:27-29; Mark 14:23-25; Luke 22:17-20)*

(5) *Wine Offered to Jesus at the Crucifixion (Matt. 27:32-55; Mark 15:23).*

These claims are outrageous! None of these Scriptures prove in the slightest degree that our Lord approved of fermented wine (for a full treatment of these arguments, see part 2, chapter 2). However, there are certain dangerously distorted points here that must be commented on. These points are as follows:

(a) On the subject of putting new wine in old bottles, let the reader consider the contents of the parable for themselves, which reads:

> *And he spake also a parable unto them; No man putteth a piece of a new garment upon an old; if otherwise, then both the new maketh a rent, and the piece that was taken out of the new agreeth not with the old. And no man putteth new wine into old bottles; else the new wine will burst the bottles, and be spilled, and the bottles shall perish. But new wine must be put into new bottles; and both are preserved. No man also having drunk old wine straightway desireth new: for he saith, The old is better.* (Luke 5:36-39)

Notice that Jesus mentions **nothing** about personally preferring fermented wine. R.B. Grindrod explains this fact, when commenting on verses 37, and 38, of the above:

> *It is, however, an illustration derived merely from certain customs of the country, and cannot with justice be quoted in evidence of the Saviour's approval of intoxicating liquor.*

After actually reading the Scriptures, one is amazed how Bustanoby, and others like him, could draw such a conclusion from our Lord's statement which suggests that He in any way approved of drinking! In John 3:20 Jesus stated:

> *For every one that doeth evil hateth the light, neither cometh to the light, lest his deeds should be reproved.*

256

Shall we then suggest that because Jesus Himself made this statement, that He approves of evil? This kind of reasoning would be absurd, but this is exactly what Bustanoby has done with the above passage of Scripture. What he fails to mention is that the above passage testifies to the use of new wine (unfermented), as well as old wine (fermented). Grindrod again explains:

> *It applies, indeed, with equal fitness to wine in its unfermented state. The juice of the grape when put into strong vessels and kept from exposure to the air, would readily remain unfermented, and particularly after it had been submitted to a certain degree of heat.*

(b) The account that "The Son of man is come eating and drinking," which we looked at earlier, had no reference to alcoholic drinks whatsoever, but was a statement which contrasted the open life style of our Lord to the secluded life of John the Baptist. Albert Barnes correctly explains the meaning of the term used in Matt 11:19 and Luke 7:34, "The Son of man came eating and drinking":

> *That is, living as others do; not practising austerity; and they accuse him of being fond of excess, and seeking the society of the wicked.*

On this point, Adam Clarke adds:

> *That is wheresoever he was invited to eat a morsel of bread, and observed no rigid fasts...*

On the issue of Christ being called a winebibber by His enemies, Bustanoby seeks to use this as evidence that our Lord was a drinker of alcoholic wine. His argument is built upon what appears to be a serious and deliberate manipulation of the word translated "winebibber" (oinopotes). Again, as we learnt earlier, the word simply means a winedrinker. It is derived from two Greek words, oinos (wine), and potes (a drinker). Bustanoby states that the word means a drunkard, because it fits his biased view that Christ must have been a regular drinker of alcoholic wine for His enemies to call Him a drunkard. He makes this viewpoint clear on page 72, when he states:

> But if wine drinking was so reprehensible to God, why did Jesus not use these occasions of eating and drinking together as opportunities to point out this most heinous sin? What is more, if others drank wine and Jesus did not, his example would have been enough to make the charge of drunkenness ridiculous.

In order to pass of his views for fact, he also quotes a Bible translation that suits his view, which in actual fact inaccurately translates the word rendered "winebibber" in the Authorized Version. On page 71, he quotes the New International Version translation of Luke 7:31-34, which states:

> To what, then, can I compare the people of this generation? What are they like? They are like children sitting in the marketplace and calling out to each other:
>
> `We played the flute for you, and you did not dance; we sang a dirge, and you did not cry.'
>
> For John the Baptist came neither eating bread nor drinking wine, and you say, `He has a demon.' The Son of Man came eating and drinking, and you say, `Here is a glutton and a drunkard, a friend of tax collectors and "sinners."' But wisdom is proved right by all her children.

We will now examine some reputable authorities on the Scriptures, which make plain the truth concerning the word wrongly translated "drunkard" here (oinopotes). Young's Analytical Concordance states:

> Wine drinker.

Robinson's Lexicon of the New Testament:

> a wine-drinker, wine-bibber.

Vine's Expository Dictionary of New Testament Words:

a wine-drinker.

Thayer's Greek-English Lexicon of the New Testament:

a wine-bibber, given to wine.

Strong's Exhaustive Concordance:

a tippler:-winebibber.

For those unfamiliar with the term "tippler," the Oxford Dictionary explains:

Drink intoxicating liquor habitually. Drink (liquor) repeatedly in small amounts.

Having established the obvious meaning of this compound word, we will now observe some of the Bible translations, which *do* translate this word correctly:

The Son of man came eating and drinking, and they say, Behold a man gluttonous, and a winebibber, a friend of publicans and sinners. But wisdom is justified of her children. (Matt 11:19 AV)

The Son of man came eating and drinking, and they say, Behold, a gluttonous man, and a winebibber, a friend of publicans and sinners! And wisdom is justified by her works. (Matt 11:19 RV)

The Son of man came eating and drinking with others and they say, Behold, a glutton and a wine drinker, a friend of tax collectors and especially wicked sinners! Yet wisdom is justified and vindicated by what she does (her deeds) and by her children. (Matt 11:19, Amplified Bible)

the son of Man came eating and drinking, and they say, Lo, a man, a glutton, and a wine-drinker, a friend of tax-gatherers and sinners, and wisdom was justified of her children.' (Matt 11:19, Young's Literal Translation)

The Son of Man came eating and drinking, and they say, Look at him! a glutton and a drinker, a friend of tax gath-

erers and sinners!" And yet God's wisdom is proved right by its results. " (Matt 11:19, New English Bible)

And I, the son of Mankind, feast and drink, and you complain that I am `a glutton and a drinking man, and hang around with the worst of sinners!' But brilliant men like you can justify your every inconsistency! (Matt 11:19, Living New Testament)

Here even the Living Bible (a paraphrase rather than an accurate word for word translation) correctly brings out the truth that the word often translated "winebibber" in the AV, means someone who *drinks* alcoholic or fermented wine. Note how even Jesus' enemies realize how evil drinking was and labels it on par with the other sins they falsely accuse Him of. What is amazing, is that Bustanoby accuses Him of the same thing!

It should also be understood that all these wild accusations levelled at Jesus in Matthew 11:19, and Luke 7:34, respectively, are false. Jesus plainly refutes these charges, which when examined all violate the Old Testament. These accusations along with their Old Testament prohibitions, are summarized as follows:

(1) The accusation that Jesus was a glutton, would violate Proverbs 23:21, "For the drunkard and the glutton shall come to poverty..."

(2) The accusation that Jesus was a wine drinker would violate Proverbs 20:1, "Wine is a mocker strong drink is raging..." Also Proverbs 23:20, "Be not among winebibbers..." (wine drinkers)

(3) The charge that Jesus was a friend of publicans and sinners was also false, contrary to the views of some, such as Bustanoby who show a total misunderstanding of the subject. On page 72, he states:

The Pharisees were right about one thing. Jesus was not austere. And he was the friend of sinners.

His misunderstanding of this point is further displayed as he seeks to use this "example" of Christ to nullify or over-throw the clear commandments of Scripture. The inspired commandment in 1 Tim 3:3, and Tit 1:7, that overseers should not be given to wine (Greek paroinos, one alongside of wine), which is the same as Prov 23:20, "Be not among winebibbers (wine drinkers)..." Here the commandment is that one should not even be among those who drink, let alone drunkards! But on page 85-86, Bustanoby subjectively refutes these commandments, on the grounds of the slander-ous accusations of Jesus' enemies! He states:

It is difficult to believe that a Christian should stay away from anyone who gets drunk. The example of Jesus as the friend of sinners and the rapport he had with them argue against this kind of separatistic thinking.

This statement is simply nonsense. Jesus was not the friend of sinners. If this were true, it would militate against Psalms 1:1:

Blessed is the man that walketh not in the counsel of the ungodly, nor standeth in the way of sinners, nor sitteth in the seat of the scornful.

Psalms 101:4, reads:

A froward heart shall depart from me: I will not know a wicked person.

Amos 3:3, states:

Can two walk together, except they be agreed?

These divinely inspired principles are comprehensively echoed in the New Testament:

Be ye not unequally yoked together with unbelievers: for what fellowship hath righteousness with unright-eousness? and what communion hath light with darkness? And what concord hath Christ with Belial? or what part hath he that believeth with an infidel?

261

And what agreement hath the temple of God with idols? for ye are the temple of the living God; as God hath said, I will dwell in them, and walk in them; and I will be their God, and they shall be my people. Wherefore come out from among them, and be ye separate, saith the Lord, and touch not the unclean thing; and I will receive you, And will be a Father unto you, and ye shall be my sons and daughters, saith the Lord Almighty. (2 Corinthians 6:14-18)

If these inspired commandments do not reflect separatistic thinking, then what does?!!!

Again we read:

Ye adulterers and adulteresses, know ye not that the friendship of the world is enmity with God? whosoever therefore will be a friend of the world is the enemy of God. (James 4:4)

We will now examine what the Master Himself Has to say about this issue. In John 8:12, Jesus states:

I am the light of the world...

In John 3:19,20, Jesus makes it plain how sinful men respond to Him who is The True Light:

And this is the condemnation, that light is come into the world, and men loved darkness rather than light, because their deeds were evil. For every one that doeth evil hateth the light, neither cometh to the light, lest his deeds should be reproved.

He further states:

The world cannot hate you; but me it hateth, because I testify of it, that the works thereof are evil. (John 7:7)

In Matthew 12:30, Jesus leaves no room for ambiguity:

He that is not with me is against me; and he that gathereth not with me scattereth abroad.

In His classic discourse to His disciples in the fifteenth chapter of John, our Lord again categorically states in no uncertain terms, that He considers only those who are His true disciples to be His friends:

Ye are my friends, if ye do whatsoever I command you. Henceforth I call you not servants; for the servant knoweth not what his lord doeth: but I have called you friends; for all things that I have heard of my Father I have made known unto you. (John 15:14,15)

These words of our Lord are in perfect harmony with all the other Scriptures, which we have examined on this point. The present author has found it necessary to labour this point, because it highlights the dangerous approach that Bustanoby has taken in dealing with this subject.

Christ was not a liberalistic religious man who was ready to compromise the standards of righteousness in order to win friends. But was and is the Spotless Son of God who came to confront man about his sinful fallen state, and to reveal to him the absolute holiness of God. God cannot compromise His love at the expense of His righteousness and justice!

Throughout Bustanoby's book, many of his arguments for drinking have not been based on the solid principles of Scripture, but on his own subjective and narrow minded interpretation of it, as we have just noted above. We again note this on page 72, when he states:

When entertained by wealthy tax collectors like Matthew and Zacchaeus, a better wine undoubtedly was on the bill of fare. But to suggest that Jesus drank only grape juice is impossible to believe, particularly when it was not the season of grape harvest and there was no handy grape press offering fresh juice. Though it is quite possible that Jesus drank a nonintoxicating beverage, I find it difficult to believe that the sinners he drank with were teetotalers.

On reading this statement, one is amazed by the prejudice. First of all, to make a categoric statement that no fresh grape juice was available to Jesus, because it was not the season of harvest is incredible! It is true that Jesus' stay at Zacchaeus' house was shortly before the Passover and hence out of the grape harvest season. But if one reads the text (Luke 19:1-10), it says nothing about a big feast being prepared for Jesus as was the case with Matthew (Luke 5:29). Therefore any comments on our Lords actions at that time, however "rational," is nothing more than sheer speculation.

However, in the case of the feast with Matthew (Levi), we know that it was at the beginning of Jesus' public ministry. According to Thomas and Gundry's excellent work, *A Harmony of the Gospels,* this would have taken place at the "middle or latter part of year." Therefore there was every possibility that our Lord's feast with Levi took place at the time of harvest, when fresh, ripe fruit was in abundance. Not that this had to be the situation for the drinking of unfermented drinks, because methods were known for preserving fruits and unfermented juices. Also, water drinking was widespread, whatever the season! This example demonstrates how Bustanoby seeks to pass of his inventive speculations for fact to the non-inquiring reader. Speculations, which are, clearly designed to accommodate his prejudicial views on drinking.

After reading Bustanoby's book, it is not hard to see why so many professed Christians associate Jesus with all sorts of sinful practices, based on their own shallow interpretations of what they think the Scriptures should say. It is indeed true that Jesus and His disciples did eat and drink with publicans and sinners on some occasions, as the Bible makes clear. But to suggest that He condescended to their sinful practices because He was in their company is another thing. It is clear from the Scriptures that these situations took place only when He was invited or welcomed by these sinners to minister to their sick spiritual state. In Luke 5:31-32, Jesus states:

They that are whole need not a physician; but they that are sick. I came not to call the righteous, but sinners to repentance.

Jesus here describes these so-called friends of His, as sick sinners in need of repentance. This is the *only* kind of rapport He had with them!

Our Lord's actions can only be determined by the divine principles of Scripture, and not by subjective and narrow-minded speculations, or the evil accusations of His enemies.

We have already seen that the Old Testament disapproved of drinking:

Be not among winebibbers (winedrinkers)...(Proverbs 23:20)

Also Proverbs 20:1:

Wine is a mocker, strong drink is raging...

Jesus Himself warned against drinking and drunkenness, and of being in the company of those who do (Matt 24:45-51; Luke 12:45,46). With these facts before us, there is no need for any speculations whatsoever. It is safer to build our arguments on what we *do* know, rather than what we don't know, or on what we think should be. We can be certain therefore that Jesus was not a drinker, that is why even His enemies call Him this (Matt 11:19; Luke 7:34). This is contrary to Bustanoby's liking, but the very fact that our Lord does not use the ordinary word for drunkenness (methe) makes this an absolute fact. Berry's Dictionary of New Testament Greek synonyms makes this point clear by stating:

Methe is the ordinary word for drunkenness.

The significance of the specific and inspired use of the Greek word oinopotes (winedrinker) by Jesus in Matthew 11:19, and Luke 7:34, is explained by Parsons:

*It should be observed that the word rendered "winebibber," simply means a "**wine-drinker**;" yet in this passage a **wine-drinker** and a glutton are placed on a **par**, plainly*

265

showing that in those days it was a disgrace for a man to be a habitual drinker of wine...

(c) Concerning the point of Jesus drinking vinegar at His crucifixion being evidence of Him approving of fermented wine, Bustanoby also states that by this Jesus taught moderation. On page 78, he states:

> *Later, when he was thirsty, he did accept some wine vinegar in a sponge...The lesson we learn about wine from Jesus is not abstinence. It is moderation.*

This subject is also dealt with more fully in Part 2, Chapter 2, *Jesus and wine.* It is necessary however, to emphasize that everything Jesus went through on the cross was a form of punishment. The Psalmist in lamentable style prophesies this:

> *They gave me also gall for my meat; and in my thirst they gave me vinegar to drink.* (Psalm 69:21)

If fermented wine was so acceptable to Jesus in moderation, why was it given to Him as punishment?! Such reasoning is ridiculous! Mr. Bustanoby's view of Christ is hazy to say the least.

THE "BEST" WINE

In John 2:10, the governor of the feast said to the bridegroom concerning the wine Jesus made, "thou hast kept the good wine until now." This has led to endless debates regarding the nature of the good or best wine. There are those who insist that the wine was intoxicating, due to general familiarity and personal preference. On the other hand, as we learnt earlier, we know that this would be impossible, in the light of the Old Testament passages, which clearly condemns the use of alcoholic beverages.

In commenting on the wine Jesus produced, Bustanoby quickly rules out any idea in his own mind that it was unfermented grape juice. On page 75, he states:

> *In chapter 4 we saw that the "best" wine to those living*

in those days was not grape juice...The best wine was aged wine.

Commenting earlier on what was considered the "best" wine in ancient times, he states the following on page 22:

However, we shall see that only the best wine was fully aged and high in alcohol content.

Here in the above comments, Bustanoby indirectly charges our Lord Jesus Christ of creating a dangerous, poisonous, and intoxicating beverage of high alcoholic content in order to manifest His glory. An act which would clearly breach the Old Testament commandments. This is a very serious charge indeed, which has far reaching consequences, of which even Bustanoby himself seems to be aware of, but finds great difficulty in explaining away. This point is made apparent on page 55, when he contradicts himself by stating the following concerning the "wines on the lees," mentioned in Isaiah 25:6:

*Isaiah in the passage quoted above (25:6) sees God feasting with his people-not on grape juice but on fine, clarified wine of low alcohol content. God gives his people only the **best** wine.*

Bustanoby can't seem to make his mind up! One moment he states that the "best" wine was high in alcoholic content, and in the next, he states it was low in alcoholic content!

In replying to a statement in David Wilkerson's book, "Sipping Saints," which stated that unfermented grape juice was considered the best wine among the ancients, he includes the following in his arguments on page 43:

There is no evidence in extra biblical literature that unfermented wine was considered by the Jews, Greeks, or Romans as the best wine. The contention that grape juice was considered the best wine is simply a myth.

This statement is totally false. We have learnt earlier in our studies that there is ample evidence (if one looks for it) that there were those among the ancient Jews, Greeks, and Romans who considered unfermented grape juice to be better than alcoholic wine. Having said this, the truth of the matter is that what one considered the "best" wine was a matter of personal preference. In Luke 5:39, Jesus said:

> No man having drunk old wine straightway desireth new: for **he saith,** The old is better.

Here Jesus makes it plain that those who were used to drinking fermented wine (old) would not immediately desire unfermented wine (new), due to familiarity. Amazingly enough, in answer to statements that unfermented grape juice was considered by the Jews to be superior to fermented wine, Bustanoby himself brings out this point. On page 39-40, he states:

> There is no question that the ancients drank a variety of beverages, both fermented and unfermented. But to say that the unfermented juice of the grape or boiled wine was considered the best wine simply is fiction. That is like comparing Coca-Cola and Chianti. Each is "the best" in its class if Coke is your preference in a soft drink and Chianti is your preference in wine. But they cannot be compared, because they are different types of beverages. Declaring that the unfermented juice of the grape was regarded as superior to carefully fermented aged wine makes the same mistake. There is no comparison. Each is in a class by itself.

The main thought of this statement is basically correct, but again he contradicts himself. After making conflicting statements that the best wine was first high in alcoholic content and afterwards stating that it was low in alcoholic content, and then repudiating the fact that grape juice was considered the best. He here makes a more reasonable statement, conceding the fact that the ancients used unfermented beverages and that alcoholic and non-alcoholic wines could be classed separately. Bustanoby's reasoning is confusing to say the least! This demonstrates to us how tragic it becomes when one uses human reasoning rather than the solid principles of Scripture to determine the will of God.

In order to determine the nature of the wine Jesus created, there is a vital and paramount truth that must be understood, and that is we should not pay too much attention to whether men considered grape juice or alcoholic wine to be the best, but we should consider what God considered to be good wine. From our detailed study of the Old Testament we know that this certainly was not alcoholic wine but the "pure blood of the grape," which was unfermented grape juice. Just exactly what the sweetness, thickness etc., of the wine was we do not know, but we do know that it was good and perfect because Jesus Had supernaturally produced it.

Even if those at the wedding had been used to drinking alcoholic wine previously, the drinking of the fresh uncontaminated grape juice, which Jesus created, would be no problem. If we again look at our Lord's parable in Luke 5:39, we will see this explained:

> *And no one after drinking old wine immediately desires new wine, for he says, The old is good or better.* (Amplified Bible)

This parable is often used by liberals as an argument for the use and superiority of alcoholic wine, but if one reads it carefully, it is in fact one of the strongest texts in favour of the superiority of unfermented grape juice. The clear implication of the parable is that one who drinks alcoholic wine will not automatically desire non-alcoholic wine, but if they were to try it, they would discover that unfermented grape juice was better, just like His doctrine that He was offering to Israel. Our Lord could not have used a better analogy than this to describe the response to His message of the Kingdom. According to Jesus' words in John 3:19, *men loved darkness rather than light, because their deeds were evil.*

Today as in Jesus' day, the great majority of men think that sin is better than righteousness, but that does not mean that this is so! God knows that the cravings of sinful men are usually to their detriment. The wine that Jesus created was not necessarily what *man* considered to be good, but that which was good for man! And we know from the Scriptures that this was certainly not a fermented wine of high or low alcoholic content, but a wine that was absolutely pure and harmless just like our Lord and Saviour.

THE ARGUMENT OF ANAEROBIC FERMENTATION

The most convincing and conclusive evidence as far as the Bible is concerned, that unfermented grape juice and not alcoholic wine was used at the Lord's Supper of which the Passover was a type, was the prohibition of all fermented things at the Passover (for a complete treatment of this subject see section in Part 2 chapter 2, *The Lord's Supper*). How Bustanoby seeks to get around this Biblical truth is really incredible. Before taking a look at Bustanoby's arguments, the reader is advised not be intimidated or too overly concerned with the technical jargon he uses. These merely have a show of wisdom, but all they really amount to is a play on words of irrelevant information which has no Scriptural support whatsoever. On page 29, he states:

> *Anaerobic fermentation, or fermentation without free oxygen, is a marvelous process that was not understood until modern times. To denigrate fermented wine as decay and symbolic of death shows no understanding of anaerobic fermentation-life without free oxygen.*

He then goes on to state that this kind of fermentation also takes place in the human body when glucose is degraded to pyruvic acid, which in turn is converted by the muscle cells into lactic acid and energy, a process known as glycolysis. He then makes a "comparison" by stating that with fermented wine in a sealed container (anaerobic conditions), yeast enzymes convert pyruvic acid to ethyl alcohol, carbon dioxide, and energy. He thus concludes from this that fermenting wine under these conditions does not indicate decay and death, but is representative of life!

In reply to this somewhat useless "comparison," it must be stated that the *Bible* makes it plain that *God Himself* regarded all kinds of fermented things as being in a state of corruption.

Young's Literal Translation makes this truth absolutely clear concerning the Passover:

> *Seven days thou dost eat unleavened things, and in the seventh day is a feast to Jehovah; unleavened things are eaten the seven days, and any thing fermented is not seen with thee; yea, leaven is not seen with thee in all thy border.* (Exodus 13:6,7, Young's Literal Translation)

We thus learn from the *Scriptures* that whether it was fermentation in bread (yeast, leaven), or fermentation in wine, or whether the wine fermented in a sealed container or not, it still *fermented* and was regarded as corrupt. God in His omniscience therefore also denigrates fermented wine as corrupt or decayed and symbolic of sin and death!

One will understand this more clearly after a more detailed study of the Scriptures which are explained in the chapter on fermentation (Part 1, chapter 8), and the section on the Lord's Supper (Part 2, chapter 2), and will see that Bustanoby's arguments are utter nonsense. If one had two bottles of milk, one with the top on and the other with the top off. If both were left to go sour over a number of days, one would not say that the one with the top on was not really sour because the souring or decaying process took place in the absence of free oxygen! This would simply be irrelevant, but this is the kind of strange unscriptural reasoning that Bustanoby employs as he clutches at straws to maintain his argument for fermented wine. In actual fact, anaerobic fermentation in wine is merely a continuation of fermentation, which had already begun, in free oxygen, which is essentially a decay process. Also, any kind of decay process can be described as having "life," whether in free oxygen or not, depending on if one is seeking to baffle one with science in order to prove a point!

We will now turn our attention specifically to the subject of the Lord's Supper and examine the far-reaching implications of Bustanoby's views. On page 77, he continues his argument for fermented wine by a principle that clearly undermines the Biblical aspect of symbolism in the Lord's Supper. He begins by quoting and dismissing Charles Wesley Ewing's good and accurate description of fermented wine, as quoted by Van Impe. It reads:

> *Fermented wine is not a product of the vine. Chemically it is entirely different from the sweet and unfermented grape juice. Fermented wine is 14% alcohol, and it has other constituents that are not found in the fresh grape juice. Alcohol does not grow on the vine. It is not a vine product. Alcohol is the product of decay, the product of fermentation. It is produced by the product of spoiling.*

Bustanoby scoffs at this statement of truth by replying:

> *Note that the legalist connects wine with decay and spoiling. To him wine is therefore not an appropriate symbol for the blood of Christ. He argues, "Fermented wine, with microbes of decay, would not picture the perfect blood of a sinless Christ." The legalist argues that since it was prophesied that Jesus would see no corruption ("decay") (Ps. 16:10), "corrupted" grape juice would be an inappropriate symbol.*

> *When the legalist speaks this way about wine he once again shows his ignorance of the chemistry of wine...wine is not connected with death and decay. It is connected with life. When must becomes true wine, it undergoes anaerobic fermentation, which is life without free oxygen.*

This arrogant statement flies in the face of Scripture, and must be destroyed with the severity it deserves according to the Scriptural mandate:

> *Casting down imaginations (reasonings), and every high thing that exalteth itself against the knowledge of God...* (2 Corinthians 10:4)

Again, Bustanoby's argument is inconsistent, because on page 34, he himself describes grape juice containing fermenting matter as "contaminated" juice! This is exactly the truth of which Van Impe himself explains the Biblical significance! That is precisely why no fermented things were permitted at the Passover, which was a type of the Lord's Supper. The innocent Passover lamb representing Jesus Christ Himself. To suggest that Jesus Christ would create a contaminated wine, and that He would use a contaminated and corrupted substance as a symbol of His precious blood, in the light of Old Testament truth, is an outrageous act of wilful ignorance.

In dealing with the subject of drinking in the Bible, Bustanoby is as one who stands with a book on wine making in one hand and a book on biochemistry in the other, with the Bible dimly in the background. But in dealing with divine truth, we are only on solid ground when we stand clutching the inspired Book in both hands! Bustanoby here in attempting to expose the so called ignorance of the "legalist" in the area of wine making, himself advertises his own ignorance of the Scriptures which is really what counts.

One needn't have a knowledge of biochemistry or wine making in order to understand God's view on this subject. All one needs to know about God and His will can be determined from a correct understanding of the Scriptures. A truth which the divinely inspired Bible declares about itself:

> *Every Scripture is God-breathed-given by His inspiration-and profitable for instruction, for reproof and conviction of sin, for correction of error and discipline in obedience, and for training in righteousness [that is, in holy living, in conformity to God's will in thought, purpose and action], So that the man of God may be complete and proficient, well-fitted and thoroughly equipped for every good work.* (2 Timothy 3:16,17, Amplified Bible)

With these inspired truths before us, one can be absolutely confident therefore that irrespective of the knowledge possessed in biochemistry or wine making, with a sound understanding of the Scriptures, one is fully equipped to answer *any* moral difficulties in the area of drink as with anything else. This has been the problem all too often, particularly in the field of creation, where Christians have felt intimidated by the impressive sounding arguments of those scientists, who flatly contradict the accounts given by God of how things should be understood. What one needs to realize is that God is the author of all scientific laws, including fermentation, and is qualified more than anyone else to state when something is corrupt and what is the spiritual significance of it. From a Biblical point of view, it must be stated categorically that fermented wine is *not* connected with life at all, but with sin, which is a process of spiritual death:

> *For thus saith the Lord God of Israel unto me; Take the wine cup of fury at my hand, and cause all the nations, to whom I send thee, to drink it. And they shall drink, and be moved, and be mad, because of the sword that I will send among them.* (Jeremiah 25:15,16)

Further references to this can be found in Psalms 60:3; 75:8; Rev 14:8,10; 16:19; 17:2; 18:3.

We have already examined the New Testament, and have conclusively learnt that Jesus Himself understood this fact:

> *No man also having drunk old wine straightway desireth new: for he saith the old is better.* (Luke 5:39)

Notice again how Jesus contrasts His doctrine to that of the religious leaders of Israel. Note how He likens His doctrine to new wine, which alone could bring spiritual life, while He likens the corrupt doctrine of the religious leaders of Israel to old wine. We will now look at ultimate proof that Jesus regarded fermented wine in the same way as leaven (fermented dough), i.e., corrupt and symbolic of sin and death. In Matthew 16:6, when again speaking of the corrupt doctrine of the religious leaders of Israel, Jesus states:

> *Take heed and beware of the leaven of the Pharisees and of the Sadducees.*

Here we have it. Our Lord uses different types of fermentation to describe sinful and corrupt doctrine. In one place He uses fermentation in wine, and in the other place He uses fermentation in dough (yeast, leaven) because *Scripturally* these perfectly typify corruption and sin. Bustanoby's statement on page 77, that this is an argument from silence, amounts to nothing more than wilful ignorance. After all his ramble about aerobic and anaerobic fermentation of which the Bible doesn't remotely mention, such a remark is hypocrisy of the highest order.

Now in returning to Bustanoby's irrelevant point on page 29, where he seeks to pass off the theory that fermenting wine in sealed containers is connected with life, because of its similarity with the energy producing process off glycolysis in the human body. It must be stated that fermenting wine in a sealed container cannot be compared with the process of glycolysis, because alcohol in wine is an end product. When alcohol is ingested it cannot be converted to anything useful, the body simply seeks to expel it! What is of primary importance is that the Bible itself symbolizes leaven (fermenation) with sin, a process of spiritual death. This is brilliantly expounded by the Apostle Paul in 1 Corinthians 5:6-8:

> *Your glorying is not good. Know ye not that a little leaven leaveneth the whole lump? Purge out therefore the old leaven, that ye may be a new lump, as ye are unleavened. For even Christ our passover is sacrificed for us: Therefore let us keep the feast, not with old leaven, neither with the leaven of malice and wickedness; but with the unleavened bread of sincerity and truth.*

These Scriptures plainly speak for themselves. All the meticulous instructions given to Israel under the Law were not just given to take up space, but had deep spiritual significance which was to be fully realised in the New Testament in Jesus Christ. If one follows Bustanoby's subjective line of interpretation, which is to ignore or reject these truths in exchange for other inventive theories, on the grounds of certain prejudices. One cheats oneself of correctly understanding the beautiful and complete picture of God's revelation of the work of Christ and His absolute holiness and majesty.

One cannot seek to overturn the truths of Scripture by a twisted interpretation of biochemistry! Even the Oxford Dictionary, certainly not written by believers, shows a correct understanding of the symbolic meaning of fermentation. Under the definition of "leaven," it states:

> Substance added to dough to produce fermentation, esp. yeast, or fermenting dough reserved for purpose; (fig.)...traces of unregenerate state (1 Cor. 5:6,7).

Today's Dictionary of the Bible states:

> The chemical definition of ferment or yeast is "a substance in a state of putrifaction, the atoms of which are in a continual motion."

In his book, Bustanoby makes a big thing of comparing fermenting wine in sealed containers with the energy producing process in the human body (glycolysis) in order to justify the use of alcoholic wine. But what about comparing it with the operation of leaven (yeast) in bread? A process which the Bible likens to corruption and sin.

The operation of leaven (yeast) in bread is fundamentally the same as the production of alcohol in fermenting wine. Virtue's New Treasury of Knowledge, Volume 4 explains:

> Bread is made in the traditional manner by adding a small quantity of baker's yeast to dough. The yeast cells feed on the traces of sugars in the wheat flour, yielding alcohol and carbon dioxide. When the bread is baked the trapped carbon dioxide expands in the dough, producing the light, spongy texture. The alcohol evaporates away.

These facts merely confirm the inspired truths we have already learnt from a God of all knowledge, through the divine revelation of Holy Scripture. True science will always uphold the facts of the Bible and not detract from it. The Scriptures we have examined are diametrically opposed to the arguments concocted by Bustanoby. We do not derive our understanding of God and spiritual things from men's interpretation of biochemistry, but from the divine principles of Scripture! Alcohol is a symbol of sin and death because the Bible says so, and that settles it.

THE PRESERVATION OF FRUIT AND
THE TESTIMONY OF JOSEPHUS

Throughout his book, Bustanoby dismisses any suggestions that the ancients preserved unfermented wine (grape juice). From our studies we have seen that it was in fact feasible, but even if Bustanoby is right on this point, the preservation of fresh fruit was an established fact. As we read earlier, the ancient Jewish historian Josephus, testifies to the fact that in the fortress called Masada, built by Herod in Palestine, fruit was found freshly ripe which had been there for one hundred years!

On page 33, Bustanoby dismisses this claim as outrageous, even though its feasibility is supported by Pliny and others, as William Whiston the translator explains. Again, as was stated previously in another chapter, even if this claim is somewhat exaggerated, in reality all that would be required at the minimum, would be to preserve any grapes to be used for making fresh grape juice, for a period just short of a year. This is indeed a fact, as Swinburn explains:

> ...in Spain they also have the secret of preserving grapes sound and juicy from one season to another.

A Mr. EC Delevan also says of Signor Pippini, who was a large wine manufacturer of Florence:

> that he had then in his lofts, for the use of his table, until the next vintage, a quantity of grapes sufficient to make one hundred gallons of wine; that grapes could always be had, at any time of the year, to make any desirable quantity; and that there was nothing in the way of obtaining the fruit of the vine free from fermentation in wine countries at any period. A large basket of grapes was sent to my lodgings, which were as delicious, and looked as fresh, as if recently taken from the vines, though they had been picked for months.

These facts would ensure that freshly squeezed grape juice could be consumed all year round, at least until the next grape harvest.

THE NATURE OF NEW WINE

In our studies we have already observed that when the Bible refers to new wine, it does *not* speak of a fermented beverage. In fact the term was used for the purpose of specifically distinguishing fermented wine from unfermented wine. Unfortunately, Bustanoby is unwilling to see this and insists that the Bible only speaks of fermented wine. An example of this is his interpretation of Acts 2:13 (for a thorough explanation of this text, see section in Part 1, chapter 7, *difficult passages*), which reads:

Others mocking said, These men are full of new wine.

Note how the inspired writer accurately records the specific word used, "new wine" (gleukos). Any reasonable person with common sense reading this text would ask the following questions:

(a) Why was the Greek word gleukos (translated "new wine") used?

(b) If the drinking of intoxicating beverages was so good and acceptable to believers in Bible times as Bustanoby suggests, why was it not simply stated in the text that "these men are drunk?"

On page 79, Bustanoby gives a misleading view concerning the last clause of this text (Acts 2:13) by quoting the NIV Translation which reads, "They have had too much wine." This translation is incorrect and should read, "These are filled with new wine" or "sweet wine," but he obviously quotes it because it suits his biased view that new wine was intoxicating.

We have already seen earlier in another chapter that the Greek word here translated "new wine" (gleukos), which derives its meaning from the Greek word Glukus, meaning sweet. We know that during the fermentation process, the sugar in the grape juice is turned to alcohol, So a very sweet juice was one that was natural, that is, unfermented. Bustanoby himself explains the alcohol producing principle. On page 27, he states:

> *Yeast, which is found naturally everywhere, converts the sugar of the grape into alcohol. The higher the sugar content of the grape, the higher will be the alcoholic content of the finished product.*

Now concerning the new wine mentioned in Acts 2:13, he makes the following contradictory claims on page 80-81:

> *This passage raises the legitimate question of whether "new wine" was intoxicating. Indeed it was! Since the grape harvest was some four to eight months past, no fresh grape juice was available. By this time the must from the most recent vintage, the "new wine," would have aerobically fermented enough to have a fairly high alcohol content.*

If this speculative statement was true, then the juice would not have been called "new wine" or "sweet wine," because much of the sugar would have been converted to alcohol! Patton's explanation appropriately refutes Bustanoby's illogical statement:

> *Science teaches that, when by fermentation the sugar is turned into alcohol, the sweetness of the juice is gone. Thus, sweet means, as the lexicons state, unfermented wine.*

These facts highlight the prejudice of Bustanoby who refuses to concede his narrow-minded views in the face of real scientific and Scriptural facts.

As we noted previously, the charge of drunkenness in Acts 2:13, was an example of cynicism. Those who made the accusation were clearly aware that these men of God did not indulge in intoxicating drinks. So they cynically accuse them of being drunk on grape juice! Indeed the use of cynical language was nothing new. Paul himself uses it in 2 Corinthians 11:5, when he states:

> *For I suppose I was not a whit behind the chiefest apostles.*

Note how Paul refers to these false apostles as being the "chiefest" or "super" apostles. Shall we thus conclude from this statement that they were indeed superior to Paul? Indeed not. For we know that Paul is speaking in a cynical sense in the same way that grape juice is cynically said to produce genuine drunkenness in Acts 2:12. This type of expression is used throughout the Bible both by the enemies and servants of God.

Peter's statement therefore, that they could not have been drunk because it was only the third hour of the day (9 am), was not an admission that sweet wine could intoxicate, because it couldn't. It was rather designed to show the utter folly of any suggestion of drunkenness. To plead innocence from the false charges of drunkenness on the grounds of their Christian character was not enough to silence these sceptical sinners. So Peter puts the argument beyond doubt. For not even drunkards got drunk at that time of day (1 Thess 5:7).

Bustanoby's statement on page 80, that Peter would not have given an explanation if the accusation of drunkenness was made in mockery or in jest, has no Scriptural support whatsoever. In Matthew 12:24, the Pharisees made an even more wild and absurd accusation against Jesus when He cast out an evil spirit. They accuse Him of casting out the spirit by Beelzebub the prince of demons, an act that was totally impossible. Jesus did not ignore their foolishness, but replied by stating:

> Every kingdom divided against itself is brought to desolation; and every city or house divided against itself shall not stand: And if Satan cast out Satan, he is divided against himself; how shall then his kingdom stand? (Matthew 12:25,26)

He then continues by giving a thorough explanation, which totally refuted their foolish allegations. If one applied the same dangerous principles employed by Bustanoby and others in interpreting Acts 2:13, to this text, i.e., basing our judgments on the words of the enemies of God, then we would conclude that Jesus did indeed cast out demons through the prince of demons!

It was just as impossible to get drunk on new wine (grape juice) as it was for Satan to cast out Satan, irrespective of what the text might appear to say, *Judge not according to the appearance, but judge righteous judgment.* (Jesus Christ, John 7:24)

DRINKING UNDER THE LAW

On page 24 of his book, Bustanoby states the following concerning this subject:

> *We should ask, then, "Why does God go into such detail in Deuteronomy about restrictions but neglect to instruct the people carefully on this immensely important issue?" I can only conclude that drinking wine was not a sin.*

This sarcastic statement clearly displays a lack of understanding of this subject. He obviously hasn't properly read through the book of Deuteronomy or the other four books of the Law! Let the reader consider the following:

> *And I have led you forty years in the wilderness: your clothes are not waxen old upon you, and thy shoe is not waxen old upon thy foot. Ye have not eaten bread, neither have ye drunk wine or strong drink: that ye might know that I am the Lord your God.* (Deuteronomy 29:5,6)

> *Butter of kine, and milk of sheep, with fat of lambs, and rams of the breed of bashan, and goats, with the fat of kidneys of wheat; and thou didst drink the pure blood of the grape.* (Deuteronomy 32:14)

These Scripture passages of which we examined earlier (see Part 1, chapter 7; *An indepth defence of the abstinence position,* for a full explanation), plainly show that the drinking of fermented beverages was unacceptable to God. For throughout the whole forty years in the wilderness the Israelites did *not* drink any, but rather, as the text immediately above states clearly, they drank the pure unfermented juice (blood) of the grape. The clear implications from this are that they did indeed receive instructions concerning the dangerous effects of intoxicating substances. This is borne out in the book of Leviticus, which states:

And the Lord spake unto Aaron, saying, Do not drink wine nor strong drink, thou, nor thy sons with thee, when ye go into the tabernacle of the congregation, lest ye die: it shall be a statute for ever throughout your generations: And that ye may put difference between holy and unholy, and between unclean and clean; And that ye may teach the children of Israel all the statutes which the Lord hath spoken unto them by the hand of Moses.
(Leviticus 10:8-11)

This inspired text makes it perfectly plain that the **drinking** of fermented beverages affected one's ability to discriminate between what was right and what was wrong. God regarded the accurate transmission of His Law so highly, that those who were charged with the responsibility of conveying it were commanded to abstain from fermented beverages when ministering on penalty of death, lest it impair their ability to propagate divine truth in an undistorted manner. Bustanoby's interpretation of this text is really incredible. On page 46, he states:

The priests, by not drinking on duty, bore witness to the fact that the duties performed in the tabernacle were out of the ordinary and required extraordinary behavior not required elsewhere.

This inventive statement is an attempt to evade the issue clearly set out in the text, and highlights the hypocrisy and prejudice of Bustanoby when it comes to the subject of drink. Our text above already states in no uncertain terms, why the priests were commanded to abstain from wine and strong drink while ministering. Adam Clake's Commentary repudiates Bustanoby's statement of undefined nonsense. In commenting on the first clause of verse 10, of the above text, *that ye may put difference between holy and unholy,* he accurately states:

This is a strong reason why they should drink no inebriating liquor, that their understanding being clear, and their judgment correct, they might be always able to discern between the clean and the unclean, and ever pronounce righteous judgment. Injunctions similar to this were found among the Egyptians, Carthaginians, and Greeks. Indeed, common sense itself shows that neither a drunkard nor a sot should ever be suffered to minister in holy things.

As Clarke states, this is a matter of common sense of which Bustanoby is blatantly ignorant. It is clear therefore, that the drinking of intoxicating beverages was regarded as sin as well as drunkenness, because it affected one's reasoning powers. Surely if drinking affected the priests ability to communicate divine truth, it would also affect the people's ability to practice it!

This truth also has a wider New Testament application, as Gleason Archer explains:

> *It is thus made clear that priests who drank were thereby prevented from carrying out their ministry of teaching the people the distinction between what was holy and what was profane.*
>
> *This has implications for the New Testament priesthood of all believers (1 Peter 2:9) and suggests that they may be seriously handicapped in carrying on the work of soulwinning if they personally indulge in the use of alcohol. By doing so, they may cause millions of fellow citizens to stumble who have become enslaved to this degrading practice and are looking for some way out of their bondage. These are scarcely apt to take seriously the Christian witness of one who has not rid himself of "everything that hinders" (Heb. 12:1), especially when he starts speaking about the victorious life of faith.*

In this section we have seen that Bustanoby is alcoholic minded. His objections to total abstinence from alcoholic beverages are not on the grounds of Scriptural facts, but on sheer prejudice!

ALCOHOL ABUSE-A CORRECT
SCRIPTURAL DEFINITION

Throughout Bustanoby's book, he gives his own subjective interpretation of what he considers to be alcohol abuse. He claims that the Bible permits the use of alcohol but not its "abuse." On page 48, he states the following:

> There is no question that alcoholic beverages are dangerous-that it is possible to be seduced by them. As we shall see, Scripture gives us ample warning about this. But Scripture also makes a distinction between the use and abuse of alcohol-a distinction that the legalistic prohibitionist refuses to acknowledge.

The question we must all ask ourselves is what does the Bible define as alcohol abuse? From our previous studies we have already learnt that the *drinking* of alcohol was unacceptable to God in the same way as drunkenness, because it deprives one of their normal reasoning powers. Therefore the *use* of alcoholic beverages constitutes alcohol abuse, but since Bustanoby claims that his arguments are backed by Scripture, we will hear his side of the story. On page 24, he states the following:

> ...the book of Proverbs gives us ample warning about limits. Israel, by this time, had sufficient experience with alcohol to require the instruction given in Proverbs. And they were instructed to be moderate, not abstinent.

These claims are absolutely outrageous! The present author challenges Bustanoby and those who hold his views, to find one passage in the whole of Proverbs, which instructs moderation in the use of alcoholic beverages!

The book of Proverbs rather commands *abstinence* and not moderation regarding alcoholic beverages. Let the reader again consider the following:

> Wine is a mocker, strong drink is raging: and whosoever is deceived thereby is not wise. (Prov 20:1)

> Be not among winebibbers; (wine drinkers)... (Prov 23:20)

Look not thou upon the wine when it is red, when it giveth his colour in the cup, when it moveth itself aright. (Prov 23:31)

It is not for kings, O Lemuel, it is not for kings to drink wine; nor for princes strong drink: Lest they drink, and forget the law, and pervert the judgment of any of the afflicted. (Prov 31:4,5)

These passages conclusively shows how important it is for one to read the plain simple message of the Scriptures for themselves, rather than what someone else says about the them! God, The Great Prohibitionist Himself, commands total abstinence from all alcoholic beverages!

In another attack on the so-called "legalist" (a label he slaps on all those who advocate the Scriptural principle of total abstinence from alcoholic beverages), Bustanoby states the following on page 16:

...the Scripture says that drunkenness is sin. The legalist declares that since drinking can lead to drunkenness, drinking is therefore sinful.

What Mr. Bustanoby fails to understand, is that this is precisely how the Bible says that drunkenness should be avoided! Let the reader again consider these wise words from the book of Proverbs:

*Who hath woe? who hath sorrow? who hath contentions? who hath babbling? who hath wounds without cause? who hath redness of eyes? They that tarry long at the wine; they that go to seek mixed wine. **Look not thou upon the wine** when it is red, when it giveth his colour in the cup, when it moveth itself aright. At the last it biteth like a serpent, and stingeth like an adder. Thine eyes shall behold strange women, and thine heart shall utter perverse things. Yea, thou shalt be as he that lieth upon the top of a mast. They have stricken me, shalt thou say, and I was not sick; they have beaten me, and I felt it not: when shall I awake? I will seek it again.* (Proverbs 23:29-35)

Let the reader note how the writer first graphically describes the effects of drunkenness, and then responds by stating, "Look not thou upon the wine..." He then goes on again to explain that despite the stupefying effects of this intoxicating wine, the drinker seeks it again. This is a clear reference to alcohol addiction. The inspired writer states that in order to avoid the damaging effects of alcohol, one should not even look at intoxicating wine, this naturally means total abstinence. This therefore is not a so-called "legalist" view as Bustanoby erroneously suggests, but a sound Biblical one!

It may be argued that this text refers to a wine of high alcoholic content, but by today's standards this "dangerous wine" as Bustanoby describes it, would be pretty ordinary. Therefore it is clear from this text that the drinking of alcoholic wine that is capable of producing drunkenness is sin.

In Proverbs 20:1, intoxicating wine in general is labelled as a mocker. So even if one uses the high alcoholic content argument to suggest that this is the only case that abstinence may be commanded, or the diluted wine theory to justify the use of alcohol, the Bible makes it plain that drinking alcoholic beverages constitutes alcohol abuse which in the light of Scripture is sin. There is no need to bend Scripture in any way to see this, as Bustanoby claims. All one simply has to do is to read it!

A BIBLICAL AND COMMON SENSE LOOK AT DRINKING

I beseech you therefore, brethren, by the mercies of God, that ye present your bodies a living sacrifice, holy, acceptable unto God, which is your reasonable service. And be not conformed to this world: but be ye transformed by the renewing of your mind, that ye may prove what is that good, and acceptable, and perfect, will of God. (Romans 12:1,2)

In this section we will see how the Scriptures militate against all Bustanoby's arguments for drinking. On further examination of his book, we will see that his arguments for drinking are riddled with numerous contradictions and Scriptural inconsistencies. The principle of drinking defies all Biblical sense. To suggest that God in the name of moderation would bestow upon man a poisonous and addictive drug is beyond all logic. It is hard to see how one can be a drinker and comply with the above Scriptural mandate which stresses the importance of one intelligently presenting their bodies in an acceptable condition before God, and having the mind renewed in order to please God to the fullest. Young's Literal Translation of the above text brings out this point even clearer:

> *I call upon you, therefore, brethren, through the compassions of God, to present your bodies a sacrifice-living, sanctified, acceptable to God-your intelligent service; and be not conformed to this age, but be transformed by the renewing of your mind, for your proving what is the will of God-the good, and acceptable, and perfect.*
> (Romans 12:1,2, Young's Literal Translation)

Concerning the study of wine drinking in the Bible, R.B. Grindrod wisely states:

> *An inquiry into the nature and qualities of the wines mentioned in the Scriptures, forms an interesting and highly important subject of investigation. Much obscurity overhangs the subject, even in the present day, and there is reason to fear that mankind have too frequently interpreted the language of Scripture with a view to extenuate sinful practices, and to gratify sensual desires.*
>
> *An investigation of this subject ought to be entered into with appropriate caution, lest the purity of the Almighty should be impeached, in representing him as sanctioning or approving of a practice which has a direct tendency to produce sin.*

Sadly, this has not been the case with Bustanoby's book. While claiming to be fighting the battle against what he calls alcohol abuse, and at the same time upholding the theory that the Bible supports and encourages drinking, he has probably done more to promote alcohol abuse than he has to stop it! Either the Bible is for the use of alcoholic beverages or it is against it. On page 61, he states:

> *Gluttony, like drunkenness, begins with a wrong attitude toward a good thing.*

Note how Bustanoby tries to legitimise drinking by putting it in the same category as food, in order to pass off his moderation theory. We know from the Bible that gluttony is sin, but alcohol is not a food but a drug, and therefore cannot be considered in the same sense as food. However, on page 63, he grossly contradicts himself by stating:

> *...I have come to the conclusion that alcohol does have a great deal of power to lead astray. I believe it is the most seductive drug there is.*

Since as he states, alcohol is "the most seductive drug there is," then why abuse it by drinking it in the first place?!!! In answering his dangerous statement which describes alcoholic beverages capable of producing drunkenness as "a good thing," we will follow the wise direction of the apostle Paul in determining truth, which he states in Romans 4:3, and Galatians 4:30, *what saith the scripture?*:

> *Wine is a mocker, strong drink is raging: and whosoever is deceived thereby is not wise.* (Proverbs 20:1)

The Bible completely contradicts Bustanoby by stating that alcoholic beverages both mocks and distorts one's personality by making them aggressive. An extract from a study on alcohol published by United Kingdom Alliance, explains in scientific terms the truth of this inspired text:

> *Because alcohol is a narcotic drug it has the same effect upon the central nervous system as morphine and anaesthetics.*

> *The first areas of the brain to be affected are the frontal lobes, or `upper brain'-the site of man's higher faculties, judgment, self control, reason and reaction time. Thus,*

because of this, alcohol is a very dangerous drink for drivers. Alcohol accounts for at least one in ten of all deaths on the road. Seventy or eighty per cent of all crimes in Britain are considered to be committed under the influence of alcohol.

Because alcohol acts on the brain as an anaesthetic, there is interference with normal brain activity, even though the drinker may not be aware of it. Under this condition, the best features of man are lost first, and his worst features brought out.

These facts make it clear that the drinking of alcoholic beverages is totally unacceptable from a Biblical and common sense perspective. R.B. Grindrod explains:

On a careful examination it will be found, that the whole tenor of Scripture is opposed to every species of intemperance. The causes and effects of this degrading vice are pointed out in the strongest possible manner, and faithful warnings are therein given against mankind in any way becoming victims of intoxicating drink. This is found to be the case, not only in the inculcation of general principles, but in the illustration of those principles by particular examples.

It is therefore a matter of Biblical and common sense that the vast quantity of wine that our Lord created at the wedding in Cana of Galilee, the fruit of the vine used at the Lord's Supper, and the wine which is spoken of as a blessing in many places in the Old Testament, must be of an unfermented nature. The Reverend B. Parsons in his studies, also labours to get an hearing in explaining this common sense truth:

In offering these remarks on the wines of Scripture, I have no where attempted to deny that inebriating liquors existed in Palestine; all I contend for is, that there were wines which did not intoxicate, and that these latter are the only ones which a God of love and mercy would recommend. He has created us with a constitution with

289

which alcohol wages the bitterest war. God has not given us a body that can long resist its attacks, and it would therefore be presumptuous to assert that he has ever approved of a liquor which must prey upon its vitals. He in a thousand ways shows the value that he sets upon human life, and the means he employs for its preservation; and most contradictory to his general benevolent proceedings would it be, if he had commanded us to use a beverage which must injure all the functions of our bodies, and at the same time enfeeble our minds and deprave our morals.

Bustanoby rejects this truth as false, and insists that "wine" in the Bible must be interpreted as a fermented or alcoholic beverage. on page 45, he makes this clear by stating:

More than anything else, false exegesis of Scripture, including false theories about unfermented wine, have both compromised the integrity of Scripture and discredited an otherwise noble cause-the battle against alcohol abuse.

Here we have another amazing and incredulous statement by Bustanoby. It must be stated in the face of this erroneous statement, that it is rather false and narrow-minded theories which state that the Bible *only* speaks of fermented wine that has led to false exegesis of Scripture. This has greatly discredited the godly battle against the sin of intemperance!

His objections against unfermented wine in the Bible context, on the grounds of compromising the so-called "integrity of Scripture," is absolutely incredible!

It must be stated again that it is views of Biblical interpretation such as Bustanoby's, that claims that the Bible supports drinking, and exclusively speaks of alcoholic wine, which has brought the high moral standard of the Bible into disrepute. RA Torrey explains:

A stock objection against the Bible, and not only against the Bible but against Jesus Christ Himself, is found in the

story of Jesus turning the water into wine at the marriage
festival at Cana of Galilee as recorded in John 2:1-11.

Even sinful people, who realise the damaging effects of alcohol, find it impossible to reconcile the principle of drinking with a holy and righteous God. Our study demonstrates that Bustanoby's views leads to endless confusion that defies all common sense, of which he is unable to explain away, as we learnt earlier. Another example of this can be found on page 50, when he states:

My personal preference is that those who rule or hold high
office in government be total abstainers. And I like the idea
of pastors being total abstainers for the sake of example.

If Jesus drank, approved of, and created intoxicating wine as Bustanoby suggests, why then should a pastor abstain as a matter of example? Should he not rather drink as an example of following the so-called conduct of his Lord and Master? Such contradictory nonsense is beyond all reason. One can't have it both ways!

In Bustanoby's book he almost scorns the idea of drinking unfermented grape juice. On pages 32-43, he relegates the drinking of grape juice to a mere myth, along with other methods used by the ancients for preserving unfermented grape juice. On page 61, he calls alcoholic beverages, which causes drunkenness, "a good thing." On page 75, he makes it clear that he considers the "good wine" that Jesus made at Cana to be an alcoholic beverage. On page 22, he states that the best wine to those living in ancient times was aged wine of high alcoholic content. On page 25, he claims that God blessed his people with this kind of wine. Today Bustanoby's book would serve as a good advertisement for the liquor industry!

This kind of inconsistency is typical of Bustanoby's book. The study on alcohol published by United Kingdom Alliance, flatly and correctly refutes Bustanoby's erroneous and dangerous statement that God blessed His people with "good" alcoholic wine. It states:

Quite contrary to the opinion of many, alcohol is not the gift of God, God, by His direct act, does not make alcohol. The laws of nature ripen grapes. If they are not eaten, they rot and decompose. The manufacture of alcohol is wholly man's device.

Because of the damaging effects that *any* alcohol has upon the human body, it must be categorically stated again that it is a matter of common sense that God did *not* bestow upon man alcoholic beverages as a so-called "blessing." It is therefore a matter of Biblical and common sense that when the Bible speaks of wine as a blessing, it is of the unfermented kind. On page 23, Bustanoby describes this as "logical gymnastics," whatever that's supposed to mean! One thing we do know, it's certainly logical!

Alcohol is in a sense no different from other dangerous hard drugs. A booklet published by The British Temperance Society, states the following concerning alcohol:

Alcohol is the only drug that causes visible damage to the brain. It tends to release inhibitions, and emotions can erupt into assault and homicide. Chronic alcoholism can destroy the personality. Alcohol is often addictive. Withdrawal is correspondingly as severe as that as barbiturates.

It is inconceivable that God in the name of moderation would sanction the use of LSD, marijuana, barbiturates etc., but this is exactly the position that Bustanoby is forced to adopt. If as he suggests, the Bible permits moderation with as he puts it, "the most seductive drug there is," then the same must also apply to the other less seductive drugs!

Alcohol damages the brain, heart, liver, and impedes the oxygen flow in the blood, it can also cause damage to the unborn, and can also affect male sperm. The important thing to note is that all this can occur without a person even becoming drunk! Concerning this anti moderation point, the booklet entitled, *Alcohol the inside story,* states (bold print the author's):

*...brain cells do not multiply and are irreplaceable, so brain damage accumulates throughout an individual's life. Every time a person takes a **drink**, he hastens this process, damaging his brain by cutting off oxygen to the vital cells.*

The booklet entitled, *Alcohol and you* also confirms this fact. It states:

*When a person takes a **drink** of alcohol, the red cells in the blood start to stick together. These red cells are then unable to pick up oxygen from the lungs and release it to other parts of the body.*

The same authority also states:

Alcohol, when taken orally, does not remain in the stomach, but is distributed to all parts of the body, and because it is a poison the body soon begins to eliminate it. Up to ten per cent is excreted through the urine, breath, saliva and sweat. The rest must be disposed of inside the body and is oxidized or burned.

He, who created our bodies, designed them to resist this poison. He whose revelation inspired these words, *I will praise thee; for I am fearfully and wonderfully made* (Psalms 139:14), in His wisdom warns against that which disrupts it, *Wine is a mocker, strong drink is raging* (Prov 20:1). This truth is beautifully expressed by Professor Moses Stuart, after a thorough Biblical study of this subject:

The use of intoxicating liquors, is as evidently forbidden by God in his arrangement of our natures, as in the volume of his revelation.

The damage that alcoholic beverages causes to our bodies, puts it beyond a shadow of a doubt that God does not approve of the so called moderate drinking of this dangerous substance.

God expects us to exercise our minds that He gave us to logically and sensibly reason things out concerning conduct, in the light of His revelation. Jesus Himself employed this principle of stimulating men's God given minds in order to determine the will of God. An example of this can be found in Luke 7:40-43, which reads:

> And Jesus answering said unto him, Simon, I have somewhat to say unto thee. And he saith, Master, say on. There was a certain creditor which had two debtors: the one owed five hundred pence, and the other fifty. And when they had nothing to pay, he frankly forgave them both. Tell me therefore, which of them will love him most? Simon answered and said, I suppose that he, to whom he forgave most. And he said unto him, Thou hast rightly judged.

In John W. Wenham's book, *Christ and the Bible*, he states the following concerning Jesus, under the heading, *The right use of reason*:

> Jesus condemns neither minuteness of study nor the excercise of reason. His condemnation comes when the wickedness of men so perverts their reason or their methods of study that they become blind to the inner principles of divine revelation. He himself knew how to stimulate the excercise of reason and repeatedly he encouraged his hearers to go beneath the externals of Scripture language and think out its underlying principles.

It was for this very same cause that our Lord so harshly rebuked the Pharisees in Luke 11:39-40:

> And the Lord said unto him, Now do ye Pharisees make clean the outside of the cup and the platter; but your inward part is full of ravening wickedness. Ye fools, did not he that made that which is without make that which is within also?

In defining what defiles a man, Jesus includes foolishness in a catalogue of heinous sins:

> That which cometh out of the man, that defileth the man. For from within, out of the heart of men, proceed evil

thoughts, adulteries, fornications, murders, Thefts, covetousness, wickedness, deceit, lasciviousness, an evil eye, blasphemy, pride, foolishness: All these evil things come from within, and defile the man. (Mark 7:20-23)

In Ephesians 5:15,16, Paul also warns against this:

See then that ye walk circumspectly, not as fools, but as wise, Redeeming the time, because the days are evil.

To suggest that God would bestow upon man alcoholic beverages as a blessing is indeed foolishness. The very principles of Scripture argue against such absurd "reasoning," and are an insult to a God of love and omniscience. The Rev. B. Parsons sensibly states the following, concerning this kind of thinking:

No one who has carefully examined the effects of inebriating wines will say that there is a blessing in them, unless a diseased stomach, a shattered frame, an injured intellect, inflamed passions, and a premature death, for which, in most cases, the unhappy victim is unprepared, can be termed blessings.

Bustanoby's insistence that the Bible exclusively speaks of alcoholic wine is indeed illogical. This unreasonable stance is clearly designed to screen out the abstinence argument. If he admits that unfermented wine was used even once in the Bible context, he would be forced to concede that it could have been used in numerous other instances. This would seriously threaten the whole shaky foundation on which he has built his "Christian liberty" theory, and would eventually bring his whole argument crashing to the ground!

So in obstinately pursuing this viewpoint, he has created numerous problems for himself and others. For instance, if one accepts Bustanoby's opinion that the Bible encourages drinking (this has to be the case, since he claims that God blessed His people with alcoholic wine), then every Christian should be a supporter of the liquor industry. If as He suggests, Christ created alcoholic wine, and that alcoholic wine was used at the Lord's

Supper, then everyone should be encouraged to drink, including teenagers. His statement on page 107, is thus a contradiction, when he states:

> *Christian liberty may permit adults to drink, but adolescents by law may not drink. The adolescent who drinks any amount of alcohol is breaking the law, and adults who abet this drinking are also guilty.*

Again, if we accept all that he says about alcohol and the Bible, then this statement would be invalid. Adolescents would indeed be at liberty to drink, despite what the law states, because this would mean that adolescent Christians would not be permitted to participate in the Lord's Supper! Breaking the law would not be wrong, for Acts 5:29, states:

> *We ought to obey God rather than men.*

In continuing the argument based on Bustanoby's reasoning, it would mean that every Christian should encourage the advertisement of alcoholic drinks. Christians should then sound a message out to the world that they should moderately enjoy God's blessing! Anyone with any common sense would realise that this kind of thinking would be potentially disastrous. But if one suggests that Jesus created a vast amount of alcoholic wine, then this should certainly be the attitude that Christians should adopt. It is obvious that this kind of thinking is senseless, because one simply cannot abuse their bodies in moderation!

On page 50, Bustanoby's claims that Christian liberty permits responsible drinking, is completely refuted in the booklet entitled, *Alcohol and you*, which states:

> *Remember, there is no such thing as responsible drinking-only degrees of irresponsibility.*

From what we know about alcohol, the human body, and the nature of God revealed to us through Holy Scripture, this statement is absolutely correct.

It is a pity that in the area of drink, Bustanoby's reasoning has been influenced more by this world's sinful mentality rather than the Word of God. One's mind must be renewed by the Word of God, and not by the views of sinful men, as our opening text of Romans 12:1,2 makes clear.

Although well intentioned, Bustanoby's book is dangerous because he elevates his own subjective philosophy above the plain and simple commandments of Scripture. In his book he devotes three whole chapters to dealing with alcohol problem cases. Much of which consists of his own opinions, and is extremely shallow in Scriptural content, as is indeed the case with the rest of his book. Although his material may help some, he would have saved himself a lot of trouble and counselling time if he had focused on Scriptures such as the following:

> *Wine is a mocker, strong drink is raging: and whosoever is deceived thereby is not wise.* (Proverbs 20:1)
>
> *Be not among winebibbers; among riotous eaters of flesh.* (Prov 23:20)
>
> *Look not thou upon the wine when it is red, when it giveth his colour in the cup, when it moveth itself aright. At the last it biteth like a serpent, and stingeth like an adder.* (Prov 23:31,32)

The above Scriptures clearly condemn the *use* of alcoholic beverages. If one sensibly adheres to these wise words he would totally abstain, and would hence never have a problem with alcohol. This truth is endorsed in the excellent booklet entitled, *Alcohol and you.* It states:

> *Frequent drinking can lead to a powerful habituation which is beyond control of the person. There are those who sincerely believe that this could never happen to them. They believe that it is only people with severe mental problems who become alcohol-dependent; people who have good character, education and health and general will-power can, they think, drink without danger. This is not true.*

Alcohol dependence strikes people in all walks of life...The only one hundred per cent safe course by which this danger can be avoided is never to use alcohol.

God's way is always the best way, because it is the most simple, plain and effective. One realizes the good work done by many organizations devoted to helping those with alcohol and other drug related problems etc. Indeed they are to be commended for this; but those organizations or individuals that do not base their work whole heartedly on Scriptural principles, deprive themselves of much success.

The present author would strongly advise anyone reading this book, on the authority of the Word of God, to abstain totally from alcoholic beverages, because they certainly aren't good. And are totally unnecessary as far as good health is concerned.

Much counselling, heartache, expense, and loss of time would be avoided if these wise, common sense and Biblical principles were heeded.

A BIBLICAL LOOK AT LEGALISM
AND CHRISTIAN LIBERTY

In Bustanoby's literature, there is a lot of talk about not declaring something unlawful which the Bible declares lawful, as if this is the only side to legalism. In his pseudo zeal for Christian liberty on the issue of drink, he forgets that one must not declare something lawful which the Bible declares unlawful either! Let us consider what Jesus, the Master Himself, has to say about this aspect of legalism:

> *For laying aside the commandment of God, ye hold the tradition of men, as the washing of pots and cups: and many other such like things ye do...Making the word of God of non effect through your tradition, which ye have delivered: and many such like things do ye.* (Mark 7:8,13)

Now bearing this truth in mind, let us now again consider the clear and unquestionable commandments of the following inspired Scriptures:

Wine is a mocker, strong drink is raging: and whosoever is deceived thereby is not wise. (Prov 20:1)

Be not among winebibbers... (Prov 23:20)

Look not thou upon the wine when it is red, when it giveth his colour in the cup, when it moveth itself aright. (Prov 23:31)

These are clear commandments to abstain from alcohol. How in the face of these plain Scriptures and many others in the New Testament, Bustanoby can state on page 21, that "the issue of alcohol use is not that clear in Scripture," is absolutely amazing?!! Obviously he either hasn't taken the time to read the Scriptures properly, or is wilfully ignorant of the facts for reasons that suit him.

Bustanoby's argument that Christian liberty permits drinking is entirely without substance, as the Scriptures themselves make clear. The serious charges which he makes against those who advocate total abstinence by branding them as "legalists," is outrageously false and libellous.

The whole theme of Bustanoby's book seems to be geared to undermining the truth of total abstinence, in order to provide a platform for him to display his "expertise" in dealing with those already affected with alcohol.

We have already observed from our studies, that his attempts to explain away those Scriptures, which condemn drinking, are totally unsatisfactory from a Scriptural perspective. It also appears that he has an axe to grind with the so-called "legalist." This may be largely responsible for his insulting, thoughtless, narrow- minded, and unreasonable approach to this subject.

Ironically, when we examine the Scriptures, we learn that it is Bustanoby himself who is the legalist, because he is clearly guilty of "making the word of God of non effect" by what he calls the "traditional interpretation"! We also learn that he is guilty of blatant hypocrisy in his interpretation of the Scriptures, and of manipulating the Christian liberty issue to accommodate his drinking bias.

The fact is, that the more one reads Bustanoby's book, the more it becomes evident that he himself doesn't really understand the Christian liberty issue. This is quite apparent from his statement on page 24, which reads:

> *The Bible is very clear in naming sin in act or principle. Therefore, the apostle Paul can be very confident in teaching us that we are free to do anything the Bible does not declare sin. All things not sinful are lawful* (1 Cor. 10:23).

This statement is correct, but sadly for Bustanoby, the Bible very clearly names drinking as sin, both in act and in principle. Having already established without a shadow of a doubt from our studies, the fact that alcohol is a poison and a pollutant of the human body, let us take note of what the apostle Paul, "the great champion of liberty" as Bustanoby himself describes him, has to say concerning this principle:

> *Having, then, these promises, beloved, may we cleanse ourselves from every pollution of flesh and spirit, perfecting sanctification in the fear of God.* (2 Corinthians 7:1, Young's Literal Translation)

This text very clearly condemns the principle of drinking. Here we have an implicit command to abstain from alcoholic beverages and any other thing impure! Therefore all Bustanoby's ramble about the ins and outs of legalism and his fine-spun arguments concerning wine making, are totally irrelevant as far as this subject is concerned. Paul the inspired apostle states in no uncertain terms the requirements for holy living and these requirements excludes the use of all drug abuse, including alcohol. When Bustanoby states that the Bible is very clear in naming sin, he grossly contradicts himself and destroys his whole argument at the very roots.

We will now take another look at how Bustanoby grossly contradicts himself concerning the subject of Christian liberty. On page 21, he states the following:

> *...we ought not to encourage the abstainer to use alcohol.*

Such an act would be insensitive to his scruples and a clear violation of Romans 14:1, which says, "Accept him whose faith is weak, without passing judgment on disputable matters." Since this matter is disputable, the abstainer's scruples are to be respected.

We have already established in our studies that the use of alcohol is *not* a "disputable" matter, but even if this were the case, Bustanoby again grossly contradicts his above statement. On pages 73-74, he gives an account of how he and some of his Christian friends were given beer to drink as a toast at a feast hosted by an unbeliever, many years ago. He explained that one of the Christian group, a Baptist seminary student, was an abstainer from alcohol and was deeply offended by the gesture although well meaning, and refused to drink.

Bustanoby recalls how he was deeply distressed, even to this day by the action of the Baptist student. He claims that this "did not help the cause of Christ but rather diverted attention from the gospel to beer!" And that it spoiled a good relationship because he was making "an issue over a non-issue." This is an amazing contradiction to what he states on page 21, that "the abstainer's scruples are to be respected." He draws his argument for this view from a serious misinterpretation of 1 Corinthians 10:27-30, which reads:

If any of them that believe not bid you to a feast, and ye be disposed to go; whatsoever is set before you, eat, asking no question for conscience sake. But if any man say unto you, This is offered in sacrifice unto idols, eat not for his sake that shewed it, and for conscience sake: for the earth is the Lord's, and the fulness thereof: Conscience, I say, not thine own, but of the other: for why is my liberty judged of another man's conscience? For if I by grace be a partaker, why am I evil spoken of for that which I give thanks?

Note that this text specifically refers to the subject of the offering of food as a sacrifice to idols or demons by the gentiles, which is an issue of conscience. Whether the food was offered to idols or not, it made no difference at all to the actual condition of the food. Paul earlier made this point clear in verse 19, of the same chapter:

> *What say I then? that the idol is any thing, or that which is offered in sacrifice is any thing?*

Indeed 1 Corinthians 10:27-30, does not apply to the issue of alcohol whatsoever. To interpret it that way would be to take the Scripture out of context. This is exactly what Bustanoby has done, he has taken the passage out of context to accommodate his views on drinking. His interpretation of this text is erroneous. The believer is not obligated to consume any pollutant placed before him by the unbeliever for the so-called cause of maintaining a good relationship.

Now in returning to the main crux of the argument for a correct Scriptural explanation, we will see that Bustanoby's conduct was definitely wrong, and that in the light of Scripture, the abstinent action of the Baptist Christian was positively correct. First of all, when the abstaining Christian displayed embarrassment and offence when suddenly confronted with the dilemma of drinking beer, to use his own words, Bustanoby was totally insensitive to the scruples of his fellow brother in Christ. On page 74, he insensitively and somewhat belittlingly describes the conduct of his brother in Christ, who clearly did not know how to handle the awkward situation that he found himself in:

> *The Baptist seminary student looked as though he could have died! I knew what his problem was. This devout Baptist would not let alcohol touch his lips. He put his hands together, as in prayer, bowed deeply, and would not look at the superintendent, who was dumbfounded. Undoubtedly he wondered why his honored guests would not join in his toast.*

We have already learnt from our studies that the Bible condemns drinking. This means that the Baptist Christian was vindicated in his conduct of obeying the Scriptures, but again even if one viewed this from the Christian liberty perspective, he would still be Biblically correct in his convictions. Romans 14:22-23 makes this absolutely clear:

> *Hast thou faith? have it to thyself before God. Happy is he that condemneth not himself in that thing which he alloweth. And he that doubteth is damned if he eat, because he eateth not of faith: for whatsoever is not of faith is sin.*

Any attempt therefore by another to cause offence to this stance would also be sin. Romans 14:21 explains:

> *It is good neither to eat flesh, nor drink wine, nor any thing whereby thy brother stumbleth, or is offended, or is made weak.*

Bustanoby clearly violates this text and deliberately causes offence to his brother, as he himself unashamedly proclaims on page 74:

> *I quickly picked up my glass, raised it in toast, and took a sip. My buddies followed suit, but the seminarian just remained bowed.*

The Scriptures further condemns Bustanoby's overt hypocrisy:

> *But when ye sin so against the brethren, and wound their weak conscience, ye sin against Christ. Wherefore, if meat make my brother to offend, I will eat no flesh while the world standeth, lest I make my brother to offend.* (1 Corinthians 8:12,13)

Bustanoby found it more convenient to violate the Scriptures, and to cause offence to his brother, than to simply explain the situation to the unbeliever! The welfare of our brethren is our priority:

> *As we have therefore opportunity, let us do good to all men, especially unto them who are of the household of faith.* (Galatians 6:10)

Bustanoby's behaviour in this situation was indeed disgraceful. One is amazed that he doesn't feel ashamed to mention the incident (Apart from the subject in hand, see also part 2, chapter 9, for a treatment of 1 Peter 4:3, which condemns Christians indulging in intoxicating drinks as toasts etc!). Indeed an apology to the offended brother would be the least he could do!

This is yet another example, which highlights the fact that Bustanoby's views on Christian liberty in the area of drink are contradictory, confusing, unchristian, and unscriptural, to say the least.

The fact of the matter is that in reading Bustanoby's book, one finds great cause for concern at the cynical, sarcastic, and insulting attitude which he displays towards those Christians who do not share his views.

A good example of this can be found on pages 60-61, where he implies that those (prohibitionists, as he calls them) whom he considers to be overweight who take a stand against alcohol, are nothing more than hypocritical gluttons. One won't waste any time in quoting his cynical and sarcastic remark on this. Or in discussing how one should correctly define a glutton in the light of Scripture (Taking into consideration that God made all of us *different*, with our own distinct and unique profiles. Such as metabolism, physique, etc.), in order to counteract his slanderous remarks. But what must be said however, is that to suggest that someone is a glutton because in his eyes they are overweight, is not only outrageously unfair, but is also wicked. One could be the most riotous glutton and be as thin as a rake! Any reasonable person would find Bustanoby's remarks intolerable.

It is a little wonder then that on close examination, much of his statements have been found to be unscriptural. For it is hard to see how anyone can fairly and Biblically discuss a subject with love and concern for those who are supposed to be in error, when one's attitude has plummeted to that level!

The subject of Christian liberty must be understood in its proper Biblical context. Galatians 5:13 states:

> *For brethren, ye have been called unto liberty; only use not liberty for an occasion to the flesh, but by love serve one another.*

This inspired text makes it clear that Christian liberty does not permit sins of the flesh, such as drinking and other drugs. The apostle Peter also echoes this truth:

Dearly beloved, I beseech you as strangers and pilgrims, abstain from fleshly lusts. which war against the soul. (1 Peter 2:11)

Concerning this text, Albert Barnes states:

The meaning is, that indulgence in these things makes war against the nobler faculties of the soul; against the conscience, the understanding, the memory, the judgment, the exercise of a pure imagination. There is not a faculty of the mind, however brilliant in itself, which will not be ultimately ruined by indulgence in the carnal propensities of our nature. The effects of intemperance on the noble faculties of the soul is well known...

Christian liberty does not give one the license to indulge in sensual appetites. Many people misunderstand the fact that Christian liberty gives one the freedom to keep the strict commandments of the God. Jesus said:

...but if thou wilt enter into life, keep the commandments. (Matthew 19:17b)

In 1 Corinthians 7:19, the apostle Paul states:

Circumcision is nothing, and uncircumcision is nothing, but the keeping of the commandments of God.

Concerning Galatians 5:13, Adam Clarke states:

The gospel proclaims liberty from the ceremonial law; but binds you still faster under the moral law. To be freed from the ceremonial law is the gospel of liberty; to pretend freedom from the moral law is antinomianism.

So we see from the Scriptures that although we are free in Christ, there are still great restrictions upon us as believers. If one doesn't understand this truth, the subject of Christian liberty can be used as a cloak of permissive liberalism, which engulfs all kinds of sins of the flesh, including drinking or intemperance.

The solid principles laid down in the commandments of Galatians 5:13, automatically refutes Bustanoby's arguments that Christian liberty permits drinking. Or that those who take a stand against alcohol are legalistic prohibitionists, who are writing their own Talmud with their self imposed rules.

On pages 14 and 15, we see him try to uphold these views by seriously taking Colossians chapter 2 way out of context. If one takes the time to study the book of Colossians, they will learn that the contents bear no relation to the issue at hand. Basically, the heresies taught at Colosse were an attack upon the person of the Lord Jesus Christ. That is why when we read the book of Colossians Jesus Christ is so central, and is given His rightful place of authority, dominion, and creative power.

What Bustanoby has done is to take the apostle Paul's strong denunciations of the false man made teachings at Colosse, and have laid them to the charge of those who rightly teach Biblical authority for abstinence from alcohol, as if they were guilty of the same sins. This is nothing more than a smoke screen that is designed to shock and outrage the reader into a state of prejudice. For maximun effect, he puts those who advocate total abstinence from alcohol as a Biblical principle, on parallel with the false teachers at Colosse, by stating that the Colosssian heretics also taught abstinence from wine.

The fact of the matter, is that this statement has no significance whatsoever. Just because the false teachers at Colosse also taught abstinence from wine does not detract from the Biblical argument for such a case, for even the legalists in Jesus' day were commended by Him for some of the practices they embraced. In Matthew 23:23, He states:

> Woe unto you, scribes and Pharisees, hypocrites! for ye pay tithe of mint and anise and cummin, and have omitted the weightier matters of the law, judgment, mercy, and faith: these ye ought to have done, and not to leave the other undone.

Here in the midst of His rebukes, our Lord commends the scribes and Pharisees for tithe paying because this act complied with Scripture. It is a pity that Bustanoby didn't take a leaf out of our Lord's book in determining what is acceptable in God's eyes. Drinking alcohol was clearly condemned in the Old Testament, as we have observed on numerous occasions in our studies. Therefore Bustanoby's "subtle" attempt to superimpose the Colossian heresy on to the alcohol issue is absolutely scandalous. In fact as previously stated, teaching or permitting practices forbidden by Scripture is also a form of legalism, of which Bustanoby himself is clearly guilty. Colossians 3:5 destroys Bustanoby's one tracked view of legalism in the Colossian letter, by stating:

> *Mortify therefore your members which are upon the earth; fornication, uncleanness, inordinate affection, evil concupiscence, and covetousness, which is idolatry.*

The Amplified Translation of this text reads:

> *So kill (deaden, deprive of power) the evil desire lurking in your members-those animal impulses and all that is earthly in you that is employed by sin: sexual vice, impurity, sensual appetites, unholy desires, and all greed and covetousness, for that is idolatry [the deifying of self and other created things instead of God].*

This text makes it clear that although one is free from man made restrictions, he is also restricted from sinful lustful cravings, and the destructive drug of alcohol, as well as any other drug, must also apply here!

On page 14, Bustanoby seeks to use Colossians 2:21, as a rebuke to the so-called legalist today for claiming Biblical authority for censoring the use of alcoholic beverages. Speaking of the Colossian heretics, he states:

> *Not only were these people prideful, they were also guilty of unbiblical asceticism with their "Do not handle! Do not taste! Do not touch!" (Col. 2:21).*

These serious allegations cannot be transposed to the alcohol situation, because he fails to quote the key point of the apostle Paul's above statement, which is the last clause of verse 22:

...after the commandments and doctrines of men?

From our studies we have already learnt that abstinence from intoxicants is a concept which comes from God Himself. And is *not* a man made doctrine, as Bustanoby would have us believe. Therefore as far as the alcohol issue is concerned, his attempt to use Colossians 2:21, to refute the abstinence cause is totally irrelevant and invalid.

In summing up God's view concerning the evil practices among the Colossians, the apostle Paul states:

Such regulations indeed have an appearance of wisdom, with their self imposed worship, their false humility and their harsh treatment of the body, but they lack any value in restraining sensual indulgence. (Colossians 2:23, NIV)

Let us note from the text, that it is positively God's desire that the sensual desires of the flesh be restrained. God's method for dealing with the flesh is that men keep His strict commandments. Contrary to Bustanoby's thinking, one doesn't have to invent any legalistic rules to enforce total abstinence from alcoholic beverages. For the abstinence truth is already clearly outlined in Scripture, both specifically and in principle. Bustanoby's attempt on page 15, to transpose the criticisms of the above text on to the so-called "legalists" for their calls for total abstinence is absolutely scandalous. Also, his statement at the bottom of page 14, concerning Paul's condemnation of the Colossian heretics for harshly treating their bodies in the above text, again does not and cannot apply to the alcohol issue For abstinence from the poisonous drug of alcohol, can hardly be described as harsh treatment of the body!

Christians therefore can be confident in upholding total abstinence from alcoholic beverages as being Biblically based, without feeling threatened by Bustanoby's inventive arguments. In the midst of all the talk of legalism and man made laws etc., the most important thing that one must remember is the law of love. God's love for human beings is expressed in His strict commandments. These are designed to protect us from our own sinfulness. We in turn are required to express this love towards each other. This principle is the heart of the Law. In Matthew 22:37-40, Jesus said:

> *Thou shalt love the Lord thy God with all thy heart, and with all thy soul, and with all thy mind. This is the first and great commandment. And the second is like unto it, Thou shalt love thy neighbour as thyself. On these two commandments hang all the law and the prophets.*

If a person loves God and his neighbour, he will not drink alcohol or encourage his neighbour to drink. This act would violate the Scriptures. Habakkuk 2:15, clearly explains:

> *Woe unto him that giveth his neighbour drink, that puttest thy bottle to him, and makest him drunken also...*

Gleason Archer also refutes Bustanoby's erroneous talk that total abstinence from alcohol is a form of legalism. He states:

> *If we really care about the souls of men, and if we are really in business for Christ rather than for ourselves, then there seems (to this writer, at least) to be no alternative to total abstinence-not as a matter of legalism, but rather as a matter of love.*

In the light of this truth, it is fitting to end our study of this topic with the Apostle Paul's inspired explanation of the purpose of the Law:

> *Owe no man any thing, but to love one another: for he that loveth another hath fulfilled the law. For this, Thou shalt not commit adultery, Thou shalt not kill, Thou shalt not steal, Thou shalt not covet; and if there be any other commandment, it is briefly comprehended in this saying, namely, Thou shalt love thy neighbour as thyself. Love worketh no ill to his neighbour: therefore love is the fulfilling of the law. (Romans 13:8-10)*

CHAPTER 8

NEW TESTAMENT WORDS AND BIBLE TRANSLATIONS RELATING TO ABSTINENCE

...ye have not spoken of me the thing which is right...
(Job 42:8)

Robert Young in his preface to his literal translation of the Bible states the following:

> *...there can be no reasonable ground for denying the inspiration of the New Testament by any one who holds that of the Old, or who is willing to take the plain unsophisticated meaning of God's Word regarding either.*

> *This inspiration extends only to the original text, as it came from the pens of the writers, not to any translations ever made by man, however aged, venerable, or good; and only in so far as any of these however aged, venerable, or good; and only in so far as any of these adhere to the original-neither adding to nor omitting from it one particle-are they of any real value, for, to the extent that they vary from the original, the doctrine of verbal inspiration is lost, so far as that version is concerned.*

In this chapter we will look at various Bible translations with regard to the subject of total abstinence. We will also look at the uses of different words in this area, along with many of the arguments.

We will see that unfortunately, many Bible translations have failed to fully communicate the truth of total abstinence. This is due to a number of reasons such as words changing their meaning, the translations of different Greek words etc. Not of all of the Bible translations have been deliberately misleading, but some have been negligent or passive in bringing out the complete truth of total abstinence. And as Young states above, only the original meaning of the words which the Holy Spirit intended the writer to convey, can truly be classed as inspired.

When expounding this subject, there are also those who are guilty of the charges mentioned in our above Scriptural text, in that they have not spoken of God, "the thing which is right." When dealing with this subject or any other, maximum effort should be made to bring to light the full idea that the writer through the Holy Spirit of God was expressing when he wrote the inspired text. This is extremely important, especially when it comes to translations of the Bible. Sadly, whether with translating or commentary exposition, many scholars regard the truth regarding drink as insignificant, and as we will see later in another chapter, study in this area has been termed by some as "treacherous and doubtful exegesis."

We will now begin by taking a look at the correct meaning of some English words that relate to drink. We will then compare these meanings with various Bible translations, to see how clearly the language conveys the meaning of the original Greek words when translated in the New Testament (key words from translations or commentaries will be highlighted in bold print for emphasis).

The first word we will look at is the word "temperance" or "temperate." Unfortunately, this word is terribly misunderstood by many Christians today. When referring to this word with respect to alcoholic drinks, many think that it means to drink but don't get drunk. There are those who even try to give further strength to their excuses for indulging in alcoholic or intoxicating drinks, by quoting Galatians 5:22,23, which reads:

> *But the fruit of the Spirit is love, joy, peace, longsuffering, gentleness, goodness, faith, Meekness, temperance...*

Some scholars of reputable character even try to use the "temperance" argument to explain away Jesus' action of turning water into wine. Again it is unfortunate, that many fail to realize the fact that the word "temperance" or "temperate" can also mean to abstain from alcoholic drinks. Let us note carefully the definition of the word "temperate" according to the Oxford Illustrated Dictionary:

> *Moderation, self-restraint, in speech, conduct, etc., esp. in eating and drinking; moderation in use of, **total abstinence** from, alcoholic liquors as beverages; (attrib.) non-alcoholic, aimed at the restriction or prohibition of alcoholic drinks...*

The fact that this word can refer to total abstinence from alcoholic drinks may come as a shock to some. It may also come as a further shock that in most cases in the New Testament where the word "temperate" or "temperance" is used it means exactly that, total abstinence! Let us take for example the statement made by the apostle Paul in 1 Corinthians 9:25, which reads:

> *And every man that striveth for mastery is temperate in all things. Now they do it to obtain a corruptible crown; but we an incorruptible.*

The word translated "temperate" in this passage amongst other things, includes total abstinence from strong wine, and any other alcoholic or intoxicating substances. Albert Barnes' lengthy notes on this passage gives us a thorough understanding of this point:

> *The word which is rendered "is temperate" denotes **abstinence** from all that would excite, stimulate, and ultimately enfeeble; from wine, from exciting and luxurious living, and from licentious indulgences. It means that they did all they could to make the body vigorous, active, and supple. They pursued a course of entire temperate living...The phrase "in all things" means that this course of temperance or abstinence was not confined to one thing, or to one class of things,*

but to every kind of food and drink, and every indulgence that had a tendency to render the body weak and effeminate.

Regarding this word in relation to the practice of the ancient Greeks striving to obtain a corruptible crown, he goes on to state:

*So much **temperance** would heathens practise to obtain a fading wreath of laurel, pine, or parsley...If the heathens practised temperance to obtain a fading laurel, should not we to obtain one that never fades? How much their conduct puts to shame the conduct of many professing Christians and Christian ministers. They set such a value on a civic wreath of pine or laurel, that they were willing to deny themselves, and practise the most rigid abstinence. They knew that indulgence in WINE and in luxurious living unfitted them for the struggle and for victory; they knew that it enfeebled their powers, and weakened their frame; and, men intent on an object dear to them, they abstained wholly from these things, and embraced the principles of **total abstinence**. Yet how many professed Christians, and Christian ministers, though striving for the crown that fadeth not away, indulge in wine, and in the filthy, offensive, and disgusting use of tobacco; and in luxurious living, and in habits of indolence and sloth! How many there are that WILL not give up these habits, though they know that they are enfeebling, injurious, offensive, and destructive to religious comfort and usefulness. Can a man be truly in earnest in his professed religion; can he be a sincere Christian, who is not willing to abandon any thing and every thing that will tend to impair the vigour of his mind, and weaken his body, and make him a stumbling-block to others? The value of **temperance** is here presented in a very striking and impressive view. When even the heathens wished to accomplish any thing that demanded skill, strength, power, vigour of body, they saw the necessity of being* *temperate, and they were so. And this **proves** what all experiment has proved, that if men wish to **accomplish** much, they must be temperate. It **proves** that men can do **more** without intoxicating drink than they can with it...A little experience from men like the Grecian wrestlers, who had something that they wished to do, is much better than a great deal of philosophy and sophistical reasoning from men who **wish** to drink, and to find some argument for drinking that shall be a salvo to their consciences. Perhaps the world has furnished no stronger argument in favour of **total abstinence** than the example of the Grecian Athletae.*

After looking at these enlightening facts and sensible Biblical reasoning. It is obvious from Paul's statement, *they do it to obtain a corruptible crown; but we an incorruptible,* that Paul and his fellow workers followed a course of total abstinence from alcoholic drinks, and expected the Corinthian brethren to do the same!

AN IMPORTANT NOTE FROM THE VULGATE TRANSLATION

There are further important truths that can be learnt from the Vulgate (an early Latin translation) concerning the subject of temperance. Grindrod explains its importance:

A more extended examination of learned authorities, in reference to the words translated temperance and sobriety, will add considerable light to this important branch of our inquiry. A reference also to the high authority of the Vulgate (Latin) Translation, will be highly interesting, inasmuch, as it was executed at a very early period, and probably at a time when many of the primitive customs had been transmitted from the apostolic age, in an uncorrupted state.

Concerning the word translated "temperance" (egkrateia) in 2 Peter 1:6, he continues:

In 2 Peter 1.6, this version is still more unequivocal, and the same word is rendered abstinentia. "Add to knowledge temperance," or, according to the vulgate, abstinence.

The word translated "temperate" (enkrateuomai) in 1 Corinthians 9:25, is rendered by the Vulgate as follows:

And every man that striveth for the mastery is abstinet (abstinent, temperate, self restrained) in all things.

The truths contained in this word make this a very powerful text for total abstinence from intoxicating beverages.

These facts will come as a deadly blow to those who advocate "temperate" indulgence in alcoholic drinks. In the KJV or AV New Testament, more than one Greek word is translated "temperate," but the basic meaning is that of self-control. Or as Young's Analytical Concordance puts it, "self restraint." Only in one other case does it mean anything different and that is in Titus 2:2, where it means "sound mindedness." The Bible does not make any room whatsoever through the words translated "temperate" or "temperance," for the indulgence in alcoholic drinks but that of self restraint, i.e., total abstinence!

The next word that we will look at is the word "sober." Many people think this word only means to not be in a state of drunkenness. Because this word is used fairly frequently throughout the New Testament, many therefore believe that the Bible makes allowances for drinking as long as one does not get drunk, but this is simply not the case. In the English language the word "sober" does not always only refer to a state of non intoxication, but can also mean a state of being totally free from the influence of intoxicating drinks. Virtue's Encyclopaedic English Dictionary states the following regarding the word "sober":

Temperate in the use of intoxicating liquors; abstemious; not intoxicated; not drunk; not wild, visionary, or heated with passion; having the regular exercise of cool, dispassionate reason; dispassionate; calm; serious; grave; not bright, gay, or brilliant in appearance; dull-

looking. To make sober; to cure of intoxication; to make temperate, calm, or solemn. To become sober, staid, or sedate...

It goes on to give the definition of the word "sobriety," which means a state of being sober. It reads:

Temperate in the use of intoxicating liquors; abstemiousness; moderation; freedom from the use of strong drink; calmness; coolness; seriousness; gravity.

Let us now take a look at the New Testament and examine some of the passages where the word "sober" is used, or where the original Greek refers to it. We will then take a look at various Bible translations to determine how well the truth of total abstinence is projected when the original Greek word specifically demands it. We will also examine how well the truth of total abstinence has been declared or veiled by some Bible scholars and commentators. The first passage we will examine is from the Authorized or King James Version. It reads:

A bishop then must be blameless, the husband of one wife, vigilant, sober, of good behaviour, given to hospitality, apt to teach. (1 Timothy 3:2)

The word translated "vigilant" (nephalion) as we saw earlier, means to abstain from intoxicating wine. The word translated "sober" (sophron) means to be clear or sound minded. Unfortunately, the Authorized Version in using the word "vigilant" (watchful) does not bring out the true or full meaning of the word. Because of this problem, the reader or student of the Bible is dependant upon good Bible translations (even though the AV translation is of a very high standard), lexicons, (word study dictionaries), and Bible commentaries, to fairly and accurately present the meaning of the original. Sadly in the abstinence area, this has not always been the case. If an individual was trying to determine more than the superficial meaning of the word translated "vigilant" in the above text, this is what he or she would find from the following Bible Commentaries:

Jamieson, Fausset and Brown's Bible Commentary:

> `sober'; ever on the watch, as sober men alone can be; keenly alive, so as to foresee what ought to be done.*

Matthew Henry's Bible Commentary:

> *He must be vigilant and watchful against Satan.*

The Bible Knowledge Commentary:

> `well-balanced'.*

Vincent's Word Studies of the New Testament:

> *The kindred verb nephein means to be sober with reference to drink, and, in a metaphorical sense, to be sober and wary; cool and unimpassioned...In N.T the meaning of the verb is always metaphorical, to be calm, dispassionate, and circumspect.*

Let the reader notice here how Vincent does not admit or mention that the word translated "vigilant" (nephalion) means to abstain from intoxicating drinks, but barely mentions it by stating that the root verb "means to be sober with reference to drink" (which in the English language can be ambiguous). He then subjectively makes sure that there cannot be any literal command through this word to abstain from intoxicants, by stating that it is only used in a metaphorical sense in the New Testament. This is incorrect. Let the reader judge for himself on the reliability of this kind of Biblical "exegesis"! Albert Barnes, one of the few commentators who presents the full truth of this word, wisely and fairly gives the definition concerning the word translated "vigilant" in 1 Timothy 3:2, from Robinson's Lexicon of the New Testament. He states:

> *It means, properly, sober, temperate, abstinent, especially in respect to wine.*

Joseph H. Thayer's Greek-English Lexicon of the New Testament although an excellent work, tampers with the meaning of the word translated "vigilant" in 1 Timothy 3:2. It states the meaning of the word as:

sober, temperate; abstaining from wine, either entirely (Joseph.antt.3,12,2) or at least from its immoderate use: 1 Tim 3:2,11; Tit 2:2.

The point that the reader must note here is that the last clause of Thayer's quote reading, "or at least from its immoderate use," is an incorrect addition to the meaning of the word. The correct meaning of the word is to *entirely abstain* from intoxicating beverages especially wine. No sense of immoderation is attached to this word whatsoever.

Let the reader again note how Thayer himself quotes the Jewish historian Josephus, who used this same word when stating that the priests under the Law of Moses, were *not* permitted to drink wine while ministering in their sacred garments (Joseph.antt.3, 12,2). But note how he goes on to say that the word could also mean moderation on the strength of 1 Tim 3:2,11 and Titus 2:2, none of which give the slightest hint of the idea of moderation. The word translated "vigilant" (nephalios) is used in these passages, but *never* does it change its meaning. When referring to intoxicating drinks, never does it mean anything other than total abstinence. Thayer himself when referring to ancient authorities on this word goes on to state:

...of things free from all infusion or addition of wine, as vessels, offerings, etc.

This shows us that some scholars when confronted with the truth of total abstinence, ignore, deliberately masquerade, or tone down the truth. This is unfortunate because others following their work often perpetuate the same ideas. An example of this is Wuest's Word Studies of the New Testament. Concerning the word translated "vigilant" in 1 Timothy 3:2, he states:

abstaining from wine, either entirely or at least from its immoderate use.

This is obviously a direct quote from Thayer which due to the untruth added to the first part which is correct, i.e. that one should abstain entirely, will cause those who read it without investigating it for themselves, to think that there is no direct command to

318

abstain from intoxicating drinks, but merely an option. Adam Clarke's Bible Commentary brings out the meaning of the word translated "vigilant" (Greek, nephalios or nephaleon, the meaning is the same) in 1 Timothy 3:2, perhaps more clearly and fairly than any other. It states:

> He must be vigilant; nephaleon, from ne, not, and pio, to drink. Watchful; for one who drinks is apt to sleep, so he who abstains from it is more likely to keep awake, and attend to his work and charge.

Here we learn that 1 Timothy 3:2, gives a clear command to abstain from alcohol. A fact which most Bible scholars and commentators do not bring out or make obvious to the mind of the reader, as we saw from numerous examples earlier. It is also unfortunate that the Authorized or King James Version (AV or KJV) does not make the case for total abstinence clear. Dr. William Patton explains this problem:

> It should be constantly borne in mind that the Authorized Version was translated when the drinking usages were well-nigh universal. The attention of Christians and thoughtful men had not been called to the pernicious influence of alcoholic drinks. though drunkenness existed, still no plans were devised either for its prevention or its cure. It was regarded as an evil incident to hospitality and social cheer.
>
> The translators, with the most honest purpose, faithfully, according to their ability, rendered into English the original Scriptures, but were nevertheless unintentionally and unconsciously influenced by the philosophy and usages of their day. As the river carries in its waters that with which absolute certainty tells of the soil through which it has flowed, so the translators must carry into the renderings which they give evidences of the prevailing usages and modes of thought of their day. Thus innocently, though naturally, shades of meaning have been given to particular passages. These have come down to us with feelings of

319

sacred reverence. To give a new rendering seems almost to be sacrilege. With this feeling every department of science has to contend when it would throw new light upon the sacred page. Astronomy and geology have met this difficulty, and it is not strange that the cause of temperance should have to contend with this feeling, notwithstanding the convictions of temperance men are the result of experience and diligent, patient investigation.

The same problem also applies to many modern translations. Indeed the temperance (abstinence) truth has been one of thorough and open-minded investigation (hence the need for this book) which is certainly warranted, because this precious truth to a large extent has been veiled. We saw earlier that the words translated "temperate" and "sober" in the AV (1 Tim 3:2, "vigilant") when referring to drink means total abstinence.

Even though Bible translations which use the words "sober" or "temperate" in the passages where abstinence applies are technically correct, the abstinence truth is still not fully projected because many readers of the Bible do not understand these words to mean total abstinence, but moderation. As is stated on the cover of Harold J. Berry's book on Word Studies in the Greek New Testament:

Everything you believe depends on what you think they mean.

Bible translations therefore generally speaking, have not dared to state the abstinence truth in no uncertain terms. Out of the entire Bible translations, only Young's Concise Bible to the knowledge of this author, has consistently made the truth of total abstinence crystal clear, with no room for doubt or ambiguity.

We will now look at some of the major passages which declares the abstinence message and compare what some of the common translations have to say regarding this, along with Young's Bible (key words will be highlighted in bold print). The following Bible translations will be used, with the abbreviations for each in brackets:

The King James or Authorized Version (KJV); The Amplified Bible (AMP. BIB.); The Living Bible (LB); The Revised Standard Version (RSV); The Revised Version (RV); The New English Bible (NEB); The Moffatt Translation (MOF-FATT); The New American Standard Bible (NASB); The New International Version (NIV); Young's Concise Bible (YOUNG'S BIB.). The major passages concerning total abstinence from intoxicants are as follows:

> *A bishop then must be blameless, the husband of one wife, **vigilant sober**, of good behaviour, given to hospitality, apt to teach.* (1 Timothy 2:3, KJV)

> *Now a bishop (superintendent, overseer) must give no grounds for accusation but must be above reproach, the husband of one wife, **circumspect** and **temperate** and **self-controlled**...* (AMP BIB)

> *For a pastor must be a good man whose life cannot be spoken against. He must be **hardworking and thoughtful**, orderly, and full of good deeds...* (LB)

> *Now a bishop must be above reproach, the husband of one wife, **temperate, sensible**, dignified, hospitable, an apt teacher.* (RSV)

> *The bishop therefore must be without reproach, the husband of one wife, **temperate, soberminded**, orderly, given to hospitality, apt to teach.* (RV)

> *Our leader, therefore, or bishop, must be above reproach, faithful to his wife, **sober, temperate**, courteous, hospitable, and a good teacher.* (NEB)

> *Well, for the office of a bishop a man must be above reproach; he must be married only once, he must be **temperate, master of himself**...* (MOFFATT)

> *An overseer, then, must be above reproach, the husband of one wife, **temperate, prudent**, respectable, hospitable, able to teach.* (NASB)

*Now the overseer must be above reproach, the husband of but one wife, **temperate, self-controlled**, respectable, hospitable, able to teach.* (NIV)

`*the overseer, therefore, it behoves to be unlaid-hold-upon, husband of one woman (only), **not drinking, soberminded**, seemly (in behaviour), a friend of strangers, apt to teach.*` (YOUNG'S BIB.)

We can see here how Bible translations vary. The words we are particularly interested in, have been put in bold print to help the reader easily follow the subject. These words refer to abstinence from strong drink, and clear mindedness respectively (Greek, nephalion and sophron). In other words, in order for one to be soberminded he must not drink. Clarke's comments on 1 Timothy 3:2, regarding the command that a bishop must be amongst other things, sober (Greek, sophron; meaning sober or sound mindedness), explains this truth:

...a man of a sound mind; having a good understanding, and the complete government of all his passions.

Let us not ignore the fact that most of the above translations are quite commendable, but as was earlier stated, only Young's Bible leaves no room for conjecture. Another point to be noted is that the Living Bible goes nowhere near bringing out the truth of the original text. This shows us how cautious we must be with Bible translations. We would do well to heed the old phrase that only the original text is inspired and not any translations of that text.

The next comparative Bible translations on abstinence or temperance we will look at is 1 Timothy 3:11, they read:

*Even so must their wives be grave, not slanderers, **sober**, faithful in all things.* (1 Timothy 3:11, KJV)

*[The] women likewise must be worthy of respect and serious, not gossipers, but **temperate** and self controlled...* (AMP BIB.)

*Their wives must be thoughtful, **not heavy drinkers,** not gossipers, but faithful in everything they do.* (LB)

*The women likewise must be serious, not slanderers, but **temperate,** faithful in all things.* (RSV)

*Women in like manner must be grave, not slanderers, **temperate,** faithful in all things.* (RV)

*Their wives, equally, must be women of high principle, who will not talk scandal, **sober** and trustworthy in every way.* (NEB)

*Their wives must be serious too; they must not be slanderers, they must be **temperate** and absolutely trustworthy.* (MOFFATT)

*Women must likewise be dignified, not malicious gossips, but **temperate,** faithful in all things.* (NASB)

*In the same way, their wives are to be women worthy of respect, not malicious talkers but **temperate** and trustworthy in everything.* (NIV)

*`women (i.e. deaconesses it behoves to be venerable, not devils, (i.e. `thrusters through,') **not drinking,** steadfast.'* (YOUNG'S BIB.)

Here we can see that the Greek word which means to abstain from intoxicating drinks (nephalious) is generally translated "temperate," and twice translated "sober." Again the Living Bible is in error, because the word generally translated "temperate" does not refer to drinking in moderation but to abstinence, which again Young's Bible clearly defines.

The next comparative translations on abstinence to be looked at is Titus 2:2, which reads:

*That the aged men be **sober,** grave, **temperate,** sound in faith, in charity, in patience.* (Titus 2:2, KJV)

*Urge the older men to be **temperate,** venerable (serious), sensible, **self-controlled;** sound in the faith...* (AMP BIB.)

*Teach the older men to be **serious** and unruffled; they must be **sensible**, knowing and believing the truth...* (LB)

*Bid the older men be **temperate**, serious, **sensible**, sound in faith, in love, and in steadfastness.* (RSV)

*that aged men be **temperate**, grave, **sober-minded**, sound in faith, in love, in patience.* (RV)

*Let the older men know that they should be **sober**, high-principled, and **temperate**, sound in faith...* (NEB)

*Older men are to be **temperate**, dignified, **sensible**, sound in faith, in love, in perseverance.* (NASB)

*Teach the older men to be **temperate**, worthy of respect, **self controlled**, sound in faith, in love and in endurance.* (NIV)

*`aged (or elders, elderly) men to be **not-drinking**, reverent, **sound-minded**, healthy in the faith, the love, the endurance.'* (YOUNG'S BIB.)

Here again two words generally are put in bold print. As stated earlier, one means to be abstinent or temperate, and the other means to be sober-minded or self-controlled. The Apostle Paul under the inspiration of the Holy Spirit uses these words together because each is independent on the other. That way he could not be mistaken over his strict rules for abstinence from strong or intoxicating beverages. Again, Young's Concise Bible makes this truth clear in no uncertain terms.

We will continue our study of comparative Bible translations by taking a look at some of the passages where the Greek word nepho (usually translated "sober" in KJV) is used. Robinson's Lexicon of the New Testament gives us the meaning of this word:

*to be **sober**, temperate, abstinent, espec. in respect to wine.*

Although some of the passages we are about to look at have been looked at in another chapter, the purpose here is to *compare* Bible translations. The passages read:

*Therefore let us not sleep, as do others; but let us watch and be **sober**.* (1 Thessalonians 5:6, KJV)

*Accordingly then, let us not sleep, as the rest do, but let us keep wide awake (alert, watchful, cautious and on guard) and let us be **sober** (calm, collected and circumspect).* (AMP BIB.)

*So be on your guard, not asleep like the others. Watch for His return and stay **sober**.* (LB)

*So then let us not sleep, as others do, but let us keep awake and be **sober**.* (RSV)

*so then let us not sleep, as do the rest, but let us watch and be **sober**.* (RV)

*We do not belong to night or darkness, and we must not sleep like the rest, but keep awake and **sober**.* (NEB)

*Well then, we must not sleep like the rest of men, but be wakeful and **sober**.* (MOFFATT)

*so then let us not sleep as others do, but let us be alert and **sober**.* (NASB)

*So then, let us not be like others, who are asleep, but let us be alert and **self-controlled**.* (NIV)

*`therefore, then, we may not sleep at all, as also the rest, but may we be wakeful and **sober**,' (lit. **not drinking**).* (YOUNG'S BIB.)

All the translations here with the exception of the NIV, translate the Greek word nepho as "sober." Young's Bible expands on the word by stating that it means literally (lit.) "not drinking." Thus we have more clear evidence that when the Scriptures refer to sobriety in the case of drink, it refers to a mind which is totally alert, which means total abstinence from strong drinks.

The same word we just looked at (nepho) is also translated "sober" in 1 Peter 1:13, by many Bible translations. As we have just compared translations, it is not necessary to quote multiple verse by verse translations again, but Young's Bible again makes the abstinence truth clear:

> `have girded up for yourselves the full loins of your mind, being not drinking, hope perfectly upon the grace being borne to you in an uncovering of Jesus Christ.'* (1 Peter 1:13, Young's Bible)

This same word is used in 1 peter 5:8, which is again generally translated "sober." We will finish our study on this particular word by making a brief Bible translation comparison. We will only view the relevant part of the respective translation that relates to abstinence, to see how well the thought is conveyed. These read as follows:

> *Be sober...* (1 Peter 5:8, KJV)
> *Be well-balanced-temperate, sober-minded...* (AMP BIB.)
> *Be careful...* (LB)
> *Be sober...*(RV)
> *Awake!...* (NEB)
> *Keep cool...* (MOFFATT)
> *Be of sober spirit...* (NASB)
> *Be self-controlled...* (NIV)
> *be not-drinking...* (YOUNG'S BIB.)

The next point that we will look at regarding Bible translations, is Paul's statement in 1 Tim 3:8, and Titus 2:3, "not given to much wine." Although these are not direct commands to abstain, it is important to examine how they are translated, because there are those who believe that these are texts that permit moderate drinking of intoxicating wine. We saw earlier in part 2, chapter 4 (see for full explanation), that this was *not* a license for moderate drinking of intoxicating wine.

The original Greek in these passages simply means, "not to be addicted to much wine" and "not a slave to much wine" respectively. We also saw earlier, that there was every possibility that Paul could have been referring to the practice of excessive indulgence in unfermented grape juice. There is no justification whatsoever for translating these clauses as "not a drunkard." Had the writer intended to allow moderate drinking of alcoholic wine, this would have been made clear in no uncertain terms. Any translation therefore which translates the statements in 1 Tim 3:8, and Titus 2:3, "not given to much wine" as "not a drunkard" or "not a heavy drinker," is no longer translating but interpreting. Again we will only compare what various translations say about the relevant clause, "not given to much wine." The first comparison we will look at is from 1 Tim 3:8, which reads:

> ...*not given to much wine*... (KJV)
> ...*not addicted to much wine*... (RSV)
> ...*not given to much wine*... (AMP. BIB.)
> ...*They must not be heavy drinkers*... (LB)
> ...*not given to much wine*... (RV)
> ...*given neither to excessive drinking*... (NEB)
> ...*nor addicted to drink*... (MOFFATT)
> ...*or addicted to much wine*... (NASB)
> ...*not indulging in much wine*... (NIV)
> ...*not holding to much wine*... (YOUNG'S BIB.)

Here the Living Bible, New English Bible, and Moffatt translations interpret rather than translate. Hence the result is misleading, because the Bible does not make allowances for moderate drinking of alcoholic drinks.

Although the KJV states "not given to much wine" in 1 Tim 3:8, and Titus 2:3, the original Greek is slightly different, even though the thought is still the same. The original text of 1 Tim 3:8, says that one should not be addicted to much wine, and Titus 2:2, says that one should not be slaves to much wine. For arguments sake, we will also compare translations of this clause from Titus 2:3. They read:

> ...*not given to much wine*... (KJV)
> ...*not..slaves to drink...* (AMP BIB.)
> ...*must not be heavy drinkers*... (LB)
> ...*nor enslaved to much wine*... (RV)
> ...*not to be..slaves to drink*... (RSV)
> ...*not..slaves to strong drink*... (NEB)

...not..slaves to drink... (MOFFATT)

...nor enslaved to much wine... (NASB)

...or addicted to much wine... (NIV)

...not having been in bondage to much wine...

(YOUNG'S BIB.)

The translations that are most in error here, are the Living Bible and the New English Bible. By stating that one must not be a heavy drinker, the Living Bible gives the impression that the text allows for moderate drinking of intoxicants. This is not what the text says or means at all. This "translation" is merely a paraphrase or interpretation. As for the New English Bible, this translation takes gross liberties with the inspired text, which does not state or imply that the wine which was not to be over indulged in was alcoholic. The idea therefore of strong drink, again is not a translation but an interpretation. Nowhere in the New Testament does it permit so called moderate drinking of alcoholic drinks.

The final passage we will compare as far as translations are concerned, are the commands in 1 Timothy 3:3 and Titus 1:7, translated "not given to wine" (me paroinos). The first passage we will compare is 1 Tim 3:3. Again we will only quote and examine the relevant part of the verse concerned, which reads:

Not given to wine... (1 Timothy 3:3, KJV)

Not given to wine... (AMP BIB.)

He must not be a drinker... (LB)

no drunkard... (RSV)

no brawler... (RV)

he must not be given to drink... (NEB)

not a drunkard... (MOFFATT)

not addicted to wine... (NASB)

not given to much wine... (NIV)

not given to wine... (Young's Literal Translation)

It is worthwhile commenting on these translations in order of their accuracy. The King James Version or Authorized Version, Amplified Bible, and Young's Literal Translation, are the most precise in their rendering into English the original Greek. Surprisingly, the Living Bible and New English Bible, are good and accurate translations in terms of projecting the abstinence thought, but not quite so accurate in literality. Although a command not to drink, would naturally also include abstinence from intoxicating wine. These translations therefore are certainly acceptable.

The New American Standard Bible gives a reasonable translation but it is not accurate enough, this is because the word "addicted" does not truly reflect the meaning of the original Greek. Most would probably understand this text to be a warning against drunkenness instead of its correct meaning of "not alongside wine," or "not given to wine."

The New International Version gives a poor translation here. No such idea of quantity with respect to wine is attached to this word whatsoever. If the inspired Apostle had intended to say "not given to much wine," he would have stated this as he did in verse 8 of this same chapter (see part 2, chapter 4, for a discussion of this verse).

The Moffatt Version also gives a poor translation. Again, if the writer had intended to warn against drunkenness, he would have used the Greek word whose root conveyed that idea (methe) as he did in Ephesians 5:18; 1 Corinthians 5:11; and Galatians 5:21.

Finally, the most inaccurate and unjustifiable translation is that of the Revised Version which we already examined in another chapter (see again part 2, chapter 4). The footnote of the RV also gives an alternate rendering of this clause, which reads, "Or, not quarrelsome over wine." This also, in the opinion of the present author, is an extremely liberal translation. What is even more hypocritical and unfair of the RV in this area, is that the Greek word nephalios (translated "temperate" in 1 Tim 3:2,11; Titus 2:2 RV) which means to abstain from intoxicating drinks, should also be footnoted with the note "Or not a drinker," but no such attempt is made to bring the abstinence truth to light, either in the text or in the footnote! But note how in the above text of the RV, the extreme meaning of the Greek word paroinos, is given in the translation as "no brawler." Again in the RV footnote another extreme meaning "Or, not quarrelsome over wine," is given without even stating the primary meaning of the word in the clause, which should be translated as "not given to wine" or "not alongside of wine."

Unfortunately, it is this attitude of highlighting points that detract from the abstinence truth, and ignoring the obvious ones, which contribute to it that brings the Bible into disrepute and misleads many people. Therefore total faith should not be placed in any particular Bible translation. This is because some of them are not really true translations of the original, but merely the opinions or interpretations of men!

We will now turn to Titus 1:7, where this same Greek word is used in its identical sense (me paroinos), and again compare Bible translations of the relevant clause for consistency. These read:

> ...*not given to wine...* (KJV)
> ...*or given to drink...* (AMP BIB.)
> ...*they must not be drunkards...* (LB)
> ...*he must not be..a drunkard...* (RSV)
> ...*no brawler...* (RV)
> ...*he must be no drinker...* (NEB)
> ...*he must not be...a drunkard...* (MOFFATT)
> ...*not addicted to wine...* (NASB)
> ...*not given to drunkenness...* (NIV)
> ...*not given to wine...* (Young's Literal Translation)

The translations which vary from that of 1 Timothy 3:3, are the Amplified Bible, Living Bible, and New International Version. The Amplified Bible and New International Versions are not significantly different from their translations of 1 Tim 3:3. The Amplified Bible still gives an accurate projection of the abstinence truth, and hence this translation is acceptable. The New International Version here, and in 1 Tim 3:3, is inaccurate and does not reflect the original Greek as was stated earlier.

The Living Bible, although a paraphrase, is grossly inconsistent in projecting the truth of these two identical texts. The Living Bible's "translation" of the above text is obviously incorrect, whereas the one of 1 Tim 3:3, is acceptable. This again demonstrates the need for caution when using various versions of the Bible.

We have learnt from thoroughly examining various translations of the Bible in this chapter, that the many texts for total abstinence from intoxicating drinks are truths that are laid buried in many Bible translations!

Throughout our study we have seen that the commands to abstain from alcoholic or intoxicating drinks have been given as a must to bishops (overseers) and deacons. This is not because these commands are exclusively for them, but that God desired them to abstain so that they could bring everyone up to the same standard, as the inspired account of Ephesians 4:11-13 declares:

> *And he gave some, apostles; and some, prophets; and some, evangelists; and some, pastors and teachers; For the perfecting of the saints, for the work of the ministry, for the edifying of the body of Christ: Till we all come in the unity of the faith, and of the knowledge of the Son of God, unto a perfect man, unto the measure of the stature of the fulness of Christ.*

It is sad that Bible translations generally speaking do not make the abstinence truth more crystal clear. Especially when many of the modern translations contain extensive footnotes etc., and even bracket and expand on the meaning of words, as is the case with the Amplified Bible. Expositors of the Bible have a tremendous and awesome responsibility of not shunning to declare, "all the counsel of God," and how too frequently in the area of drink has this been the problem!

There is indeed the need to fear and tremble in the face of the sacred text and to heed the warnings of our Lord, who states:

> *For unto whomsoever much is given, of him shall be much required: and to whom men have committed much, of him they will ask the more.* (Luke 12:48b)

In this chapter we have looked at words, Commentaries, and Bible translations in the New Testament concerning drink. It is greatly hoped that these will have served as a great help to those sincerely seeking truth on this subject. Even if one may have found it difficult to follow all of the arguments, at least comparing Bible translations will be a very simple, quick and stimulating way of arriving at truth in this neglected field.

CHAPTER 9

OTHER REFERENCES TO DRINKING IN THE NEW TESTAMENT

We will now look at the remaining passages that refer to drinking in the New Testament. The first of which reads:

> *Let us walk honestly, as in the day; not in rioting and drunkenness, not in chambering and wantonness, not in strife and envying. But put ye on the Lord Jesus Christ, and make not provision for the flesh, to fulfil the lusts thereof.* (Romans 13:13,14)

This passage is very interesting. The Greek word translated "rioting" is komos. Thayer explains the meaning of this word:

> *a revel, carousal, i.e. in Greek writers properly a nocturnal and riotous procession of half-drunken and frolicsome fellows who after supper parade through the street with torches and music in honour of Bacchus or some other deity, and sing and play before the houses of their male and female friends; hence used generally, of feasts and drinking parties that are protracted till late at night and indulge in revelry.*

Here we see the Apostle Paul warns against drinking and the resulting evils of it, and then warns against drunkenness itself. Concerning the warning, "And make not provision for the flesh," Clarke states:

> *By flesh we are here to understand, not only the body, but all the irregular appetites and passions which led to the abominations already recited. No provision should be made for the encouragement and gratification of such a principle as this.*

The word translated "provision" is pronoia, which means "forethought." Kenneth Wuest quotes Denney on the meaning of this word:

> *an interest in it which consults for it, and makes it an object.*

The last clause of verse 14, could therefore read, "and make no forethought for the flesh, to fulfil the lusts thereof." The NIV states:

> *...and do not think about how to gratify the desires of the sinful nature.*

Here we can see that one is not even to think about purchasing or obtaining alcoholic beverages which are used to satisfy the lusts of the sinful nature, let alone drinking it and being so-called "moderate" with it!

Since this chapter ends with the command, "and make not provision for the flesh, to fulfil the lusts thereof;" it is clear therefore that both drinking and drunkenness, as well as everything else mentioned, are works of the flesh.

The next passage of Scripture is probably the most misunderstood in Christian circles regarding total abstinence. It reads:

> *It is good neither to eat flesh nor to drink wine, nor anything whereby thy brother stumbleth, or is offended, or is made weak.* (Romans 14:21)

Some Christians have quite well intentionally written that this verse is a case for total abstinence from alcohol, but this is *not* the case. The Apostle Paul had already dealt with this in the previous chapter (13:13,14), as he is writing a systematic and orderly epistle. Here in Romans chapter 14, he is dealing with an entirely different subject.

Others have been more ignorant, and have stated that this is the *only* case for abstinence from alcohol. This again is totally incorrect. This erroneous view from the Hastings Bible Dictionary, is also endorsingly quoted in F.N. Peloubet's Bible Dictionary, which states:

the apostle Paul has stated the case for total abstinence in Romans 14 in a way that does not need the treacherous aid of doubtful exegesis for it's support.

This is quite a bold statement, which in itself is doubtful and has no Scriptural support whatsoever. As stated previously, Romans 14, is not the only case for total abstinence from alcohol at all, as we have seen, and will see again from Scripture. The exegesis is not doubtful or treacherous, as the authorities above would have us believe. For the truths come straight from the mouth of God Himself:

Every Scripture is God-breathed... (2 Timothy 3:16, Amplified Bible)

The opening three verses of Romans chapter 14, declares exactly what the chapter is all about:

Him that is weak in the faith receive ye, but not to doubtful disputations. For one believeth that he may eat all things: another, who is weak, eateth herbs. Let not him that eateth despise him that eateth not; and let not him which eateth not judge him that eateth: for God hath received him. (Romans 14:1-3)

First of all, we should note before we look at verse 21, the verse that concerns us most, that the apostle is *not* dealing with the case of total abstinence from alcohol. Because this is *not* a "doubtful disputation" but Scriptural. The apostle had only just written against those who indulged in drinking and the resulting evils associated with it, moments before in the previous chapter which we just examined (Rom 13:13,14).

What the apostle Paul sets out to do here in chapter 14, is to clear up the disputes regarding certain customs and practices in the church. This is the sole purpose of the chapter. Alan F. Johnson explains:

It should be clear from what follows that Paul is not talking about any specific commands of God or biblical prohibitions such as adultery, lying, and idolatry. The argument was over the use of certain material things and the observance of social customs.

Here we have the point. These things were not important; the ones who found fault in eating or drinking certain things, were not to pass judgment on those who did. And those who did, were to do likewise to those who did not. The apostle Paul then goes on in verse 17, to state the most important and crucial aspect of the Christian life:

For the kingdom of God is not meat and drink; but righteousness, and peace, and joy in the Holy Ghost.

The first term here, "righteousness," has to do with the believer's relationship with God. He is to be obedient to the commandments of God if he is to enjoy the peace and joy in the Holy Ghost.

Abstinence from alcohol is not an option, but a Scriptural command. Proverbs 23:31, makes this absolutely clear:

Look not thou upon the wine when it is red, when it giveth his colour in the cup...

The conception therefore, that the apostle Paul only endorses total abstinence from alcohol on the account of the feelings of a fellow brother or sister, is not valid. A key verse, which explains this even further, is verse 20, which states:

For meat destroy not the work of God. All things indeed are pure; but it is evil for that man who eateth with offence.

The word translated "meat" here properly denotes food. The NIV states:

Do not destroy the work of God for the sake of food.

Alcohol is *not* food but a poisonous drug, which is used for satisfying the desires of the flesh, and therefore again does not and cannot apply here. The booklet entitled, *Alcohol and you,* explains this fact:

Alcoholic drinks contain no significant amounts of protein or fat, and can therefore not make good the bodily *requirements lost through wear and tear nor build tissue anew, so in that sense cannot be classed as food. Food, by definition, must build and restore cells and be storable as reserves against future use. A drug by definition, is any substance which brings about a chemical change in the functioning organs of the body, and on the basis of this definition alcohol should be classed as a drug. It is true that since alcohol is oxidized in the body, thereby supplying energy and perhaps, to a very small extent, allowing the organism to save its fat and protein, it can be regarded as a `fuel' food-but its toxic and tissue destroying properties by far exceed its slight fuel value.*

The wine that Paul was referring to in verse 21, was obviously not alcoholic. Paul was speaking of wholesome *food* and drink in general, which would naturally include the juice of the grape. Albert Barnes' Commentary on this text explains:

Wine was a common drink among the Jews, and usually esteemed lawful. But the Nazarites were not allowed to drink it (Numb. vi.3), and the Rechabites (Jer.xxxv.) drank no wine, and it is possible that some of the early converts regarded it as unlawful for Christians to drink it. Wine was moreover used in libations in heathen worship, and perhaps the Jewish converts might be scrupulous about its use from this cause...Besides, the wines which are now used are different from those which were common among the ancients. That was the pure juice of the grape. That which is now in common use is mingled with alcohol, and with other intoxicating ingredients.

We should note again that had the apostle been referring to alcoholic wine he would not have made the statement in verse 20, "All things indeed are pure." He would be thus saying that alcoholic wine was pure, harmless, and legal just like any other food. This would contradict Proverbs 20:1 which states, "Wine is a mocker."

To determine whether the Bible speaks of wine in its fermented or unfermented state must be judged from the context.

And the context here in Romans 14, makes it clear that Paul was *not* permitting the use of fermented or alcoholic wine.

It is unfortunate for those who usually use Romans 14:21, as a text for total abstinence from intoxicating wine, but there are many other Scripture passages which we have already examined that support this godly cause.

For those who declare that the sole reason for total abstinence from alcoholic wine is due to the objections of a brother or sister on the "authority" of this verse, there are also many other passages that command unconditional *total abstinence!*

The next passage that we will look at concerning drink, is found in 1 Corinthians 5:11, it reads:

> *But now I have written unto you not to keep company, if any man that is called a brother be a fornicator, or covetous, or an idolater, or a railer, or a drunkard, or an extortioner; with such an one no not to eat.*

Here drunkenness is ranked equally alongside these other vices mentioned. The true believer is given the commandment that he should not even eat with such a person! Such is the evil of strong drink that every person who drinks is a potential drunkard. They run the risk of being completely overtaken in this ungodly habit, thereby bringing upon themselves the condemnation of God. Notice how the apostle Paul concludes these instructions in the latter part of verse 13, by stating, "Therefore put away from among yourselves that wicked person." That is, the one who was guilty of fornication and any of the evils listed above.

In the following chapter, the apostle Paul mentions some of the same things again:

> *Know ye not that the unrighteous shall not inherit the kingdom of God? Be not deceived: neither fornicators, nor idolaters, nor adulterers, nor effeminate, nor abusers of themselves with mankind, Nor thieves nor covetous, nor drunkards, nor revilers, nor extortioners, shall inherit the kingdom of God.* (1 Corinthians 6:9,10)

Here we see that hell is reserved for the vile, which includes the drunkard. One might say that nothing is said here against drinking, but this argument is lacking because the Bible never speaks favourably concerning intoxicating drinks. It simply states the culminating evil of it, i.e. drunkenness. D.L. Moody states the following concerning this subject:

> *Now let those mothers who have sons who are just commencing a dissipated life, wake up; and rest not day nor night until their boys are converted by the power of God's grace, because no drunkard shall inherit the kingdom of God. Many of these moderate drinkers will become drunkards; no man ever became a drunkard all at once. How the devil blinds these moderate drinkers! I do not know of any sin more binding than the sin of intemperance; the man is bound hand and foot before he knows it.*

The next passage that we will look at concerning drink is very interesting indeed, it reads:

> *Now the works of the flesh are manifest, which are these; Adultery, fornication, uncleanness, lasciviousness, Idolatry, witchcraft, hatred, variance, emulations, wrath, strife, seditions, heresies, Envyings, murders, drunkenness, revellings, and such like: of the which I tell you before, as I have told you in time past, that they which do such things shall not inherit the kingdom of God.*
> (Galatians 5:19-21)

Before we look more closely at this passage, it is interesting to note that the term "the works of the flesh are manifest," means those which are more open or obvious. The NIV states, "The acts of the sinful nature are obvious..." We know that this is very true of drunkenness (the subject which concerns us here). It is more obvious or open when a person is drunk than when he is indulging to a lesser extent. In the light of the text therefore, one who drinks must be still yielding to the lusts of the flesh.

In verse 21, the word translated "revellings" is komos, which is the same word used in Romans 13. It means a half-drunken orgy. It is also worth noting how in verse 21, the apostle uses the term "and such like." Meaning that those things which were similar to drunkenness, i.e. revellings (drinking parties etc.), along with all the other vices of the flesh mentioned, would cause exclusion from the Kingdom of God. Concerning drunkenness and revellings, the Bible Knowledge Commentary states the following:

> *Two sins associated with alcohol fall in a fourth category of evils. Drunkenness (methai) refers to excessive use of strong drink by individuals, and orgies (komoi) probaly refers to the drunken carousings commonly associated with such things as the worship of Bacchus, the god of wine.*

Here we have a further view concerning the evil of a alcohol. The believer should guard himself against this lustful practice of which drunkenness is the culmination, because, "they which do such things shall not inherit the kingdom of God."

The next passage reads:

> *And be not drunk with wine, wherein is excess; but be filled with the Spirit.* (Ephesians 5:18)

The NIV Translation reads:

> *Do not get drunk on wine, which leads to debauchery. but be filled with the Spirit.*

While Ephesians 5:18, is a warning against drunkenness, notice the marked steps in depravity. Drinking leads to drunkenness, which in turn leads to debauchery. In his explanation on the meaning of the word translated "excess," Barnes ably brings out this point:

> *The word means that which is unsafe, not to be recovered; lost beyond recovery; then that which is abandoned to sensuality and lust; dissoluteness, debauchery, revelry. The meaning here is, that all this follows the use of wine. Is it proper then for Christians to be in the habit of drinking it?*

340

The next passage that we will look at concerning drinking reads:

> *For the time past of our life may suffice us to have wrought the will of the gentiles, when we walked in lasciviousness, lusts, excess of wine, revellings, banquetings, and abominable idolatries.* (1 Peter 4:3)

When Peter refers to "the time past," he is speaking of their previous conduct before they were acquainted with Christ. Wuest states:

> *The tense used implies that the course is closed and done, and looked back upon as a standing and accomplished fact. Thus should a Christian view his life previous to salvation, namely, as a closed matter. He died with Christ, and has been raised to newness of life. Old things have passed away. All things have become new. The old habits, associates, practices, places, amusements, everything of the old life which is not in accord with the Word of God should be taboo in the new life he is now living as a Christian.*

In the light of these facts it is very strange why some Christians desire alcoholic beverages, and will do everything possible to justify the use of it, even if it means taking the Bible out of context.

Let us now look closely at the verse and some of the key words used. The word translated "lusts" means any kind of sinful desire. The other three words used in this verse, which specifically relate to sins associated with alcohol, are quoted below. Berry gives us the Greek words with their definitions:

> *"excess of wine"-"oinophlugia" is a prolonged condition of drunkenness, a debauch.*

> *"revellings"-"komos" includes riot and revelry, usually as arising from drunkenness.*

> *"banquetings"-"potos" is rather concrete, a drinking carousing.*

Here we can see the manifold influences that alcohol has on evil practices. Barnes expands on the first of these words, which is translated "excess of wine":

The word here used (oinophlugia) occurs nowhere else in the New Testament. It properly means overflowing of wine, (oinos, wine, and phluo, to overflow;) then wine-drinking; drunkenness. That this was a common vice need not be proved. Multitudes of those who became Christians had been drunkards, for intemperance abounded in all the heathen world. It should not be inferred here from the English translation, `excess of wine,' that wine is improper only when used to excess, or that the moderate use of wine is proper. Whatever may be true on that point, nothing can be determined in regard to it from the use of this word. The apostle had his eye on one thing-on such a use of wine as led to intoxication; such as they had indulged in before their conversion. About the impropriety of that, there could be no doubt. Whether any use of wine, by Christians or other persons, was lawful, was another question. It should be added, moreover, that the phrase `excess of wine' does not precisely convey the meaning of the original. The word excess would naturally imply something more than was needful; or something beyond the proper limit or measure; but no such idea is in the original word.

Here we can see that this word referred to wine drinking as well as drunkenness. Robinson's Lexicon of the New Testament defines this word as:

wine-drinking, drunkenness, vinolency.

We have already examined the word translated "revellings" (see also comments on Rom 13:13,14 and Gal 5:19-21). Barnes again expands on the word here translated "banquetings" (Greek, potos; key points relating to abstinence highlighted in bold print):

*The word here used (potos) occurs nowhere else in the New Testament. It means properly **drinking; an act of*** *drinking; then a drinking bout; drinking together. The thing forbidden by it is an assembling together for the purpose of drinking. There is nothing in this word referring to eating, or to banqueting, as the term is now commonly employed. The idea in the passage is, that it is improper for Christians to meet together for the purpose of drinking-as wine, toasts, &c. The prohibition would apply to all those assemblages where this is understood to be the main object. It would forbid, therefore, an attendance on all those celebrations in which drinking toasts is understood to be an essential part of the festivities, and all those where hilarity and joyfulness are sought to be produced by the intoxicating bowl. Such are not proper places for Christians.*

Young's Concise Bible, also bears out the point that this text is loaded with points which condemn the *drinking* of intoxicating or alcoholic drinks. It reads:

*having come alongside for itself of the life is sufficient to have wrought thoroughly for ourselves the will of the nations, having passed on in lasciviousnesses, overdesires, boilings of wine, revelries, **drinking**, and unlawful idolatries.* (1 Peter 4:3, Young's Bible)

The truths contained in the text above clearly speaks for itself. In the light of the above text, it is impossible for Christians to justify the use of alcoholic beverages, a practice which the inspired text associates with sinners.

Before we conclude our study of this text, there is something worth noting of great importance. In the previous verse of the above text in consideration (1 Pet 4:2), it states:

That he no longer should live the rest of his time in the flesh to the lusts of men, but to the will of God.

Barbieri states concerning this verse:

The man who does not know God is driven by his desires to satisfy his own appetites. But the Christian who has the

343

proper perspective on life enjoys a singleness and clarity of purpose that the unsaved individual can never experience. The Christian does not live to gratify fleshly desires, but to accomplish the will of his Father in heaven.

Since the apostle goes on in the next verse that we just examined to condemn drinking, no one can deny that this is one of the lusts of the flesh referred to here. Therefore when the apostle earlier states in 1 Peter 2:11, "abstain from fleshy lusts, which war against the soul," it was a clear command to abstain from alcohol!

We will now turn our attention to the book of Revelation where we will find many references to wine and drunkenness. The first reference to wine is found in Revelation 6:6, which reads:

And I heard a voice in the midst of the four beasts say, A measure of wheat for a penny, and three measures of barley for a penny; and see thou hurt not the oil and the wine.

There are many views concerning this verse, but it is clear that the servant of God (the voice in the midst of the four beasts) is giving instructions that during the famine, the oil (olive oil plant) and the wine (vine) was not to be affected. Here we have another clear indication that the juice in the grape cluster was regarded as "wine" equally as well as when it was in its fermented state, because everything else is spoken of in its natural state (note, wheat and barley not bread). This verse surely reflects to some degree Isaiah 65:8:

Thus saith the Lord, As the new wine is found in the cluster, and one saith, Destroy it not; for a blessing is in it: so will I do for my servants' sakes, that I may not destroy them all.

The following passages in the Revelation of Jesus Christ, shows God's view towards intoxicating wine. It is used as a symbol of His wrath against sin:

And there followed another angel, saying, Babylon is fallen, is fallen, that great city, because she made all

nations drink of the wine of the wrath of her fornication.
(Revelation 14:8)

Let the reader note that Babylon is condemned for making all nations *drink* of the intoxicating wine of her fornication. Here we can see by the symbolic language, that God regards the drinking of intoxicants as being just as evil as drunkenness, which is mentioned later in the chapter. Young's Bible states:

> *...Fall, fall did Babylon the great (city), because she has caused all nations to drink (some) of the wine of (the wrath of) her whoredom.*

Drinking carousals and sexual impurity were often closely associated. This was a common practice especially in Babylon, so it is used here metaphorically to more fully illustrate how spiritually she polluted the nations. Clarke's Commentary states:

> *There is an allusion here to a custom of impure women, who give philtres or love potions to those whom they wish to seduce and bind their will; and these potions are generally of an intoxicating nature, greatly inflaming the blood, and disturbing the intellect.*

Barnes in his notes, also comments on the nature of this wine:

> *There seems an incongruity in the use of this word here, and Professor Stuart proposes to render it "the inflammatory wine of her fornication;" that is, inebriating wine; wine that excited the passions and that led to uncleanness.*

Here we can see how much God hates intoxicating wine, because of its destructiveness to the body and mind and the vices associated with it. This truth is brought out in the other passages relating to wine in Revelation. They read:

> *The same shall drink of the wine of the wrath of God, which is poured out without mixture into the cup of his indignation; and he shall be tormented with fire and brimstone in the presence of the holy angels, and in the presence of the Lamb.* (Revelation 14:10)

> *And the great city was divided into three parts, and the cities of the nations fell: and great Babylon came in remembrance before God, to give unto her cup of the wine of the fierceness of his wrath.* (Rev 16:19)

> *With whom the kings of the earth have committed fornication, and the inhabitants of the earth have been made drunk with the wine of her fornication.* (Rev 17:2)

> *For all nations have drunk of the wine of the wrath of her fornication, and the kings of the earth have committed fornication with her, and the merchants of the earth are waxed rich through the abundance of her delicacies.* (Rev 18:3)

In Revelation 18:13, wine is named as one of the luxuries that Babylon was famous for:

> *And cinnamon, and odours, and ointments, and frankincense, and wine, and oil, and fine flour, and wheat, and beasts, and sheep, and horses, and chariots, and slaves, and souls of men.*

We will now look at another aspect of God's wrath, that of the treading of the winepress. This was used in the Old Testament as a symbol of God's wrath in executing judgment upon sinners (Isaiah 63:3; Joel 3:13). This is fulfilled in the following passages of Revelation by our Lord Jesus Christ who will execute righteous judgment upon the unbelieving:

> *And the angel thrust in his sickle into the earth, and gathered the vine of the earth, and cast it into the great winepress of the wrath of God. And the winepress was trodden without the city, and blood came out of the winepress, even unto the horse bridles, by the space of a thousand and six hundred furlongs.* (Rev 14:19,20)

> *And out of his mouth goeth a sharp sword, that with it he should smite the nations: and he shall rule them with a rod of iron: and he treadeth the winepress of the fierceness and wrath of Almighty God.* (Rev 19:15)

We have now looked at every passage in the New Testament concerning wine drinking and such like. We have learnt that it is impossible that Jesus could have approved of the use of intoxicating or alcoholic beverages. We have also seen that both alcoholic and non-alcoholic wines respectively, were used. The lesson we learn very clearly from this is that our Lord only gave His approval to wine that was pure, unfermented, non-alcoholic, and unintoxicating.

In our study of the book of Revelation we see that, "Jesus Christ the same yesterday, and to day, and forever," abhorred intoxicating wine. That is why it is used as a symbol of God's divine wrath. It is utterly ridiculous therefore to suggest that our Lord used wine of this same nature as a symbol of His precious blood, which was given as an atonement for the sins of mankind.

Today the believer faces many pressures from the World to indulge in this socially accepted drug, but the Christian is to be different from the world as the Scripture admonishes:

> *And be not conformed to this world: but be ye transformed by the renewing of your mind, that ye may prove what is that good, and acceptable, and perfect, will of God.* (Romans 12:2)

BIBLIOGRAPHY

Alford, Henry. *The Greek New Testament* (London: Rivingtons, Waterloo Place; & Deighton, Bell, and Co., Cambridge, 1856).

Ali, Maulana Muhammad. *The Quran, Arabic Text; English Translation and Commentary* (Speciality Promotions Co. Inc. Chicago, Illinois, 1973).

Archer, Gleason L. *Encyclopedia of Bible Difficulties* (Zondervan Publishing House, Grand Rapids, Michigan, 1982).

Arnold, Paul. *"...not after drinking..."* (UK Band of Hope, London).

Barbieri, Louis A. *First and Second Peter* (Moody Press, Chicago, 1981).

Barclay, William. *New Testament Words* (SCM Press Ltd, London, 1964).

Barnes, Albert. *Notes on the Old and New Testament* (London: Blackie & Son, Paternoster Buildings, Glasgow and Edinburgh, 1884-85).

Berry, George Ricker. *A Dictionary of New Testament Greek Synonyms* (Zondervan Publishing House, Grand Rapids, Michigan, 1979).

Berry, Harold J. *Gems from the Original* (Back to the Bible, Lincoln, Nebraska, 1972).

British Temperance Society, *Alcohol The Inside Story* (The British Temperance Society, Watford, Herts.).

Bryant, T.A. *Today's Dictionary of the Bible* (Bethany House Publishers).

Bustanoby, Andre S. *The Wrath of Grapes* (Baker Book House, Grand Rapids, Michigan, 1987).

Clark, Gordon H., et al. *Can I Trust My Bible?* (Chicago: Moody Press, 1963).

Clarke, Adam. *Commentary and Critical Notes on the Bible* (London: William Tegg, 1824).

Cottrell, Jack. *The Authority of Bible* (Baker Book House, Grand Rapids, Michigan, 1978).

Dempsey, Michael W. *Virtue's New Treasury of Knowledge, Volumes 1 & 4* (Macdonald & Co. Publishers Ltd. Great Britain, 1974).

Derk, Francis H. *The Names of Christ* (Bethany Fellowship, Inc. Minneapolis, Minnesota, 1969).

Douglas, Alban. *100 Bible Lessons* (O.M.F. Publishers, Mandaluyong, Metro Manilla, 1966).

Dow, Rev. James L. *Collins Gem Dictionary of the Bible* (William Collins Sons & Co. Ltd., 1974).

Edersheim, Alfred. *The Life and Times of Jesus the Messiah* (MacDonald Publishing Company, Mc Lean, Virginia 1987).

Edersheim, Alfred. *The Temple* (WM. B. Eerdmans Publishing Company, Grand Rapids, Michigan, 1983).

Edwards, Brian H. *Nothing but the Truth* (Evangelical Press, Welwyn, Hertforshire, 1978).

Encyclopedia Britannica Inc. Volume 1 (University of Chicago).

Ewing, John Wesley. *The Bible and its Wines* (Denver: Prohibition National Committee, 1949).

Fausset, A.R. *Fausset's Bible Dictionary* (Zondervan Publishing House, Grand Rapids, Michigan, 1949).

Gaebelein, Frank E. *The Expositors Bible Commentary* (Zondervan Publishing House, Grand Rapids, Michigan, 1978)

Geisler, Norman L. & Nix, William E. *A General Introduction to the Bible* (Moody Press, Chicago).

Gesenius, W. *Hebrew and Chaldee Lexicon* (Baker Book House, Grand Rapids, Michigan, 1984 ed.).

Gray, James M. *Bible Problems Explained* (Moody Press, Chicago, 1941).

Grindrod, Ralph Barnes. Bacchus. *An Essay on the Nature, Causes, Effects, and Cure, of Intemperance* (London: J. Pasco, 1839).

Thomas, Robert L. & Gundry, Stanley N. *A Harmony of the Gospels* (Moody Press, Chicago, 1978).

Harris, R. Laird; Archer, Gleason L; and Waltke, Bruce K. *Theological Wordbook of the Old Testament* (Moody Press, Chicago, 1980).

Hendriksen, William. *The Gospel of John* (The Banner of Truth Trust, Edinburgh, 1982 ed.).

Henry, Matthew. *Commentary on the whole Bible* (Marshall, Morgan and Scott, 1960).

Jamieson, Robert; Faussett, A.R. and Brown, David. *Commentary on the Whole Bible* (Zondervan Publishing House, Grand Rapids, Michigan, 1982 ed.).

Johnson, Alan F. *Romans the Freedom Letter* (Moody Press, Chicago, 1974).

Keil, C.F. & Delitzsch, F. *Commentary on the Old Testament* (WM. B. Eerdmans Publishing Company, Grand Rapids, Michigan, 1986).

Leupold, H.C. *Exposition of Genesis* (Evangelical Press, London, 1972).

Leupold, H.C. *Exposition of Isaiah* (Baker Book House, Grand Rapids, Michigan, 1968).

Lion Publishing. *The Lion Concise Bible Handbook* (Lion Publishing plc. Icknield Way, Tring, Herts, England, 1983).

Marshall, Alfred. *The Interlinear Greek-English New Testament Literal English Translation* (Samuel Bagster and Sons Ltd, 1958).

Masters, Peter. *Should Christians Drink? The case for total abstinence* (The Wakeman Trust, London, 1992).

Moody, D.L. *Heaven* (Inspirational Promotions, Burlington, Ontario, Canada).

Moore, John N. & Slusher, Harold S. *A Search for Order in Complexity* (Zondervan Publishing House, Grand Rapids, Michigan, 1974).

Morris, Henry M. *Studies in the Bible and Science* (Baker Book House, Grand Rapids, Michigan, 1978).

Oxford *Illustrated Dictionary* (Oxford University Press, 1962, 1975).

Lees, Dr. F.R. *Carefully Revised Historical and Explanatory Notes on Dr. Nott's Ten Lectures on Bible Temperance* (People's Edition).

Packer, Tenney, and White. *Marshall's Bible Handbook* (Marshall, Morgan & Scott, London, 1980).

Parsons, Rev. B. Anti-Bacchus: *An Essay on the Crimes, Diseases, and other Evils connected with the use of Intoxicating Drinks* (Published by John Snow, London).

Patton, William. *Bible Wines or Laws of Fermentation and Wines of the Ancients* (Sane Press, Oklahoma City).

Patterson, Richard F. and Dougall, John. *Virtue's English Dictionary, Encyclopaedic Edition* (Blackie & Son Limited, 1977).

Peloubet, F.N. *Everyday Dictionary of the Bible* (Zondervan Publishing House, Grand Rapids, Michigan, 1967).

Pentecost, J. Dwight. *The Parables of Jesus* (Zondervan Publishing House, Grand Rapids, Michigan, 1982).

Pentecost, J. Dwight. *The Words and Works of Jesus Christ* (Zondervan Publishing House, Grand Rapids, Michigan, 1982).

Prohst, *Grape juice manufacturers* (Produced and exported by Braueri Rob. Leight AG, Stuttgart W.-Germany).

Ravenhill, Leonard, *Why Revival Tarries* (Send the Light Trust, 1972).

Robinson, Edward. *A Greek And English Lexicon of the New Testament. Revised by Alexander Negris and John Duncan* (T. & T. Clark Publishers, Edinburgh, 1844).

Shepard, J.W. *The Christ of the Gospels* (Grand Rapids: Eerdmans, 1946).

Shloer, *Grape juice manufacturers* (Beecham Products. Brentford, Middlesex, United Kingdom).

Smith, W. *Dictionary of the Bible* (A Spire Book. Published by Jove Publications, Inc., for Fleming H. Revell Company, Old Tappan, New Jersey, 1982).

Smith, W.M. *Greek and Roman Antiquities* (London: Taylor and Walton, 1842).

Stein, Robert H. *Wine Drinking In New Testament Times* (Christianity Today, June 1975).

Strong, James. *Exhaustive Concordance of the Bible* (Dugan Publishers, Inc. Gordonsville, 1894).

Tatford, F.A. *Exposition of Joel* (Prophetic Witness Publishing House, Eastbourne, Sussex, 1974).

Teacher's Advisory Council, *Alcohol Basic facts* (Published by the Teacher's Advisory Council on Alcohol and Drug Education, Manchester, 1980).

Tenney, Merril C. *The Zondervan Pictorial Bible Dictionary* (Zondervan Publishing House, Grand Rapids, Michigan, 1977).

Thayer, Joseph H. *A Greek-English Lexicon of the New Testament* (Baker Book House, Grand Rapids, Michigan, 1977).

Thomson, A.R. *Black's Medical* Dictionary (Butler and Tanner, 1979).

Torrey, R.A. *Difficulties in the Bible* (Moody Press, Chicago, 1907).

Trench, R.C. *Notes on the Miracles of Our Lord* (Baker Book House, Grand Rapids, Michigan, 1983).

United Kingdom Alliance, *Alcohol and you.* (Published by United Kingdom Alliance, Alliance House, London).

Unger, Merrill F. *Dictionary of the Bible* (Moody Press, Chicago 1983).

Van Impe, Jack, and Campbell, Roger F. *Alcohol: The Beloved Enemy* (Thomas Nelson Publishers, Nashville, Camden, New York, 1980).

Vincent, M.R. *Word Studies in the New Testament* (MacDonald Publishing Company, 1888).

Vine, W.E. *An Expository Dictionary of New Testament Words* (Fleming H. Revell Company, Old Tappan, New Jersey, 1966).

Walvoord, John F., and Zuck, Roy B. *The Bible Knowledge Commentary of the Old Testament* (Victor Books, a division of SP Publications, Inc. 1985).

Walvoord, John F., and Zuck, Roy B. *The Bible Knowledge Commentary of the New Testament* (Victor Books, a division of SP Publications, Inc. 1983).

Weiss, G. Christian. *A Greater than Solomon* (Back to the Bible, Lincoln, Nebraska, 1964).

Wenham, John W. *Christ and the Bible* (Tyndale Press, London, 1972).

Whiston, W. *Josephus: Complete* Works (Published by Pickering & Inglis Ltd., Glasgow, under special arrangements with Kregel Publications, Grand Rapids, Michigan, 1981).

Wilkerson, David. *Sipping Saints* (Fleming H. Revell Publishing Company, Old Tappan, New Jersey, 1978).

Williamson, G.I. *Wine in the Bible and the Church* (Presbyterian and reformed Publishing Company, Phillipsburg, New Jersey, 1985).

Wuest, Kenneth S. *The Pastoral Epistles in the Greek New Testament* (WM. B. Eerdmans Publishing Company, Grand Rapids Michigan, 1982).

Wuest, Kenneth S. *Romans in the Greek New Testament* (WM. B. Eerdmans Publishing Company, Grand Rapids, Michigan, 1976).

Young, Robert. *Analytical Concordance to the Bible* (United Society for Christian Literature, Lutterworth Press, Guildford and London, 1979).

Young, Robert. *Concise Critical Comments on the Bible* (Edinburgh: Geo. Adam Young & Co., Publishers).

Young, Robert. *Literal Translation of the Bible* (Pickering & Inglis, London & Glasgow).

ADDITIONAL NOTES AND NEW TESTAMENT SCRIPTURAL INDEX

Frequently used Old and New Testament words and their definitions for wine and strong drink:

Hebrew Word	Greek Equivalent	Usual Translation	Definition
Yayin	Oinos	Wine	Alcoholic wine or unfermented grape juice.
Tirosh	Gleukos	New wine	Sweet, fresh, unfermented grape juice.
Shekar	Sikera	Strong drink	Sweet, unfermented juice, or strong intoxicating drink, including beer.

New Testament passages with words that command abstinence from intoxicants, literally or metaphorically:

1 Corinthians 9:25
1 Timothy 3:2,11
1 Peter 1:13; 4:7; 5:8

1 Thessalonians 5:6,8
Titus 2:2

New Testament passages which forbids one being alongside of wine:

1 Timothy 3:3

Titus 1:7

New Testament passage forbidding one from being at drinking parties:

1 Peter 4:3

New Testament definitions of key words:

Temperate/Temperance:
(1) Self-restraint
(2) Sound-minded (on one occasion)

Sober:
(1) Sound, or clear-minded
(2) To be totally free from the influence of intoxicants
(3) Watchful

Winebibber: A wine drinker

Fruit of the vine: Freshly pressed grape juice

Vinegar: Sour wine

Definitions of the symbolic use of wine in the Bible:

Alcoholic wine: Sin, spiritual death and the wrath of God

Unfermented grape juice: Peace, prosperity, and Jesus' precious blood of the New Testament, which gives spiritual life

New Testament references to literal drunkenness and chapters commenting on them:

	Chapter	
Matthew 24:49	**Part 2, Chap 2**	
Luke 12:45; 21:3	"	"
Romans 13:13	"	**Chap 9**
1 Corinthians 5:11; 6:10	"	"
Galatians 5:21	"	"
Ephesians 5:18	"	"
1 Thessalonians 5:7	"	**Chap 5**

**An incorrect supposition
of drunkenness:** Acts 2:15   **Part 2, Chap 7**

Main Chapters dealing with every New Testament reference to wine etc.:

Titus 2:3	(a command, "not to be given to much wine")	**Part 2, Chap 4**
1 Tim 2:23	(a little wine to be taken for the stomach)	" "
1 Tim 3:3	(a command, "not to be given to wine")	**Part 2, Chap 4**
Titus 1:7	(a command, "not to be given to wine")	**Part 2, Chap 4**
I Pet 4:3	(excess/overflowing of wine)	**Part 2, Chap 9**
Rev 6:6	(wine to be spared in the famine)	**Part 2, Chap 9**
Rev 14:8	(wine of fornication)	" "
Rev 14:10	(wine of the wrath of God)	" "
Rev 16:19	(wine of the wrath of God)	" "
Rev 17:2	(wine of fornication)	" "
Rev 18:3	(wine, one of Babylon's luxuries)	" "
Rev 14:19,20	(winepress of God's wrath)	" "
Rev 19:15	(winepress of God's wrath)	" "